THE HOPE
OF ETERNAL LIFE

LUTHERANS AND CATHOLICS IN DIALOGUE XI

Common Statement of the Eleventh Round of the U.S. Lutheran-Catholic Dialogue

Edited by
Lowell G. Almen and Richard J. Sklba

Lutheran University Press
Minneapolis, Minnesota

THE HOPE OF ETERNAL LIFE
Lutherans and Catholics in Dialogue XI

The document, *The Hope of Eternal Life*, was developed as a resource by the Committee for Ecumenical and Interreligious Affairs of the United States Conference of Catholic Bishops (USCCB) and the Ecumenical and Inter-Religious Relations section of the Evangelical Lutheran Church in America (ELCA). It was reviewed by Archbishop Wilton D. Gregory, chair of the USCCB Committee for Ecumenical and Interreligious Affairs, and Presiding Bishop Mark S. Hanson of the ELCA, and it has been authorized for publication by the undersigned.

<table>
<tr><td>Msgr. David Malloy</td><td>The Rev. Donald J. McCoid</td></tr>
<tr><td>General Secretary, USCCB</td><td>Ecumenical Executive, ELCA</td></tr>
</table>

Cover: In a depiction of the resurrection, Christ as the vanquisher of death pulls Adam and Eve from their graves. This fresco is in the apse of the parecclesion, a type of narthex, of the Church of Our Saviour in Chora, a section of Istanbul, Turkey. It is believed to date from the fourteenth century. Elsewhere, many mosaics and frescoes depict Christ lifting Adam from a tomb. This one shows both Adam and Eve with Christ the Victor.

Library of Congress Cataloging-in-Publication Data
The hope of eternal life : common statement of the eleventh round of the U.S. Lutheran-Catholic dialogue / edited by Lowell G. Almen and Richard J. Sklba.
    p. cm. — (Lutherans and Catholics in dialogue ; 11)
    Includes bibliographical references.
    ISBN-13: 978-1-932688-63-4 (alk. paper)
    ISBN-10: 1-932688-63-3 (alk. paper)
    1. Lutheran Church—Relations—Catholic Church—Congresses. 2. Catholic Church—Relations—Lutheran Church—Congresses. 3. Lutheran Church—Doctrines—Congresses. 4. Catholic Church—Doctrines—Congresses. I. Almen, Lowell G., 1941- II. Sklba, Richard J.
    BX8063.7.C3H67 2011
    236—dc23
                    2011023199

Lutheran University Press, P.O. Box 390759, Minneapolis, MN 55439
Manufactured in the United States of America

Contents

CHAPTER III
Traditional Disputes within the
Context of Our Common Hope

Preface

"Blessed be the God and Father of our Lord Jesus Christ! By his great mercy he has given us a new birth into a living hope through the resurrection of Jesus Christ from the dead" (1 Peter 1:3).

"The Hope of Eternal Life" is a human yearning that is both deeply personal and widely shared. For Christians, that hope is confessed regularly. As we declare in the Apostles' Creed, "I believe in . . . the resurrection of the body, and the life everlasting." Likewise, in the Nicene Creed, we and the whole church confess, "We look for the resurrection of the dead, and the life of the world to come."

The agreements emerging in Round XI of the U.S. Lutheran-Catholic Dialogue contribute to the ongoing ecumenical journey of our churches. This dialogue has been described by Pope Benedict XVI and others as a very productive one. Indeed, the U.S. dialogue has produced substantive results since it was inaugurated on March 16, 1965, less than four months after the publication of the Decree on Ecumenism during Vatican II.

The foundation for the discussions and findings of Round XI was established by the "Joint Declaration on the Doctrine of Justification." That declaration was received officially by the Catholic Church and member churches of the Lutheran World Federation on October 31, 1999. Further, the statement of Round XI builds on the findings of the previous ten rounds of the U.S. Lutheran-Catholic Dialogue.

We are united as Christians by our baptism into Christ. We are taught by Scripture and tradition and share a common life in Christ. We affirm as Lutherans and Catholics in the dialogue process a commitment to the goal of full communion, even as we recognize that further agreements are necessary before full, sacramental communion can be restored. Matters for such consideration include the nature of the church, the ordering of ministry, patterns for the formulation of authoritative teaching, and the anthropological and ecclesial contexts for making judgments about human sexuality and other concerns.

The statement of Round XI offers fresh insights into some issues that proved contentious in the debates of the sixteenth century. Among the issues explored in this dialogue were continuity in the communion of saints, prayers for or about the dead, the meaning of death, purgation, an interim state between death and the final general judgment, and the promise of resurrection. Agreements are affirmed on the basis of new insights. Areas needing further study also are identified.

The agreements affirmed by the dialogue emerged from a shared search. The agreements do not represent a compromise between opposing views, nor do the statements ignore complex doctrinal or confessional concerns.

The members of the dialogue recognize that they do not speak officially for their respective churches. They offer their work as diligent scholars and conscientious servants of the churches. They do so with the desire that the emerging agreements may contribute in fruitful ways to the ecumenical endeavor now and in the years to come.

We hope that this statement may serve a salutary catechetical function within our churches. The findings of the dialogue may be a resource for study among clergy as well as throughout the parishes and congregations. This report also may assist individuals who provide pastoral care to the sick and dying.

During the five years of discussion in Round XI, we experienced two deeply poignant events. Two of the original members of the U.S. Lutheran-Catholic Dialogue were entrusted into the loving arms of their Creator and Redeemer. Fr. George H. Tavard died on August 13, 2007, and Dr. John H. P. Reumann on June 6, 2008. Throughout their years of service on the dialogue, they made monumental contributions to all of the dialogue's ten statements. They also offered early contributions to what emerged as the text of Round XI.

For all the conscientious and scholarly work demonstrated by each member of this dialogue, we express our gratitude as we present this report to our churches.

THE MOST REV. RICHARD J. SKLBA, *co-chair*
THE REV. LOWELL G. ALMEN, *co-chair*
All Saints' Day + November 1, 2010

Common Statement:

The Hope
OF ETERNAL LIFE

Round XI

U.S. Catholic-Lutheran Dialogue

CHAPTER I

Our Common Hope
of Eternal Life

A. Positive Developments in the Lutheran-Catholic Dialogue in Light of the "Joint Declaration on the Doctrine of Justification"

1.   An ecumenically historic moment transpired in an old church at Augsburg, Germany, on October 31, 1999. In the Church of St. Anna, which dates from 1321, official representatives of the Catholic Church and the member churches of the Lutheran World Federation signed the "Joint Declaration on the Doctrine of Justification."

2.   Their signatures attested to the official reception in our churches of the fruit of years of ecumenical dialogue on the topic of justification, one of the central issues of contention in the Lutheran Reformation of the sixteenth century. That solemn ceremony marked a "decisive step forward on the way to overcoming the division of the church."[1]

3.   The consensus expressed in the "Joint Declaration" is assumed in this report of the eleventh round of the U.S. Lutheran-Catholic Dialogue. The findings, statements of consensus, and even expressions of certain divergent convictions related to "The Hope of Eternal Life" are built upon what Lutherans and Catholics confessed together in the "Joint Declaration" in 1999: "By grace alone, in faith in Christ's saving work and not because of any merit on our part, we are accepted by God and receive the Holy Spirit, who renews our hearts while equipping and calling us to good works."[2]

4.   The method of the "Joint Declaration" is reflected in this report. Lutheran-Catholic differences are not denied, but those differences are

---

[1] "Joint Declaration on the Doctrine of Justification," (hereinafter cited as JDDJ), October 31, 1999, ¶44.

[2] JDDJ, ¶15.

placed in the context of an extensive consensus in faith and practice. Seen in the light of that consensus, the remaining differences need not stand in the way of communion between our churches.

5.	Lutherans and Catholics in the United States have engaged in ongoing, substantive dialogue for almost half a century. Beginning in 1965, this official dialogue addressed doctrines and issues of great importance for our churches. Acknowledged have been points of agreement and convergence. Addressed, too, have been matters that have separated our churches since the sixteenth century. The ten rounds of discussion have focused on the Nicene Creed (Round I); baptism (Round II); the Eucharist (Round III); the ministry of the Eucharist (Round IV); papal primacy (Round V); teaching authority and infallibility (Round VI); justification (Round VII); the one mediator, the saints, and Mary (Round VIII); Scripture and tradition (Round IX); and the church as *koinonia* of salvation–its structures and ministries (Round X). The summaries of findings and joint or common statements—accompanied occasionally by supporting studies—have contributed significantly to wider ecumenical discussion and fostered greater mutual understanding between our churches.[3]

6.	This round of our dialogue has taken up a cluster of themes that remained for further deliberation after our earlier discussions and following the reception of the "Joint Declaration." Both Lutherans and Catholics affirm that the justified who die in the faith will be granted eschatological perfection. Further, the faithful in both churches affirm that death does not break the time-transcending communion of the church. The justified in this life are one in Christ with those who have died in Christ.

---

[3] Lutherans and Catholics in Dialogue, 10 volumes: (1) *The Status of the Nicene Creed as Dogmas of the Church* (1965) [L-C, I]; (2) *One Baptism for the Remission of Sins* (1966) [L-C, II]; (3) *The Eucharist as Sacrifice* (1967) [L-C, III]; (4) *Eucharist and Ministry* (1970) [L-C, IV]; (5) *Papal Primacy and the Universal Church* (1974) [L-C, V]; (6) *Teaching Authority and Infallibility in the Church* (1980) [L-C, VI]; (7) *Justification by Faith* (1985) [L-C, VII]; (8) *The One Mediator, the Saints, and Mary* (1992) [L-C, VIII]; (9) *Scripture and Tradition* (1995) [L-C, IX]; *The Church as Koinonia of Salvation—Its Structures and Ministries* (2005) [L-C, X]. Volumes 1–4 originally were published by the Bishops' Committee for Ecumenical and Interreligious Affairs, Washington, D.C., and the U.S.A. National Committee of the Lutheran World Federation, New York, N.Y. Volumes 5–9 were published by Augsburg Fortress, Minneapolis. Volumes 1–3 also were reprinted in one volume by Augsburg Fortress as was volume 4 (1979). Volume 10 was published by the U. S. Conference of Catholic Bishops, Washington, D.C.

7.   Yet the members of the dialogue pondered how our respective traditions have spoken of the transformation of the faithful to eschatological perfection. We probed the meaning of prayers for the dead. We wrestled with descriptions of the contemporary character of indulgences in Catholic practice, especially in the light of the "Joint Declaration." And we explored how funeral practices reflect actual beliefs and even serve catechetically to remind the faithful of the hope of resurrection through Jesus Christ.

8.   The "Joint Declaration" affirms that the "Lutheran churches and the Roman Catholic Church will continue to strive together to deepen this common understanding of justification and to make it bear fruit in the life and teaching of the churches."[4] We offer now this report as one step in the movement toward greater mutual understanding and as a shared witness to our common "hope of eternal life."[5]

B. Hope in our Time

9.   Contemporary cultural attitudes toward death are ambivalent at best. The 2008 Pew U.S. Religious Landscape Survey found that almost three-quarters of Americans say they believe in life after death. Even among those the survey identified as religiously unaffiliated, almost half agreed with such belief.[6] Such beliefs can take many forms, however, from the sophisticated to the sentimental, and are surrounded by a wide range of understandings of death embodied in our culture.[7] Ernest Becker's

---

[4] JDDJ, ¶43.

[5] The U.S. Conference of Catholic Bishops engaged with the Evangelical Lutheran Church in America and its predecessor bodies and also with The Lutheran Church–Missouri Synod (LCMS) in the first nine rounds of the U.S. Lutheran-Catholic Dialogue, beginning in 1965. With the 1999 signing of the "Joint Declaration on the Doctrine of Justification" by the Catholic Church and the member churches of the Lutheran World Federation, a new context was created for the dialogue. The "Joint Declaration" informed and guided the deliberations of both Round X and Round XI. The Lutheran Church–Missouri Synod is not a member of the Lutheran World Federation, nor was the LCMS a signatory of the "Joint Declaration." The LCMS, however, was invited to participate in this round of discussions. Procedurally, the dialogue functioned in keeping with the protocol document established for Round XI (see Appendix I).

[6] Pew Forum on Religion & Public Life, *U.S. Religious Landscape Survey: Religious Beliefs and Practices: Diverse and Politically Relevant* (Washington, D.C.: Pew Research Center, 2008), 31–32.

[7] See the survey by Paul Fiddes, *The Promised End: Eschatology in Theology and Literature* (Oxford: Blackwell Publishers Ltd., 2000).

Pulitzer Prize winning study *The Denial of Death* began with the assertion: "The idea of death, the fear of it, haunts the human animal like nothing else; it is a mainspring of human activity."[8] "New Atheists" call belief in life after death "dangerous nonsense" and charge that this "nonsense" provides support for fanaticism and terrorism.[9] Dylan Thomas's famous poem urges us not to "go gentle into that good night," but to "rage, rage against the dying of the light."[10]

10.   Christian faith hinges on the belief that death is not the end of life for the individual, for humanity, or the universe. "If for this life only we have hoped in Christ, we are of all people most to be pitied" (1 Cor. 15:19). For every Christian, "to live is Christ, and to die is gain" (Phil. 1:21). Death is not the last word, for "death has been swallowed up in victory" (1 Cor. 15:54). This hope is not only for ourselves, but for all things: "For the creation waits with eager longing for the revealing of the children of God . . . in hope that the creation itself will be set free from its bondage to decay and will obtain the freedom of the glory of the children of God" (Rom. 8:19, 21). In the midst of our culture's mixture of messages on death and the future, the gospel proclaims that life is the destiny of humanity and of the world.

11.   This hope is the common heritage of Christians. Disagreements on the Christian hope of eternal life have not touched the core of our common confession. Christians need to make that confession together before the world with confidence and joy. Members of this dialogue desire that our work may contribute not only to the ongoing reconciliation of our Lutheran and Catholic traditions, but also to the proclamation of that message of hope.

12.   *Together we confess: Life does not end in death. God in Christ offers everyone the hope of eternal life.*

C. Presentation of What Is to Follow

13.   What follows is presented in three major sections: Chapter II describes the common convictions that shape the hope of both Catholics and Lutherans. The text examines a series of individual topics: death and

---

[8]   Ernest Becker, *The Denial of Death* (New York: Free Press, 1973), ix.

[9]   See, e.g., Richard Dawkins, "Religion's Misguided Missiles," *Guardian* (London), Sept. 15, 2001.

[10] Dylan Thomas, *The Poems of Dylan Thomas*, revised ed. (New York: New Directions, 2003), 239.

intermediate states (i.e., the condition of the dead prior to the resurrection), judgment, hell and the possibility that all might be saved, and heaven and the final kingdom. In each case, biblical, doctrinal, and theological material is surveyed and the heart of our common convictions stated. Even in a statement as extensive as this one, all aspects of all topics cannot be addressed. We have focused on those most important for Catholic-Lutheran relations.

14.   Chapter III takes up the two most important Lutheran-Catholic controversies over last things: purgatory and prayer for the dead. The invocation of saints was covered in an earlier round of this dialogue.[11] Again, biblical and doctrinal material is surveyed and the controversy analyzed. These controversies take on a new appearance when seen against the background of our common hope and in the light of developments in our understandings of the communion of saints and in our liturgies. In each case, we find that our remaining differences, while not to be denied, need not in themselves block communion between us. The final section, Chapter IV, affirms our common hope of eternal life.

---

[11] H. George Anderson, J. Francis Stafford, and Joseph A. Burgess, eds., *The One Mediator, the Saints, and Mary: Lutherans and Catholics in Dialogue VIII* (Minneapolis: Augsburg, 1992); this statement is cited hereinafter as *The One Mediator, the Saints, and Mary.*

CHAPTER II

Called to the One Hope: Our Common Doctrinal Heritage

A. The Hope That Unites Us

1. Our Common Hope

15. Catholics and Lutherans are united not only by "one Lord, one faith, one baptism" (Eph. 4:5), but also by "the one hope" to which we are called (Eph. 4:4). We live "in the hope of eternal life that God, who never lies, promised before the ages began" (Titus 1:2). This hope is not peripheral within the Christian life, but at its center: "faith, hope, and love abide" (1 Cor. 13:13).

16. Our shared hope is not vague or uncertain, for it focuses on Jesus Christ. "For as by a man came death, by a man has come also the resurrection of the dead. For as in Adam all die, so also in Christ all shall be made alive" (1 Cor. 15:21-22). Christ "abolished death, brought life and immortality to light" (2 Tim. 1:10). Christ is not simply the reason we hope; he is the content of our hope. Our hope parallels Paul's desire "to be with Christ" (Phil. 1:23). Jesus is not only the "first-born of the dead" (Col. 1:18), the first to rise, he is himself the resurrection: "I am the resurrection and the life. Those who believe in me, even though they die, will live" (John 11:25). We cannot know the details of this future: "No eye has seen nor ear heard, nor the human heart conceived what God has prepared for those who love him" (1 Cor. 2:9). Nevertheless, we know that Jesus is our future.

17. Our shared Scripture provides numerous images for the hope of eternal life. Eternal life can be described as life in the kingdom of God (Mark 9:47), as a heavenly banquet (Matt. 8:11; Rev. 19:9), as paradise gained (Luke 23:43; Rev. 2:7), as the heavenly Jerusalem (Heb. 12:22; Rev. 3:12), as a place of rest (Heb. 4:1, 9), and as an arena of unending light (Rev. 22:5). These diverse images are brought into focus by their relation to God's act in Christ, an action that has already reached a kind of fulfillment in the death and resurrection of Christ and the pouring out of the Spirit, but which awaits its consummation in the new heaven and new earth (Rev. 21:1), in which God will be "all in all" (1 Cor. 15:28).

18.   Catholics and Lutherans alike witness in worship to our common hope. Both Lutherans and Catholics proclaim in the celebration of the Eucharist: "Christ has died; Christ has risen; Christ will come again."[12] The Nicene-Constantinopolitan Creed, used in both churches, concludes its second, Christological article with the statement: "He [Jesus Christ] will come again in glory to judge the living and the dead, and his kingdom will have no end." The final article declares: "We look for the resurrection of the dead, and the life of the world to come."

19.   Hope is particularly expressed in our funeral liturgies. Lutherans pray, "Give courage and faith to all who mourn, and a sure and certain hope in your loving care . . ."[13] and "Give us faith to see that death has been swallowed up in the victory of our Lord Jesus Christ, so that we may live in confidence and hope until, by your call, we are gathered to our heavenly home in the company of all your saints."[14] Catholics pray, "We are assembled here in faith and confidence to pray for our brother/sister N. Strengthen our hope so that we may live in the expectation of your Son's coming."[15]

2. Shared Hope as the Context of Dialogue

20.   This hope of eternal life was not a primary focus of controversy between Lutherans and Catholics during the Reformation. For the most part, the understanding of last things that had developed in western theology during the patristic and medieval periods was received by Lutherans without fundamental change. Controversy arose on matters of eschatology when Lutherans believed that some Catholic teaching or related practice (e.g., Masses for the dead) compromised the proclamation of free justification of the sinner or when Catholics believed Lutherans were undercutting the assistance Christians can give to one another even across the boundary of death.

21.   In this chapter, we present the heritage of hope that Catholics and Lutherans hold in common. There are variations between our two traditions in these areas, but they have rarely been held to be church-

---

[12] Evangelical Lutheran Church in America, *Evangelical Lutheran Worship*, Pew Edition (Minneapolis: Augsburg Fortress, 2006), 109.

[13] *Evangelical Lutheran Worship*, Leaders Desk Edition (Minneapolis: Augsburg Fortress, 2006), 670.

[14] *Evangelical Lutheran Worship*, Leaders, 668.

[15] Order of Christian Funerals in *The Rites of the Catholic Church as Revised by the Second Vatican Ecumenical Council*, Study Edition (New York: Pueblo Publishing Co., 1990), vol. 1, 979.

dividing. In the next chapter, we will look at those subjects in this area that have been more vigorously disputed between Catholics and Lutherans.

22.   Because many of the topics considered here were not disputed at the time of the Reformation, neither the Catholic nor the Lutheran texts from the Reformation era give a full picture of the shared eschatological faith. The Catholic magisterial tradition includes, in addition to sixteenth century materials, both pre-Reformation statements[16] and a variety of rich post-Reformation expositions.[17] Since Lutheranism has no widely received doctrinal texts beyond the *Book of Concord* (with the possible exception of the JDDJ), Lutheran resources for a presentation of our common heritage are less extensive. Therefore, reference will be made to material from particular Lutheran churches, even though they have not received universal Lutheran acceptance.

23.   An important background for this presentation is the JDDJ. There, Catholics and Lutherans together affirmed that "a consensus in basic truths of the doctrine of justification exists."[18] The faith we hold in common "includes hope in God and love for him."[19] We thus begin our discussions in confidence based on a shared foundation and context.

24.   What we hope for is a gift, which will be ours only through the grace of Christ. The agent who will bring that for which we hope is always God, active in Christ and the Holy Spirit. As Benedict XVI said in the encyclical on hope, *Spe salvi*: "The Kingdom of God is a gift, and precisely because of this, it is great and beautiful, and constitutes the response to our hope."[20] Only God is the adequate foundation for a sure hope. "This great hope can only be God, who encompasses the whole of reality and who can bestow upon us what we, by ourselves, cannot attain. The fact that it comes to us as a gift is actually part of hope. God is the foundation of hope: not any god, but the God who has a human face and who has

---

[16] These, however, are not extensive and address only the Western-Eastern dispute over purgatory and the fourteenth century controversy whether souls prior to the resurrection enjoy the beatific vision. See J. Neuner and J. Dupuis, eds., *The Christian Faith in the Doctrinal Documents of the Catholic Church* (New York: Alba House, 1982), 682–686.

[17] Particularly important are the *Catechism of the Catholic Church* and the encyclical of Benedict XVI, *Spe salvi [On Christian Hope]*, 30 November 2007. This encyclical is noted hereinafter as *Spe salvi* with paragraph numbers.

[18] JDDJ, ¶40.

[19] JDDJ, ¶25.

[20] *Spe salvi*, ¶35.

loved us to the end, each one of us and humanity in its entirety."[21] This common statement on hope for eternal life is an extension of common confession that salvation is a matter of God's gracious initiative.

3. The Bible in Our Discussions

25.　　We begin each topic with a discussion of the biblical material that is foundational for both our traditions, followed by a presentation of doctrinal material. The Bible constitutes both the ground for ecumenical agreement and a focus of continuing investigation and theological argument. The use of Scripture involves a number of questions: How do we relate a reading of biblical texts in relation to their historical setting to a reading that takes the total canon as the primary context of interpretation? Just what is the composition of the canon? What is the hermeneutical significance of our common belief in divine inspiration? What authority resides in the church's tradition of interpretation? What is the "literal sense" of a text and how does it relate to other possible senses?

26.　　This dialogue's discussion of biblical texts seeks to illumine the scriptural foundations and background of our churches' respective teachings on the hope of eternal life without completely settling these hermeneutical questions.[22] Judgments whether particular biblical texts adequately ground particular beliefs about heaven, hell, purgatory, etc., often involve judgments on these larger questions. Sometimes our churches have drawn different conclusions from the same biblical texts (e.g., 1 Corinthians 3 and Matthew 12:32, which will be discussed below in a section on purgatory).

B. Death and Intermediate States

27.　　The most immediate and empirically certain of last things is physical death. As the Wisdom literature of the Old Testament emphasizes, death comes alike to all, rich and poor, wise and foolish. "Who can live and never see death?" (Ps. 89:48). For Christians, however, death is never simply a natural event. Death is a consequence of sin. As Paul says: "The wages of sin is death" (Rom. 6:23). Central to the Christian message of hope is the conviction that death is not final: "O death, where is thy victory? O death, where is thy sting?" (1 Cor. 15:55). In God's kingdom, "death shall be no more" (Rev. 21:4).

---

[21] *Spe salvi,* ¶31. See discussion of merit in Chapter II.C.3: Judgment and Justification, below.

[22] See Appendix III, "On the Interpretation of Biblical Texts."

28.   What happens in the death of a human being? Is death the annihilation of the entire self? Does some aspect or part of the person continue to exist? If so, how and on what basis? Herein lies the question of "intermediate states." What is the status of the self between death and resurrection? This question was not a focus of controversy during the sixteenth century, although a few Lutheran theologians (most notably, Luther) were willing to entertain possibilities excluded by Catholic teaching. More recently, the question of intermediate states has been debated within each of our traditions. How these questions are answered affects the discussion of other topics, e.g., purgatory.

1. Biblical

29.   The early books of the Old Testament use a variety of terms to speak about the state of the dead, e.g., being gathered to the fathers (Num. 27:13, Judges 2:10) and Sheol (Gen. 37.35). As Judaism developed during the Second Temple period, descriptions of the state of the dead became more detailed. 1 Enoch 22 (a non-canonical text from the third century B.C.) portrays four chambers of the dead, with inhabitants differentiated by what they had done and suffered in this world and by the fate that they will face in the final judgment. With the Hellenization of Judaism, it becomes possible to speak of the souls of the dead as having an existence beyond death that is one of peace, purity, and immortality (e.g.,Wis. Sol. 3:1-4; 4 Macc. 18:23). We see this too in Christian eschatological discourse (e.g., Matt. 10:28; Rev. 6:9; cf. 20:4). Revelation 6:9 portrays the souls of the martyrs living in the presence of God (cf. Rev. 7:9, 15), and in the conscious expectation of the resurrection. Matthew 10:28 indicates that both the body and the soul participate in the final judgment.

30.   Although Paul does not use the term "soul" explicitly to indicate the intermediate state, he recognizes the ongoing existence of the self between death and resurrection. He describes death as a putting off of the physical body until God gives a new body in the resurrection (1 Cor. 15:38). He likens the state of death to being a naked seed awaiting a body that God shall give it (1 Cor. 15:37). While Paul's description of the state of the Christian dead is vague, it is clear that he regards them as "in Christ" (1 Thess. 4:16; 1 Cor. 15:18). Therefore, Paul speaks of death in Christ as something to be welcomed rather than feared: "My desire is to depart and be with Christ, for that is far better" (Phil. 1:23; cf. 2 Cor. 5:8).[23]

---

[23] Paul uses the euphemism of "sleep" to refer to death (1 Cor. 15:18; 1 Thess. 4:13-15; 5:10). In this metaphor he picks up Old Testament usage (cf. Dan. 12:2). Jesus also uses the euphemism (Mark 5:39; John 11:11). The euphemism of sleep implies a resurrection to come, but it says nothing about a possible state of the soul in an interim period.

31.   Some New Testament texts are less clear on the question of the state of the dead, but should be cited here. Jesus promises the repentant criminal, in Luke 23:43, a place with him in Paradise. In Jewish tradition Paradise was sometimes used to refer to the interim place for the soul before resurrection and such may be Jesus' intention, but Paradise also could be used for the age to come after the resurrection.[24] In the story of the rich man and Lazarus (Luke 16:19-31), after the two men die, the one is found in Hades and the other is found in the bosom of Abraham. Commentators disagree on whether the two men are thought to be in an interim state or in their final stations.[25] Hebrews speaks of the righteous dead of Old Testament generations having been perfected through Christ (Heb. 11:39-40; cf. 10:14; 12:23). This may suggest that these righteous dead were in a kind of interim state before the coming of Christ, but we have few details.

32.   Other New Testament texts sometimes have been used in discussions of the state of the dead in connection with Jesus' descent into the realm of the dead (1 Pet. 3:18-20; 4:6; Eph. 4:9; and Matt. 27:51b-53). Biblical scholars in recent decades have denied that these texts refer to the descent of Jesus into the realm of the dead and therefore the texts do not shed light on the question of the state of the dead.[26]

33.   In summary we may say that throughout the New Testament there is evidence for belief in an intermediate state of the dead before the

---

[24] Hermann L. Strack and Paul Billerbeck, *Kommentar zum Neuen Testament aus Talmud und Midrasch* IV/2 (Munich: Beck, 1922–1956), 1119-1120. Cf. George Foot Moore, *Judaism in the First Centuries of the Christian Era: The Age of Tannaim*, three volumes (Cambridge, Mass.: Harvard University Press, 1927–1930), 2:390–391.

[25] See I. Howard Marshall, *The Gospel of Luke* (Grand Rapids, Mich.: Eerdmans, 1978), 636–637.

[26] On 1 Peter. 3:18-20 and 4:6, see especially William Dalton, *Christ's Proclamation to the Spirits: A Study of 1 Peter 3:18-4:6* (Rome: Pontifical Biblical Institute, 1965). On Ephesians 4:9, see the commentaries. On Matthew 27:51b-53, see Donald A. Hagner, *Matthew 14-28*, WBC 33B (Dallas, Texas: Word Books, 1995), 851, where Hagner speaks of these verses as a "piece of realized and historicized apocalyptic." The document *Communio Sanctorum: The Church as the Communion of Saints*, trans. Mark W. Jeske, Michael Root, and Daniel R. Smith (Collegeville, Minn.: Liturgical Press, 2004), 73 and 88, note 4—which is the statement of the Bilateral Working Group of the German National Bishops' Conference and the Church Leadership of the United Evangelical Lutheran Church of Germany—continues the traditional interpretation of 1 Peter 3:19 and 4:6. This document is hereinafter cited as Bilateral Working Group, *Communio Sanctorum*.

resurrection, but some of the details about that state remain a mystery. Scripture is clear, however, that the self does not cease at death.[27] **Together, Lutherans and Catholics affirm that Scripture teaches the ongoing existence of the self between death and resurrection.** While some texts use the word "soul" to refer to this existence, a term that has been of great importance to both of our traditions, we acknowledge that the New Testament also can speak of this existence in other ways, which accounts for some variety of description in later tradition. Since the New Testament authors rarely speak of the intermediate state in detail, we should avoid claiming too great a certainty about our knowledge of the state of the dead on the basis of biblical evidence.

2. Doctrinal

a. Patristic Views[28]

34. The earliest Christians spoke in various ways about what follows death. Some said that departed souls sleep in Sheol, where they sense only faintly the fate to be theirs after the resurrection and their judgment by Christ.[29] Others spoke of various abodes in which the souls of the dead consciously await the final resurrection and judgment. Particular emphasis fell on the martyrs already in some way receiving their reward and rejoicing in the presence of Christ.

35. Of special importance for the development of depictions of intermediate states in Western theology were the writings of Augustine. He unambiguously states that the dead are conscious and already receive reward or punishment.

> During the time, however, which intervenes between man's death and the final resurrection, the souls remain in places specially reserved for them, according as each is deserving of rest or tribulation for the disposition he has made of his life in the flesh.[30]

36. In the centuries following Augustine, such views became more precise. Most important for later theology were the *Dialogues* of Gregory

---

[27] "Person" and "self" are used in this section as equivalent terms.

[28] For a more detailed discussion of the patristic and medieval discussion, see Appendix IV.

[29] Brian E. Daley, *The Hope of the Early Church: A Handbook of Patristic Eschatology* (Cambridge: Cambridge University Press, 1991), 73–75, 95, 114, 166.

[30] *The Enchiridion*, translated as *Faith Hope and Charity*, 29, 109, by Louis A. Arand, Ancient Christian Writers, 3 (Westminster, Md.: The Newman Bookshop, 1947), 103.

the Great. The just cannot be separated from Christ, not even by death, he said.

> Yet, nothing is clearer than that the souls of the perfectly just are received into the kingdom of heaven as soon as they leave the body. This is attested by Truth himself when he says, "Where the body lies there the eagles will gather" (Luke 17:37). For, wherever the Redeemer is bodily present, there the souls of the just are undoubtedly assembled. And St. Paul desires to have done with the present life, "and be with Christ" (Phil. 1:23). One who doubts not that Christ is in heaven will not deny that the soul of Paul is there, too.[31]

37. Conversely, the wicked are separated from God in death: "If you believe from the witness of the divine word that the souls of the saints are in heaven, you also have to believe as well that the souls of the wicked are in hell."[32]

38. Augustine, Gregory, and others continued to affirm a significant distinction between the joys of the dead prior to the resurrection and afterwards. As Gregory says: "[U]ntil then [i.e., the resurrection] they enjoy only the bliss of the soul, but afterward they will also enjoy this in the body. The flesh in which they suffered pains and torments for the Lord will also share in their happiness. . . . Just as they rejoice now only in their souls, they will then rejoice in the glory of their bodies as well."[33]

b. Medieval Views and Benedictus Deus (1336)

39. The development of scholasticism and, in particular, the adaptation of Aristotelian anthropology within Christian theology lent greater precision to medieval discussions of intermediate states, e.g., about how the soul participates in God and about the relation of the soul that subsists between death and the resurrection of the body. Greater precision brought with it, however, the possibility of more focused debate on the precise nature of the intermediate state.

---

[31] *Dialogues*, 4, 26; Fathers of the Church (New York, 1952), 39:210. The translation is modified to agree better with the original, given in Grégorire le Grand, *Dialogues*, vol. 3, A. de Vogüe, ed., Sources chrétiennes, 265 (Paris, 1980), 84.

[32] *Dialogues*, 4, 29; Fathers of the Church, 39, 225 (translation modified to agree with Sources chrétiennes, 265, 98).

[33] *Dialogues*, 4, 26; Fathers of the Church, 39, 218–219 (translation brought into better agreement with Sources chrétiennes, 265, 84–86).

40. During 1331–1334, Pope John XXII delivered a series of sermons in which he argued that the souls of the redeemed do not enjoy the face-to-face vision of God until the resurrection.[34] In the interim, they are "under the altar" (Rev. 6:9). While they are blessed through their union with the humanity of Christ, they do not yet see God. These sermons were not binding teaching and were circulated with the request for response. An intense debate was set off, with John's views both supported and criticized. On his death bed in 1334, John retracted his views.

41. John's successor, Benedict XII, called together a group of theologians to discuss the question and in 1336 he issued the constitution *Benedictus Deus*.[35] This constitution teaches, as a matter "to remain in force forever," that "immediately (*mox*) after death" the souls of the redeemed "already before they take up their bodies again and before the general judgment, have been, are, and will be with Christ in heaven, in the heavenly kingdom and paradise, joined to the company of the holy angels." In this state, they "see the divine essence with an intuitive vision and even face to face. . . . Moreover, by this vision and enjoyment the souls of those who have already died are truly blessed (*beatae*) and have eternal life and rest."

42. *Benedictus Deus* ended the debate begun by John XXII. No one in the debate denied the existence of an intermediate state; the question was the nature of the soul's participation in salvation during this intermediate state. When in the early sixteenth century a renewed Aristotelianism denied the immortality of the soul, the Fifth Lateran Council condemned "all those who assert that the intellectual soul is mortal."[36] The Council of Trent did not extend or further elaborate this tradition of teaching.

c. Reformation Teaching

43. The Lutheran Reformation had no distinctive teaching about death or intermediate states. The Lutheran Confessions simply assume

---

[34] See Appendix IV for a full discussion of this controversy and the resultant teaching.

[35] For the text of the constitution, see J. Neuner and J. Dupuis, eds., *The Christian Faith in the Doctrinal Documents of the Catholic Church*, 7th edition (Bangalore: Theological Publications in India, and Staten Island, N.Y.: Alba House, 2001), nos. 2305–2307, 1018–1019, which translates Henricus Denzinger and Adolphus Schönmetzer, eds., *Enchiridion Symbolorum, Definitionum, et Declarationum de Rebus Fidei et Morum*, 33rd edition (Freiburg, Germany: Herder, 1965), nos. 1000–1002.

[36] Neuner-Dupuis, *The Christian Faith*, 123; Denzinger and Schönmetzer, 1440-1441.

that the souls of the dead exist and are in a blessed communion with Christ.[37] No debate with Catholics or among Lutherans called for any discussion of the question and thus the Confessions do not address the nature of death or the way in which the soul survives death. In the debate over whether Christians can invoke prayers from the saints in heaven, the Confessions consistently accept as Christian teaching that the departed saints are in heaven, although we cannot know whether they are aware of our invocations of them.[38] The Apology thus states: "[C]oncerning the saints we grant that in heaven they pray for the church in general, just as they prayed for the entire church while living."[39] Luther is more reticent in the Smalcald Articles, saying that "the saints on earth and perhaps [*vielleicht*] those in heaven pray for us."[40] Authoritative statements such as *Benedictus Deus*, however, ceased to carry weight with Lutheranism.[41] As a result, questions that had been closed during the medieval period at least theoretically could be reopened. Lutheran theology of the seventeenth and eighteenth centuries continued to teach the survival of the soul beyond death and an immediate judgment, followed by acceptance into heaven or banishment to hell.[42]

---

[37] The Lutheran Confessions are cited by document, section, and page numbers contained in *The Book of Concord* as edited by Robert Kolb and Timothy J. Wengert (Minneapolis: Fortress Press, 2000); cited hereinafter as *Book of Concord*.

[38] *The One Mediator, the Saints, and Mary*, ¶68, note 70.

[39] Apology 21, §9, *Book of Concord*, 238.

[40] Smalcald Articles, Part II, Article 2, §26, *Book of Concord*, 305.

[41] The Weimar edition of Luther's works contains no reference to the constitution *Benedictus Deus*. See Martin Luther, *Werke: Kritische Gesamtausgabe* (Weimar: Hermann Böhlaus Nachfolger, 1883–1983); hereafter cited as Weimar Ausgabe, followed by volume and page number.

[42] Leonhard Hutter, *Compend of Lutheran Theology*, trans. H. E. Jacobs and G. F. Spieker (Philadelphia: Lutheran Book Store, 1868), 225-228; Nicolaus Hunnius, *Epitome Credendorum: A Concise and Popular View of the Doctrines of the Lutheran Church*, trans. Paul Edward Gottheil (Nuremberg: U. E. Sebald, 1847), 272; Karl Hase, *Hutterus Redivivus, oder Dogmatik der evangelisch-lutherischen Kirche. Ein dogmatisches Repertorium für Studierende*, 7th ed. (Leipzig: Breitkopf und Härtel, 1848), 329, citing Johann König; Heinrich Schmid, *The Doctrinal Theology of the Evangelical Lutheran Church*, 3rd ed., trans. Charles A. Hay and Henry E. Jacobs (Minneapolis: Augsburg, 1961), 626, citing Gerhard and Quenstedt. Lutheran theology did depart from pre-Reformation teaching in insisting that the redeemed who died prior to Christ (e.g., Abraham) already enjoyed heaven immediately at death and did not have to await Christ's resurrection (see Schmidt, *Doctrinal Theology*, 635, citing Gerhard). This shift was part of a general rejection of any intermediate conditions other than heaven or hell (e.g., purgatory).

44.   Luther himself often took the biblical language of death as sleep more literally than his medieval predecessors, but was unsure about what such "sleep" might be and also on other occasions used the more common language of souls in heaven.[43] In debates about purgatory and invocation of the saints, he did not make an argument that the departed are not conscious. While, as will be noted, some twentieth-century interpreters insisted that Luther consciously rejected earlier notions of an intermediate state, much contemporary scholarship denies that Luther had a settled teaching on the question.[44] The soteriology of the Lutheran Reformers, however, was dominated by language of death and resurrection: justification is closely related to participation in Christ's death and resurrection; baptism is understood in relation to death and resurrection (Rom. 6); and salvation is rising with Christ after dying with Christ. Lutheran attention was thus not focused on the soul and its intermediate state, but on resurrection as the Christian's hope.

d. Recent Discussions

45.   In the course of the twentieth century, the classical soul-body anthropology shared by Lutherans, Catholics, and others came under critique. On the one hand, this anthropology was criticized as unbiblical. The Bible, it was claimed, understood the self as essentially embodied in a way that excluded the ongoing existence of a disembodied soul. Biblical hope, it was argued, focused on bodily resurrection, not on a soul that survived death.[45] On the other hand, both science and the most widely

---

[43] For examples of Luther speaking of death as sleep, see e.g., Martin Luther, *Luther's Works*, American ed., vol. 48, Gottfried G. Krodel, ed. (Philadelphia: Fortress Press, 1963), 30; vol. 53, Ulrich S. Leupold, ed. (Philadelphia: Fortress Press, 1965), 326. For an example of his use of more traditional language of the soul in heaven, see his funeral oration on Urbanus Rhegius, in the Weimar Ausgabe, vol. 50, 400. The uncertainty of what Luther might mean by sleep can be seen in his Genesis lectures, where he speaks of Abraham as in some sense asleep, but also as "living, serving God, and ruling with him." *Luther's Works*, vol. 5, Jaroslav Pelikan, ed. (St. Louis: Concordia Publishing House, 1968), 74f.

[44] See, e.g., Bernhard Lohse, *Martin Luther's Theology: Its Historical and Systematic Development*, Roy A. Harrisville, ed. (Minneapolis: Fortress Press, 1999), 327–330; and Oswald Bayer, *Martin Luther's Theology: A Contemporary Interpretation*, trans. Thomas H. Trapp (Grand Rapids, Mich.: Eerdmans, 2008), 325–329. Luther's positive view on immortality has been argued by Fritz Heidler, *Die biblische Lehre von der Unsterblichkeit der Seele. Sterben, Tod, ewiges Leben im Aspekt lutherischer Anthropologie* (Göttingen: Vandenhoeck & Ruprecht, 1983).

[45] See, e.g., the influential study by Oscar Cullmann, *Immortality of the Soul or Resurrection of the Dead?: The Witness of the New Testament* (New York: Macmillan, 1964).

accepted philosophical outlooks with which theology was in conversation had ceased to operate with such a soul-body distinction and the metaphysics that often accompanied it. In differing ways, both Lutheran and Catholic theologians sought to engage this two-pronged critique.

1. Lutheran

46. Particularly important for the Lutheran discussion was the argument that Luther himself had rejected "the immortality of the soul," i.e., that the soul naturally possessed the characteristic of immortality.[46] Assertion of a conscious intermediate state was linked by many with an allegedly Greek soul-body dualism and criticized as undercutting the seriousness of death and the resurrection as the focus of Christian hope.[47] While some Lutheran theologians preserved versions of the traditional teaching,[48] many Lutheran theologians developed a variety of positions on intermediate states. Some affirmed that beyond death, there is no time and the dead directly enter eternity.[49] More common was an affirmation that while the self as a whole dies and has no natural immortality, the self's relation with "the God of the living" has a kind of permanence that does not pass away. A statement by Luther in his Genesis lectures is often cited and used as a theological springboard: "where and with whomever God speaks, whether in anger or in grace, that person is surely immortal."[50] Some versions of such a "dialogical immortality" did not ascribe much content to this intermediate state. For example, Werner

---

[46] Influential were the arguments of Carl Stange, *Die Unsterblichkeit der Seele* (Gütersloh: Bertelsmann, 1925), 133–144; *Das Ende aller Dinge: Die christliche Hoffnung, ihr Grund und ihr Ziel* (Gütersloh: C. Bertelsmann, 1930), 180–185. On Stange's influence, see George Vass, "The Immortality of the Soul and Life Everlasting," *The Heythrop Journal* 6 (1965): 270–288.

[47] Gerhard Sauter refers to "the battle against the concept of immortality that has dominated German Protestant theology for the last half-century." See Gerhard Sauter, *What Dare We Hope? Reconsidering Eschatology* (Harrisburg, Pa.: Trinity Press International, 1999), 188.

[48] See, e.g., the mid-century survey of Lutheran eschatology in E. C. Fendt, "The Life Everlasting," *What Lutherans Are Thinking: A Symposium on Lutheran Faith and Life*, E. C. Fendt, ed. (Columbus, Ohio: Wartburg Press, 1947), 307–322.

[49] See the discussion in Ansgar Ahlbrecht, "Die bestimmenden Grundmotive der Diskussion über die Unsterblichkeit der Seele in der evangelischen Theologie," *Catholica* 17 (1963): 1–24.

[50] *Luther's Works*, 5:76. This text is already cited by Stange in 1925 (*Unsterblichkeit*, p. 142). Most recently, it is cited at a decisive point by the Theologischer Ausschuss, Union Evangelischer Kirchen, *Unsere Hoffnung auf das ewige Leben: Ein Votum der Union Evangelischer Kirchen in der EKD* (Neukirchen-Vluyn: Neukirchener Verlagshaus, 2006), 90.

Elert would only say: "He [the departed] 'is' in judgment, in the eternal memory of God, who also will not forget him on the Last Day. There is thus good reason to write on the grave: 'He rests in God'."[51] Paul Althaus, in the most influential book on eschatology in twentieth-century Lutheranism, was more positive, but still was reticent on the character of an intermediate state: "Continuation [*Dauer*] beyond death is only a self-evident consequence of the present possession of eternal life."[52] More recent Lutheran theology, while not returning to straightforward soul-body distinctions, has been more positive in affirming intermediate states, but reserved about their precise character.[53]

47. These theological discussions have been reflected in Lutheran church documents in various ways. On the one hand, the Finnish Catechism of 1999, which was approved by the church's General Synod, repeats a traditional position regarding the soul surviving death, declaring that "our bodies will decay, but our souls await the day of resurrection when living and dead are gathered before God for judgment."[54] A 1969 statement from the Commission on Theology and Church Relations of The Lutheran Church–Missouri Synod utilizes the term "soul," while noting its biblical ambiguity. While the soul is not "by nature and by virtue of an inherent quality immortal," it is "not annihilated" in death; there is a "persistence of personal identity beyond death." Rejected is "the teaching that the soul 'sleeps' between death and the resurrection in such a way that it is not conscious of bliss."[55] On the other hand, the catechisms produced by the United Evangelical Lutheran Church of Germany in the 1970s speak more in terms of a dialogical immortality. "God created man to have communion with him. Man is

---

[51] Werner Elert, *Last Things*, trans. Martin Bertram (St. Louis: Concordia Publishing House, 1974), 42; *Der christliche Glaube: Grundlinien der lutherischen Dogmatik*, 6th ed. (Erlangen: Martin Luther Verlag, 1988), 528. Translation altered.

[52] Paul Althaus, *Die letzten Dinge: Entwurf einer christlichen Eschatologie*, 3rd ed. (Gütersloh: C. Bertelsmann, 1926), 35.

[53] See, e.g., Wolfhart Pannenberg, *Systematic Theology*, trans. Geoffrey W. Bromiley (Grand Rapids, Mich.: Eerdmans, 1998), 3:570-580; Robert W. Jenson, *Systematic Theology: The Works of God* (New York: Oxford University Press, 1999), 366-368; Hans Schwarz, *Eschatology* (Grand Rapids, Mich.: Eerdmans, 2000), 272–280.

[54] *Catechism: Christian Doctrine of the Evangelical Lutheran Church of Finland* (Helsinki: Edita, 1999), 56.

[55] Commission on Theology and Church Relations of The Lutheran Church–Missouri Synod, "A Statement on Death, Resurrection and Immortality: A Position Paper," 1969. Unpaginated.

thereby God's dialogue partner; he is addressed and he should answer. God does not revoke this relation to man—and so we are related to God in life and in death; we cannot escape him. Because the relation to God is indestructible, so is the human person."[56] An American adaptation of this catechism, *Evangelical Catechism*, which was produced under the auspices of The American Lutheran Church (a predecessor of the ELCA), is even more restrained, making no substantive affirmation about an intermediate state.[57] Most recently, the Theology Committee of the Union Evangelischer Kirchen in the Evangelical Church in Germany (not a Lutheran body, but with Lutheran participation) expressed worry about the pastoral effects of the reticence of theologians and pastors in speaking about intermediate states and interpreted the dialogical immortality of recent theology in a richer way, closer to more traditional understandings of an intermediate state.[58]

2. Catholic

48. Lutheran discussions were paralleled by Catholic discussions, especially in the German-language world. Four themes were particularly important in the period prior to 1970:[59]

---

[56] Jentsch, Werner, et al. *Evangelischer Erwachsenenkatechismus: Kursbuch des Glaubens* (Gütersloh: Gütersloher Verlagshaus Gerd Mohn, 1975), 533. The shorter, more popular version of this catechism *(Evangelischer Gemeindekatechismus.* Gütersloh: Gütersloher Verlagshaus Gerd Mohn, 1979) speaks similarly, 413. Both catechisms were produced by a Catechism Commission appointed by the church leadership of the Vereinigte Evangelisch-Lutherische Kirche Deutschlands (VELKD) [United Evangelical Lutheran Church of Germany], but neither book states that the final texts themselves were officially approved by any church body.

[57] "There are different interpretations of what happens to our conscious awareness between the time of death and the resurrection. Paul spoke of death as 'sleep' and of being 'with Christ' (1 Cor. 15:20; Phil. 1:23; 1 Thess. 4:15). Whether believers pass from death to life without being aware of the time in between, or whether they do enjoy conscious communion with Christ, we can take comfort in the promise that all who belong to Christ will be raised, as he was, in a resurrected body," according to the *Evangelical Catechism: Christian Faith in the World Today* (Minneapolis: Augsburg, 1982), 392.

[58] *Unsere Hoffnung auf das ewige Leben: Ein Votum der Union Evangelischer Kirchen in der EKD*, 24 (on problems in contemporary discussions of the departed) and 90-94 (on the intermediate state).

[59] This section assumes and does not repeat Karl Rahner's influential proposal of 1953 on the mediating role of the humanity of Christ even in the blessedness of the final vision of God. See Appendix IV, 172-174, below.

49. (1) Hans Urs von Balthasar stressed the appropriately theocentric orientation of eschatology.[60] Rather than thinking of eschatological "places" (heaven, hell, and purgatory), one should follow Augustine: "May God himself be after this life our dwelling place."[61] This inspired Balthasar to write an often cited passage:

> God is the "last thing" of the creature. Gained, he is heaven; lost, he is hell; examining, he is judgment; purifying, he is purgatory. He it is to whom finite being dies and through whom it rises to him, in him. This he is, however, as he presents himself to the world, that is, in his Son, Jesus Christ, who is the revelation of God and, therefore, the whole essence of the last things.[62]

50. (2) On separated souls in the interval between death and the end events, Henri de Lubac argued in 1938 that redeemed souls between death and resurrection, even if beholding the face of God, are affected by a twofold separation still to be overcome.[63] The disembodied soul is "cut off, in some sort, from the natural medium through which it communicates with its fellows." The saints in heaven also await the salvation of those still on earth for completion of the congregational *consortium* of the whole body of the redeemed, which is part of the beatitude of each one in the whole body of the saved.[64]

---

[60] "Eschatologie," in Johannes Feiner, Joseph Trutsch, and Franz Böckle, eds., *Fragen der Theologie heute* (Einsiedeln: Benzinger, 1957), 403–422; translated as "Some Points of Eschatology" in *The Word Made Flesh*, Essays in Theology, 1 (New York: Herder & Herder, 1964) and *Explorations in Theology*, vol. 1 (San Francisco: Ignatius, 1988), 255–277.

[61] *"Ipse [Deus] post hanc vitam sit locus noster,"* Exposition 4 of Ps 30 [= Ps 31:21], PL 36, 252; in *Exposition of the Psalms 1-32*, The Works of Saint Augustine, III/15, trans. Maria Boulding (Hyde Park, N.Y.: New City, 2000), 353.

[62] "Some Points of Eschatology," 260-61, original in *Fragen der Theologie heute*, 407-08. Balthasar's point echoes in Candido Pozo's *Theology of the Beyond* (Staten Island, N.Y.: St. Paul's, 2009; original Spanish, 1968, 4th Spanish edition, 2001), 59-60 and 530-531 (noting Balthasar in a 1999 catecheses of John Paul II); in Joseph Ratzinger's *Eschatology: Death and Eternal Life* (Washington, D.C.: Catholic University of America, 1988; original German, 1977), 234; and in Gisbert Greshake's *Leben–stärker als der Tod. Von der christlicher Hoffnung* (Freiburg: Herder, 2008; original 1976), 33–34.

[63] Henri de Lubac, "Eternal Life," Ch. 4 of *Catholicism: Christ and the Common Destiny of Man* (San Francisco: Ignatius, 1988), 112–133, especially 130–133; originally *Catholicisme: les aspects sociaux du dogme* (Paris: Cerf, 1938).

[64] Joseph Ratzinger took over from Henri de Lubac this "twofold separation" in the entry, "Auferstehung des Fleisches, VI. Dogmengeschichte," *Lexikon für Theologie und Kirche*, 2nd ed., Karl Rahner, ed. (1957), 1:1048–1052, in col. 1049, and in the entry "Himmel, III. Systematisch," *Lexikon*, vol. 5 (1960), 355–358, in 357–358. Candido Pozo affirms de Lubac's thesis as the last point of his long chapter of immortality and resurrection in *Theology of the Beyond*, 272.

51. (3) Fresh thinking resulted from Joseph Ratzinger's reading of Paul Althaus's monograph on eschatology.[65] This encounter led Ratzinger to develop his notion of human immortality as essentially "dialogical" in character. The human spirit is by the Creator's word made to live in an enduring relation with God, with the great possibility of this relation becoming the eternal dialogue of mutual love.[66]

52. (4) One new conception anticipated a topic contested in subsequent debate. Otto Karrer treated in 1956 the eschatological events and resurrection of the dead.[67] The end-events occur for each person in death and personal judgment, until the last human being dies and judgment is complete. General resurrection is not an event at the end of time. Resurrection occurs *seriatim* after Christ began the "era of resurrection." God brings human persons, after needed purgation, to perfection not as separated souls but as persons living on, as Christ lives on, in glorified spiritual "dwellings" into which they pass.

53. Beginning around 1970, Catholic theologians began arguing over proposals, like those of Otto Karrer, which telescope the traditional two-stage eschatology (individual vs. universal-cosmic) into a single-stage entry into the eternal and completed term of human life in death itself. This conception marked the "Dutch Catechism" of 1966, which said that beyond death there occurs "something like the resurrection of a new body."[68] A magisterial intervention quickly supplied the Catechism

---

[65] Ratzinger referenced Althaus's *Die letzten Dinge*, 7th ed. (Gütersloh, 1957) in a 1958 meditation, "Zur Theologie des Todes," collected in *Dogma und Verkündigung* (Donauworth: E. Wewel, 1973), 279–290, where Ratzinger adopts the Lutheran notion of death as completing the life-long realization of our baptism.

[66] Ratzinger's first account of "dialogical" immortality came in an essay, "Auferstehung und ewiges Leben," in *Liturgie und Mönchtum*, 25 (1959): 92–103, reprinted in *Dogma und Verkündigung*, 297-310, with acknowledgment of his source as Althaus, *Die letzten Dinge*, 110f and 114. Ratzinger's *Introduction to Christianity* (San Francisco: Ignatius, 2008; original 1968) features the notion on pp. 353–356 and his *Eschatology. Death and Eternal Life* (as in n. 62, above) elaborates dialogical immortality on pp. 150–157, citing Althaus on pp. 150f. Gerhard Nachtwei studied Ratzinger's conception in *Dialogische Usterblichkeit* (Leipzig: St. Benno, 1986), treating the influence of selected ideas of Althaus on pp. 13–16.

[67] "Irdische Zukunft und ewige Vollendung," in *Das Reich Gottes heute* (Munich: Ars sacra, 1956), 132-163, which was not translated with the rest of the German original in *The Kingdom of God Today* (New York: Herder and Herder, 1965).

[68] *A New Catechism: Catholic Faith for Adults* (New York: Herder and Herder, 1970), 474. Candido Pozo cites Ratzinger's dismissive observation of 1970 that the Catechism's authors were so set against dualism of soul-body that they invented mythologies likely to convince no one (see Pozo's *Theology of the Beyond*, 566).

with a corrected text, featuring two distinct eschatological phases, namely, the interim states of souls and the final, general resurrection.

54. Gisbert Greshake proposed in 1969 a single-stage eschatology centered in a conception of "resurrection in death."[69] Greshake's biblical study led him to understand "to depart and be with Christ" (Phil. 1:23) as the realization in the dying Christian of a passage like Christ's in his death and resurrection. One dies and rises into the new *aiōn*. God, the Lord of life (Rom. 4:17, 24), provides the spiritual body that lives in communion with Christ Risen.[70] Greshake claims that Benedict XII's 1336 Constitution favors his view, since its central intention, he argued, was to affirm the immediate completion of salvation with death.[71] Greshake wonders if belief in a general resurrection and "end of the world" are part of the rule of faith. If so, they could be integrated with his outlook, but only as a completion of what has already been occurring.[72]

55. Greshake's ideas had their supporters[73] and their critics.[74] Particularly incisive criticism came from Joseph Ratzinger. In the 1977 edition of *Eschatologie—Tod und ewiges Leben*, Ratzinger offered his own dialogical account of the human soul[75] and leveled a series of

---

[69] Gisbert Greshake, *Auferstehung der Toten. Ein Beitrag auf eine theologische Diskussion über die Zukunft der Geschichte* (Essen: Ludgerus, 1969), 388, a dissertation directed by Walter Kasper, which came out in the interval between the first edition of the Dutch Catechism and the corrective Supplement of 1970. Volker Busch has studied Greshake's extensive work on this topic in *In Gottes Gemeinschaft vollendet. Die Konzeption einer "Auferstehung im Tod" in der Theologie Gispert Greshakes* (Mainz: M. Grünewald, 2001).

[70] Greshake, *Auferstehung der Toten*, 257–261, 296–304, and 349–357, with the last section including a creative adoption of "dialogical immortality" from J. Ratzinger.

[71] Greshake, *Auferstehung der Toten*, 368–370.

[72] Greshake, *Auferstehung der Toten*, 399–410.

[73] See, e.g., Medard Kehl, *Dein Reich komme. Eschatologie als Rechenschaft über unsere Hoffnung,* 3rd ed. (Kevalaer: Topos, 2003), 275–279; Dermot Lane, *Keeing Hope Alive. Stirrings in Christian Theology* (Eugene, Oreg.: Wipf & Stock, n.d.; reprint, Paulist Press, 1996), 150–162.

[74] See, e.g., Juan Alfaro, S.J., "'La resurrección de los muertos' en la discussion teológica sobre el provenir de la historia," *Gregorianum* 52 (1971): 537–554; Gustave Martelet, *L'au-delà retrouvé. Christologie des fins dernières* (Paris: Desclée, 1975), 166, especially n. 2; Wolfhart Pannenberg, *Systematic Theology* (Grand Rapids, Mich.: Eerdmans, 1998; original 1993), 3:550–580.

[75] Ratzinger laid a basis in arguing with Oscar Cullmann and Otto Karrer, first, that graced life is lived now and after death *in* the indestructible life of Christ Risen and, second, that Christian faith transformed the notion of "soul" by the dynamic of dialogue with the God of the living. In passing he noted the strangeness of saying that one whose body is buried has already risen. See "Jenseits des Todes," *Internationale katholische Zeitschrift Communio,* 1 (1972): 232–244.

arguments against Greshake's proposal.[76] In later Appendices, Ratzinger criticized the Greshake thesis for manipulating resurrection language in a ghetto of academic theory that is far from ordinary faith and preaching.[77] Positively, resurrection for Ratzinger "comes only 'at the end of days' and will be the full breaking in of God's Lordship over the world."[78]

56. The Congregation of the Doctrine of the Faith, under Cardinal Franjo Šeper, laid down clear markers for Catholic discussion of the intermediate state in a Letter to the bishops of the world, issued May 11, 1979.[79] The Letter's motive was that some discussions were upsetting believers concerning the soul, life after death, and the interval before the general resurrection.

57. Of the Letter's seven main affirmations, no. 3 affirms as Catholic teaching "that a spiritual element survives and subsists after death, an element endowed with consciousness and will, so that the 'human self' subsists." There is no valid reason for not speaking of "the soul" to designate this element of the person. According to no. 5 of the Letter, the church looks for "the glorious manifestation of our Lord, Jesus Christ,"[80] which will be distinct and deferred from the state of souls immediately after death.

58. After laying down its specific doctrinal reminders, the Letter admits that we do not have from Scripture "a proper picture" of life after death. But Christians should hold firmly to two essential points, with which this section can conclude.

---

[76] Ratzinger, *Eschatology*, 109 (Greshake leaves created matter minimally sharing in final perfection); and 179 (Greshake is far from Thomas on the soul's essential ordination to the body). See also 188-189 and 192-193 (Final salvation has to include "a new earth" and Christ's return). Greshake responded vigorously to Ratzinger's book in *Theologische Revue* 74 (1978): 481–483.

[77] Ratzinger, *Eschatology*, 253–254. See also *Eschatology*, 266, with note 16 (Greshake came to admit the value of speaking of "soul," while still holding his main thesis) and 267 with note 17 ("It is wrong to speak of the soul as reaching its fulfillment in the moment of death").

[78] Ratzinger, *Eschatology*, 246, in a section on the 1979 intervention of the Congregation of the Doctrine of the Faith on eschatology.

[79] *Origins* 9 (1979): 131–133, and J. Neuner and J. Dupuis, *The Christian Faith in the Doctrinal Documents of the Catholic Church*, no. 2317, 1025–1027; original Latin text in *Acta Apostolicae Sedis* 71 (1979): 939–943.

[80] *Dei verbum [Dogmatic Constitution on Divine Revelation]*, 18 November 1965, §4. Cited in this section of *Dei verbum* are 1 Timothy 6:14 and Titus 2:13.

On the one hand they must believe in the fundamental continuity, thanks to the power of the Holy Spirit, between our present life in Christ and the future life . . . ; on the other hand they must be clearly aware of the radical break between the present life and the future one, due to the fact that the economy of faith will be replaced by the economy of the fullness of life. We shall be with Christ and "we shall see God" (1 John 3:2), and it is in these promises and marvelous mysteries that our hope essentially consists. Our imagination may be incapable of reaching these heights, but our heart does so instinctively and completely.[81]

3. Common Affirmations

59.   Our churches affirm that death cannot destroy the communion with God of those redeemed and justified. The nature of the life that the justified departed share with God cannot be described in great detail and in this life remains a great mystery. Nevertheless, Lutherans and Catholics share the sure and certain hope that the justified departed are "in Christ" and enjoy the rest that belongs to those who have run the race. As Hebrews reminds us, "Do not lose your confidence, which has a great reward" (Heb. 10:35).

60.   Our churches thus teach an ongoing personal existence beyond death, to which our divine Creator relates in saving love. This affirmation of a central aspect of our hope of eternal life is grounded in the witness of Scripture and the consensus of our authoritative traditions. This dialogue finds the understanding of a dialogical immortality that has been developed in both our traditions to be especially valuable. Those with pastoral responsibilities in our churches would do well to draw on such accounts of life in Christ that transcends bodily death when they minister to those facing death and to the grieving left behind.

61. Catholic doctrine on 1) the soul, 2) its immortality, and 3) the beatific vision prior to the general resurrection is more elaborated than

---

[81] *Origins* 9 (1979): 133. Going beyond the often terse prose of the Letter from the Congregation for the Doctrine of the Faith, the International Theological Commission offered in 1992 a fuller text, "On Certain Questions of Eschatology," published in *Irish Theological Quarterly* 58 (1992): 209–243, and in International Theological Commission, *Texts and Documents 1986-2007*, Michael Sharkey and Thomas Weinandy, eds. (San Francisco: Ignatius, 2009), 55–93. At this time Cardinal Joseph Ratzinger was president of the International Theological Commission, while Candido Pozo, S.J., led the sub-commission of nine commission members who prepared the text.

what is found in the Lutheran Confessions on these subjects. Since these teachings were not disputed in the Lutheran Reformation and not denied in the Confessions, **this dialogue finds that, in the light of the convergence shown above, official teaching on these three subjects is not church-dividing.**

C. Judgment

62.   Christian hope has always been a hope for the reign of God's justice. Isaiah says of the Lord's servant: "He will bring forth justice to the nations" (Isa. 42:1). The restitution of justice, however, involves judgment, both on humanity as a whole and on individuals. What we have been and done will come to light.

63.   All judgment, whether a yearly performance appraisal or the final judgment before the throne of God, inevitably carries with it anxiety. Hebrews speaks of "a fearful prospect of judgment" for those who "willfully persist in sin" (Heb. 10:26f). Some artistic portrayals of the last judgment easily elicit fear. For those who are in Christ, however, judgment, while sobering, is also hopeful for we know that the one who will judge us is the one who has given up his life for us on the cross. Our judge is also our advocate (1 John 2:1).

1. Judgment of Works

a. Biblical

64.   That God judges humans on the basis of their works in their earthly lives is an affirmation that we find throughout the Scriptures. From the beginning of their existence humans stand before God "naked," unable to hide from him the truth about their lives and their works (Gen. 3:7, 10-11; Heb. 4:12-13). In his law God makes clear that he punishes the guilty and rewards the righteous (e.g., Lev. 26). The prophets of Israel spoke of the coming day of the Lord, on which God would execute judgment against sinners (Isa. 13:11; Ezek. 30:3; Joel 2:1-2; Amos 5:18; Zeph. 1:14-18).

65.   The New Testament teaching of salvation through faith in Jesus Christ puts the matter of judgment in a new light, but it does not undermine the Scriptural affirmation of a final judgment. On the contrary, the New Testament consistently underlines the seriousness with which the faithful must face a final accounting of their lives before God. According to the synoptic gospels Jesus called his closest disciples to commit their lives fully to him, and he did so in such a way that ultimate things were seen to be at stake in their decision. Confession or denial of Jesus before others is said to determine one's own judgment before God (Matt. 10:32-33 and Luke 12:8-9). Moreover, according to the Gospel of Matthew, Jesus taught that humans will be judged for the deeds that they have done, with corresponding rewards and punishments (Matt. 16:27), and especially for the way that they have treated other people (Matt. 25:31-46). We are admonished to live our lives knowing that God will judge us as we have judged others (Matt. 6:14-15; 7:2; 18:23-35). While the overwhelming emphasis in the Gospel of John is on faith in Jesus Christ as *the* "work" of the Christian *par excellence* (John 6:29; cf. 6:40) and on the judgment that has *already* been passed on the world as a result of its response to Jesus (John 3:18-19; 5:24), even here a future judgment according to works in the proper sense is not excluded (John 5:29).

66. The apostle Paul apparently saw no contradiction between justification by grace through faith and judgment according to works. God sees the truth about us and will not be mocked (Gal. 6:7). Paul was well aware of the coming judgment of God (Rom. 2:6-7) and of God's wrath that would be unleashed at the end of time against evildoers (Rom. 2:5, 8; cf. also 5:9; 1 Thess. 1:10). Moreover, the deeds that we do will receive their recompense from Christ himself: "All of us must appear before the judgment seat of Christ, so that each may receive recompense for what has been done in the body, whether good or evil" (2 Cor. 5:10; cf. Rom. 14:10; 2 Cor. 11:15). On the principle that "a person reaps what he [or she] sows," Paul can even say that the one who sows to the flesh will reap corruption from the flesh, while the one who sows to the Spirit will reap eternal life from the Spirit (Gal. 6:7-8). The way that one lives in this world has eternal significance. How Paul understood the relationship between judgment according to works and justification by grace through faith will be treated below.

67. James admonishes his readers that they should "so speak and so act as those who are to be judged by the law of liberty" (James 2:12). He grounds this statement with the words, "for judgment will be without mercy to anyone who has shown no mercy" (James 2:13), echoing the teaching of Jesus that those who show mercy will receive mercy from God, while those who show no mercy cannot expect to receive mercy from God (Matt. 5:7; 18:23-35; cf. 6:14-15). In general, the focus of James on hearing and doing (1:25), on perfection (1:25), and on the commandment of love of neighbor (2:8), as well as the content of the letter as a whole, are highly reminiscent of Jesus' teaching in the Sermon on the Mount and suggest that for James the "law" by which Christians will be judged is essentially the ethical teaching of Jesus himself, or the ethical teaching of the Gospel, understood as a kind of new law, but especially the law of love.[82]

68.   The New Testament contains numerous other references to final judgment that do not require lengthy discussion here (Acts 10:42; 2 Tim. 4:1; Heb. 10:25, 27, 30; 13:4; 1 Pet. 1:17; 2:12; 4:5; 2 Pet. 2:4, 9; 3:7; 1 John 4:17; Rev. 20:12-13). This brief biblical survey is enough to show, however, that the significance of the earthly life for final judgment is a consistent biblical theme, from beginning to end.

b. Doctrinal

1. Lutheran

69.   *The Book of Concord* includes "the three chief creeds," all of which speak of Christ coming as judge. The Apostles' Creed states, "He is seated at the right hand of God, the Father Almighty. From where he will come to judge the living and the dead."[83] The Nicene-Constantinopolitan Creed expands the statement to say, "He is coming again in glory to judge the living and the dead. There will be no end to his kingdom."[84] The creed attributed to St. Athanasius implies that Christ's judgment will assess and recompense human actions or works: "He will come to judge the living and the dead. At his coming all human beings will rise with their bodies and will give an account of their own deeds. Those who have done good things will enter into eternal life, and those who have done evil things into eternal fire."[85]

70.   The principal Lutheran doctrinal text, the Augsburg Confession of 1530, affirms Christ's return as judge both in its primary Christological article[86] and its only article on eschatology: "Our Lord Jesus Christ will return on the Last Day to judge, to raise all the dead, to give eternal life and eternal joy to those who believe and are elect, but to

---

[82] See Martin Dibelius and Heinrich Greeven, *James: A Commentary on the Epistle of James*, trans. M.A. Williams and ed. H. Koester (Philadelphia: Fortress Press, 1976), 119–120; and Franz Mussner, *Der Jakobusbrief* (Freiburg: Herder, 1964), 109, 126.

[83] *Book of Concord*, 22.

[84] *Book of Concord*, 23.

[85] *Book of Concord*, 25.

[86] Augsburg Confession, Article III, *Book of Concord*, 38.

condemn the ungodly and the devils to hell and eternal punishment."[87] The *Confutatio*, the response of the Catholic theologians at Augsburg to the Confession, found nothing objectionable in these articles.[88]

71. Luther's Small Catechism (1529) states that the Risen Christ "rules eternally," but his return as judge is not mentioned.[89] The Large Catechism (also 1529) treats Christ's saving lordship as both present dominion and final act of division: "The devil and all his powers must be subject to him and lie beneath his feet until finally, at the Last Day, he will completely divide and separate us from the wicked world, the devil, death, sin, etc."[90]

72. Melanchthon's ample Article IV in the Apology implies that judgment will connect the earthly living of the righteous with their eschatological state. What one suffers and does in this life is "meritorious for other bodily and spiritual rewards, which are bestowed in this life and the life to come." In dealing with the saints, "God defers most rewards until he glorifies saints after this life. . . . And these rewards produce degrees of return, according to that passage in Paul [1 Cor. 3:8], 'Each will receive wages according to the labor of each.' These degrees are rewards for works and afflictions."[91]

73. Later Lutherans consistently affirmed judgment according to each person's actions. Since Christ is the "searcher of hearts," he will pass

---

[87] Augsburg Confession, Article XVII, *Book of Concord*, 50. Gunther Wenz comments that Articles III and XVII form a frame around the intervening articles on justification, ministry, church, and sacraments. By them, the saving process is unfolding that will climax in the definitive coming of God's reign with Christ made manifest in his glory as judge of the living and dead; see Gunther Wenz, *Theologie der Bekenntnisschriften der evangelisch-lutherischen Kirche* (Berlin, 1996), 1:575–576.

[88] "The Confutation of the Augsburg Confession," trans. Mark D. Tranvik, *Sources and Contexts of the Book of Concord*, Robert Kolb and James A. Nestingen, eds. (Minneapolis: Fortress Press, 2001), 108, 116; original in *Die Confutatio der Confessio Augustana vom 3. August 1530*, Herbert Immenkötter, ed., Corpus Catholicorum, 33 (Münster, 1979), 82–83 and 116–117.

[89] Small Catechism, *Book of Concord*, 355. Albrecht Peters, in his commentary, claims that Christ's return to judge is only "faintly discernible" (*klingt lediglich an*) in the text. Peters argues Luther's omission is due to his rejection of a medieval tradition on the creed that contrasted present grace with coming strictness of judgment. See *Kommentar zu Luthers Katechismen*, vol. 2, *Der Glaube—Das Apostolikum,* Gottfried Seebaß, ed. (Göttingen, 1991), 166–170.

[90] Large Catechism, *Book of Concord*, 435.

[91] Apology, Article IV, *Book of Concord*, 171.

judgment on "every secret word, deed, thought, desire, and purpose" of all persons.[92] With some variation on details, theologians generally agreed that works will be judged by their grounding in faith. Works that proceed from faith are approved for eternal life; those that proceed from unbelief lead to condemnation.[93]

74. Recent Lutheran official statements consistently affirm a judgment of works. Emphasis tends to fall on judgment as a final and definitive bringing to light of the quality of our lives. Faith will be manifest in how one lives.[94] This judgment underlines the need to take this life seriously. The message of judgment, however, is good news. One is freed from one's own judgment and the judgment of the persons who surround us when we know that Christ will render the decisive judgment on who we are and what we have done.[95] In addition, such judgment is part of the triumph of love and justice.[96]

2. Catholic

75. Catholic theology affirmed the same creedal texts as Lutherans. Medieval statements of faith briefly expanded on judgment. The decree "On the Catholic Faith" of the Fourth Lateran Council (1215) states that all will "receive according to their deserts, whether these be good or bad."[97]

76. The Council of Trent spoke of God's judgment of human beings in Chapter 7 of the *Decree on Justification* (1547). Righteousness granted through Jesus Christ is the garment that those reborn in baptism must

---

[92] Matthew Hafenreffer, cited in Schmidt, *Doctrinal Theology,* 655.

[93] "Therefore, faith must be the mother and the source of those truly good and God-pleasing works, which God wants to reward in this world and the next." Formula of Concord (1577), Solid Declaration, Article IV, §9, *Book of Concord,* 576. See also the references in Schmidt, *Doctrinal Theology,* 654–655; Leonhard Hutter, *Compendium,* 233; Christoph Ernst Luthardt, *Kompendium der Dogmatik,* 4th ed. (Leipzig: Dörffling und Franke, 1873), 313.

[94] *Evangelische Erwachsenenkatechismus,* 885; *Evangelical Catechism,* 390-391; *Unsere Hoffnung,* 87.

[95] *Evangelische Erwachsenenkatechismus,* 886; *Evangelische Gemeindekatechismus,* 411.

[96] *Evangelische Erwachsenenkatechismus,* 886; *Unsere Hoffnung,* 78, 88.

[97] Denzinger and Schönmetzer, no. 801; see also the Bull of Union with the Armenians of the Council of Florence, in Norman P. Tanner, ed., *Decrees of the Ecumenical Councils* (London: Sheed & Ward, 1990), 1:552.

bring unspotted before the judgment seat of Jesus Christ, so they may have eternal life.[98]

77.   The same Decree speaks of the reward of good works in Chapter 11, saying that good works of observing the commandments are required from the justified and possible for them with the help God gives them, as implied by New Testament exhortations (e.g., John 14:23; Rom. 6:22; Titus 2:12; 1 Cor. 9:24.26-27; 2 Pet. 1:10). God's reward for good works can rightly have a motivational value.[99] Trent anathematizes anyone who "says that the just ought not, in return for good works wrought in God, to expect and hope for an eternal reward from God through his mercy and the merit of Jesus Christ, if by acting rightly and keeping the divine commandments they persevere to the end."[100]

78.   Good works leading to eternal life are not accomplished independent of Christ and his grace. They depend on the predisposing, accompanying, and confirming influence of Christ as the members depend on the head and branches on the vine. Only within such dependence are Christians empowered to perform works that are meritorious and pleasing to God. These are deeds "done in God" (John 3:21), out of a righteousness not coming from us (2 Cor. 3:5), but imparted by God through Christ's merit. For the Lord gives water that in the righteous "will become a spring . . . gushing up to eternal life" (John 4:14).[101]

79.   Chapter 16 of the *Decree* completes its teaching on good works and merit with a warning against neglecting God's coming judgment on each person's life.

> No Christian should ever either rely on or glory in himself and not in the Lord (see 1 Cor. 1:31; 2 Cor 10:17), whose good-ness towards all is so great that he desires his own gifts to be

---

[98] Tanner, *Decrees of the Ecumenical Councils*, 2:674. Subsequent citations from the Councils of Trent and Vatican II will be referenced from Tanner in the text, but modified to indicate biblical sources in parentheses, not in footnotes as in Tanner. The mandate mentioned here in the *Decree on Justification* is part of the rite of baptism according to the Roman Ritual, just before those baptized are clothed with a white garment. See *The Rites of the Catholic Church* (New York: Pueblo, 1991), 102 (for baptism of adults). In the Ritual, children are to bring, with the help of family and friends, the dignity symbolized by the garment "unstained into the everlasting life of heaven" (209).

[99] Tanner, 2:676.

[100] Tanner, 2:680.

[101] Tanner, 2:678.

their merits.[102] And because "we all make many mistakes" (James 3:2), each of us ought to keep before his eyes the severity and judgment as much as the mercy and goodness; and even if one is not aware of anything in himself, a person ought not to pronounce judgment on himself (see 1 Cor. 4:3-4), for our whole life must be examined and judged not by our judgment but by that of God, "who will bring to light the things now hidden in darkness and disclose the purposes of the heart; then everyone will receive his commendation from God" (1 Cor. 4:5), who, as it is written, "will render to everyone according to his works" (Matt. 16:27; Rom. 2:6; Rev. 22:12).[103]

80. Contemporary Catholic teaching on judgment is found in the documents of the Second Vatican Council (1962-65) and the *Catechism of the Catholic Church* (1994), which integrates Vatican II into the broader Catholic tradition.[104]

81. Vatican II's Pastoral Constitution on the Church in the Modern World, in treating human dignity, speaks of us as free and responsible persons who are accountable for what we do with God's gifts. "Everyone will appear before Christ to be recompensed for the good or evil that he or she has done (cf. 2 Cor. 5:10)."[105]

82. The *Catechism of the Catholic Church* teaches that Jesus announces judgment on the Last Day, as did the prophets and John the Baptist before him (cf. Dan. 7:10; Joel 3-4; Mal. 3:19; Matt. 3:7-12). Condemnation awaits those who culpably count the offer of God's grace as nothing (cf.

---

[102] Trent makes its own an Augustinian phrase from Ch. 9 of the *Indiculus*, compiled in the early 430s, most likely by Prosper of Aquitaine, against the semi-pelagians of southern Gaul. "Tanta enim est erga omnes homines bonitas Dei, ut nostra velit esse merita quae sunt ipsius dona, et pro iis, quae largitus est, aeterna praemia sit donaturus [So great is God's goodness toward all humans that what are his own gifts he wants to be also our merits and that for gifts he has given he is going to grant eternal rewards]." Denzinger and Schönmetzer, 248. For the original context, see Augustine's Letter 194, of 418 to the presbyter Sixtus of Rome in *Letters 156-210*, The Works of Saint Augustine (Hyde Park, N.Y.: New City Press, 2004), II/3:296.

[103] Tanner, 2:678.

[104] *Catechism of the Catholic Church*, 2nd ed. (Washington, D.C.: USCC Publishing Services, 2000). Subsequent reference herein are noted by paragraph numbers.

[105] *Gaudium et spes [Pastoral Constitution on the Church in the Modern World]*, 7 December 1965, 17; Tanner, 1078. Similarly, *Lumen gentium [Dogmatic Constitution on the Church]*, 21 November 1964, 48; cited hereinafter as *Lumen gentium* with section numbers; Tanner, 2:888.

Matt. 11:20-24, 12:41-42), while our attitude to our neighbor will disclose our acceptance or refusal of God's love and grace. Jesus will say, "As you did it to one of the least of these, you did it to me" (Matt. 25:40). Still, the Son did not come to judge, but to save. But "by rejecting grace in this life, one already judges oneself, receives according to one's works, and can even condemn oneself for all eternity by rejecting the Spirit of love" (cf. John 3:18, 12:48; Matt. 12:32; 1 Cor. 3:12-15; Heb. 6:4-6, 10:26-31).[106]

83. Pope Benedict XVI's encyclical on Christian hope speaks of judgment from another perspective, that of correcting history's injustices and creating justice in ways we cannot conceive:

> There is justice. There is an "undoing" of past suffering, a reparation that sets things aright. For this reason, faith in the Last Judgment is first and foremost hope—the need for which was made abundantly clear in the upheavals of recent centuries.[107]

2. Particular and General Judgment

84. If, as the Bible depicts, a general judgment will occur at Christ's return, and if, as our churches teach, persons enter some form of heaven or hell after death, prior to Christ's return, a theological question arises about the interrelation between the *general* judgment of all humanity on the Last Day and the *particular* judgment of individuals upon their death. This has never been a church-dividing matter between our churches, but does affect issues that have been disputed, e.g., purgatory.

a. Biblical

85. New Testament texts point to both a particular judgment upon the death of an individual and a general judgment of all of humanity at the end of history. The co-existence of the two kinds of judgment is not unique to Christianity; it already existed in Judaism of the pre-Christian era. In Judaism the idea of particular judgment developed out of notions of post-mortem recompense (e.g., 1 Enoch 22), while belief in a general judgment developed out of Jewish eschatology and apocalypticism (particularly belief in resurrection of the dead) (e.g., Dan. 12:2), as well as Jewish messianism. We do not discuss here the many New Testament texts dealing with general judgment.[108] We only note that the general judgment in the New Testament is usually connected with the glorious manifestation of Christ (*parousia*) and the resurrection of the dead. The

---

[106] *Catechism of the Catholic Church*, nos. 678-679.

[107] *Spe salvi*, ¶43.

[108] Among those texts are: Acts 10:42; 2 Tim. 4:1; Heb. 10:25, 27, 30; 13:4; 1 Pet. 1:17; 2:12; 4:5; 2 Pet. 2:4, 9; 3:7; 1 John 4:17; Rev. 20:12-13.

resurrection can be understood either as a resurrection of all the dead, whereupon the righteous are given eternal life and the wicked are condemned to punishment (e.g., John 5:28-29; Acts 24:15; Rev. 20:11-15), or as a resurrection of the righteous only (Luke 14:14; 1 Thess. 4:16).

86.   Perhaps the clearest New Testament witness to a particular judgment distinguishable from the general judgment is the book of Revelation. In Revelation 6:9 the seer reports that he "saw under the altar the souls of those who had been slaughtered for the word of God and for the testimony that they had given." The fact that these martyrs are under the heavenly altar and that they are given white robes (Rev. 6:11) suggests that they have been judged worthy to be with God (cf. Rev. 3:4) and are in the presence of God. These souls look forward, however, to a later, more comprehensive judgment: "Sovereign Lord, holy and true, how long will it be before you judge and avenge our blood on the inhabitants of the earth?" Having been given the white robes, they are told to rest a little while longer until the full number of martyrs is complete. Their final judgment comes at the resurrection (Rev. 20:4-6).

87.   Paul looks forward to a union with Christ beyond death that suggests some form of particular judgment. Paul's confidence that, should he die, he will "be with Christ" (Phil. 1:23) implies a judgment on him and his faith, namely, that he is acceptable to the Lord. Similarly, in 2 Corinthians 5:8, Paul expresses his desire to be away from the body and at home with the Lord. Paul's belief in an immediate, post-mortem union with Christ, however, did not diminish his eschatological expectation of the return of Christ and of a final, general judgment (2 Cor. 5:10; Phil. 3:20-21). We may gather from Philippians 1:23-24 and 3:20-21 as well as 2 Corinthians 5:1-10 Paul's conviction that those who die in Christ before the *parousia* depart to be with Christ, even as they await the fullness of salvation that comes with the resurrection of the dead. 2 Corinthians 5:10 shows that the body remains constitutive of the self for the final judgment.

88.   The fact that Paul and the author of Revelation were able to hold both convictions together—immediate, post-mortem presence with God or Christ; and resurrection of the dead and general judgment at the end of time—should warn us against making of these two convictions false alternatives. Both convictions are biblical, and both convictions can be held with integrity.[109]

---

[109] Note also two other texts. In Luke 16:19-31, Lazarus and the rich man are depicted as going to the bosom of Abraham and to Hades respectively, apparently immediately upon their deaths. In their respective places they receive immediate recompense for their earthly lives. In Luke 23:43, Jesus tells the repentant criminal, "Today you will be with me in Paradise." These texts seem to depict a particular judgment, but the relationship to the general judgment is not clear.

b. Doctrinal

1. Lutheran

89. The Augsburg Confession does not speak of a particular judgment of each person immediately following death. Articles III and XVII refer to the general judgment on human beings carried out by Christ when he returns on the Last Day. In speaking of the saints, it presupposes that the saints are in heaven and so have already, before Christ's return, undergone judgment.[110]

90. Later Lutheran theologians consistently and explicitly taught a judgment immediately at death. The judged shall pass, then, directly to heaven or hell. The later, general judgment will publically manifest to good and evil alike both the justice of God and the vindication of the saints. In addition, only after the historical effects of our works have had a chance to run their course through history can they be fully weighed.[111]

91. Theologians differed on whether, prior to the resurrection, the dead entered the fullness of either bliss or damnation.[112] In the nineteenth century, some influential Lutheran theologians taught that humans will enjoy heaven or hell only after Christ returns and judges all of humanity. Samuel S. Schmucker, for example, noted that, in Matthew 25, the Judge says that the righteous are to *enter* the kingdom, not to *return to it*.[113] Hans Martensen, bishop of Sjaelland in the Church of Denmark, thought

---

[110] In its discussion of the invocation of the saints, the Apology to the Augsburg Confession affirms that "concerning the saints we grant that in heaven they pray for the church in general, just as they prayed for the entire church while living." Apology, Article XXI, §9, *Book of Concord*, 238.

[111] Schmidt, *Doctrinal Theology*, 645; Karl Friedrich August Kahnis, *System der lutherischen Dogmatik*, vol. 3 of *Die lutherische Dogmatik historisch-genetisch dargestellt* (Leipzig: Dörffling und Franke, 1868), 572; Theodor Kliefoth, *Christliche Eschatologie* (Leipzig: Dörffling und Franke, 1886), 74–76.

[112] Quenstedt thought that the redeemed enjoy "full and essential" [*plena et essentiali*] happiness immediately following death, but distinguished "the beginning of the plenary perception of ineffable blessings and joys" prior to the resurrection from "the fullest perception will occur after the reunion of body and soul." Gerhard similarly says that the lost, while they enter punishment immediately upon their death, do not receive these punishments "in full measure" [*non plene modo*] until they are reunited with their bodies (cited in Schmidt, *Doctrinal Theology*, 634).

[113] Samuel Simon Schmucker, *Elements of Popular Theology; With Occasional Reference to the Doctrines of the Reformation, as Avowed Before the Diet at Augsburg, in MDXXX.* 5th ed. (Philadelphia: J. S. Miles, 1845), 372.

judgment might be postponed at death for some who might benefit by further time for repentance.[114]

92. The reticence of recent Lutheran church statements to address in detail intermediate states contributes to the tendency to speak of judgment without any differentiation between immediate and final, particular and general judgment. The statements that explicitly affirm an intermediate state[115] do not directly address this question, but their affirmation that the departed either are or are not with Christ implies a particular judgment at death in distinction from the general judgment at the resurrection.

2. Catholic

93. A distinction between a particular judgment immediately at death and a general judgment at the end of history was clearly, if to a degree only implicitly, taught in the affirmation that the souls in heaven see the face of God prior to the resurrection.[116] While the precise language of judgment is not used, a separation is affirmed at death between those destined for hell and those destined for heaven, which would constitute a judgment.

94. The texts of the Council of Trent on judgment of works do not distinguish a particular judgment at death from the general judgment on the Last Day. The existence of the particular judgment is assumed, however, in Trent's several references to purgatory, which presuppose individuals were examined at death and found to be in Christ but still needing further cleansing.[117] Like the Lutheran Confessions, Trent assumes that the saints have been judged and already ushered into eternal happiness in heaven.[118]

---

[114] Hans Martensen, *Christian Dogmatics: A Compendium of the Doctrines of Christianity*, trans. William Urwick (Edinburgh: T. & T. Clark, 1892), 457–459.

[115] The Lutheran Church–Missouri Synod, "A Statement on Death, Resurrection and Immortality: A Position Paper," 1969; Finnish Catechism; UEK *Unsere Hoffnung*.

[116] See *Benedictus Deus*, 1336, discussed above, and the statements on purgatory from the councils of Lyons II (1274) and Florence (1439), discussed below.

[117] *Decree on Justification*, canon 30 (Tanner, 2:681); *Teaching and Canons on the Most Holy Sacrifice of the Mass*, Ch. II (Tanner, 2:734), and *Decree on Purgatory* (Tanner, 2:774). These passages will be examined in section II, E, below on purgation from sin.

[118] Tanner, 2:774–776.

95. *The Catechism of the Council of Trent* later specified that the Creed's article on judgment by Christ unfolds in *two times* of judgment. The "private or particular" judgment occurs at the end of life, when each one comes instantly before God for a scrutiny of all one's deeds, words, or thoughts in the life just ended. At the "universal judgment," everyone will stand together before the Judge, "[so] that in the presence and hearing of all human beings of all times each may know his final doom and sentence" through an announcement bringing pain to the wicked and consolation to the just.[119]

96. The *Catechism* of Trent presents arguments of fittingness (*rationes convenientiae*) for the general judgment in addition to each one's particular judgment.[120] Judgment at the end will show the good or bad influences that persons' actions have had over time on others and the world. For the virtuous, misrepresentations they endured in the world will be set right, with undeserved good reputations gained by sinners unmasked before all. All will grasp that God's providence has governed the world justly and wisely.[121]

97. The *Dogmatic Constitution on the Church* implicitly[122] and *The Catechism of the Catholic Church* more explicitly discuss both the particular and the general judgment. *The Catechism* notes that the New Testament "speaks of judgment primarily in its aspect of the final encounter with Christ in his second coming, but also repeatedly affirms that each will be rewarded immediately after death in accordance with his works and faith."[123] It concludes its teaching on individual judgment by quoting St. John of the Cross: "At the evening of life, we shall be judged on our love."[124]

---

[119] *Catechism of the Council of Trent for Parish Pastors*, trans. John A. McHugh and Charles J. Callan (Rockford, Ill.: TAN Books, 1982), 81.

[120] The *Catechism of the Council of Trent* follows the approach of Thomas Aquinas to the general judgment in his *Scriptum super libros Sententiarum*, IV, Dist. 47, Q. 1, Art. 1, quaestiuncula 1 (Parma edition, VII. 1132a, 1133a), which, after Thomas died, became in the *Summa theologiae, Supplementum*, Q. 88, Art. 1.

[121] *Catechism of the Council of Trent*, 82–83.

[122] *Lumen gentium*, 48–50.

[123] *Catechism of the Catholic Church*, no. 1021.

[124] *Catechism of the Catholic Church*, no. 1022. The *Catechism* references John of the Cross, *Dichos*, no. 64. See *The Collected Works of Saint John of the Cross*, revised edition, Kieran Kavanaugh and Otilio Rodriguez, eds. (Washington, D.C.: Institute of Carmelite Studies, 1991), 90, in "Sayings of Light and Love," no. 60, where the full text reads, "When evening comes, you will be examined in love. Learn to love as God desires to be loved and abandon your own ways of acting."

3. Judgment and Justification

98.   In the context of Catholic-Lutheran dialogue, the topic of the judgment of works should not go by without a brief discussion of how such a judgment relates to our justification by God's grace. If the work of Christ is sufficient for our salvation, then why should our works be judged and how does that judgment relate to our justification?

a. Biblical[125]

99.   For Paul the crucial distinction is not between faith and works abstractly conceived, as though Paul favored the former but opposed the latter. The crucial distinction is between, on the one hand, faith in Christ that alone can justify and the fruits of righteousness that result from it, and, on the other hand, works of the law done in the flesh, without justifying faith, works that cannot and do not justify. The person who lives in the flesh and without the gift of the Spirit is under slavery to sin (Rom. 7:14). A person in slavery to sin cannot please God (Rom. 8:8), because such a person is in rebellion against God (Rom. 7:22-23). In Paul's view, all of humanity outside of Christ is in this condition of slavery to sin (Rom. 3:9; Gal. 3:22); therefore no one can be justified on the basis of his or her works (Rom. 3:20). Because humans are enslaved to sin and cannot justify themselves before God, God in his own righteousness justifies the ungodly freely. He reckons righteousness to sinners as a gift, effective through faith (Rom. 3:23-26; 4:5; 5:17; Phil. 3:9). He declares sinners righteous for Christ's sake (Rom. 4:24-25).

100.   Justification, God's free act of reckoning righteousness to sinners on the basis of faith, sets the justified in a new, reconciled relationship to God (Rom. 5:1-11; 2 Cor. 5:18-19), calls forth a new creature (2 Cor. 5:17), and frees the justified from bondage to sin (Rom. 6:7). The justified, thus liberated from sin, are put on a path of producing the "fruit of righteousness" through Jesus Christ that will stand to God's glory on the last day (Rom. 6:19-22; Phil. 1:11). Paul speaks of the goal of such transformed existence in terms of wholeness, blamelessness, and completeness at the day of Jesus Christ (1 Cor. 1:8; Phil. 1:6, 10; 1 Thess.

---

[125] For an overview of ways that scholars have dealt with "judgment by works and justification by faith" in Paul, see "Rewards, But in a Very Different Sense" by Joseph A. Burgess from an earlier round of this dialogue in *Justification by Faith: Lutherans and Catholics in Dialogue VII*, H. George Anderson, T. Austin Murphy, and Joseph Burgess, eds. (Minneapolis: Augsburg, 1985), 98-100. The present treatment seeks to go beyond Burgess, who—though he correctly notes (p. 104) that for Paul eternal rewards are always a gift—does not connect in a meaningful way works and reward in Paul's theology.

3:13; 5:23). A judgment of the works of the justified remains for the end.[126]

101. According to Paul, the final judgment takes the form of recompense for deeds done in the body, whether good or evil (2 Cor. 5:10). Paul can even speak of eternal life as recompense for works done in this life (Rom. 2:6-7). Statements such as these are sometimes regarded as standing in unresolved contradiction with Paul's teaching on justification by grace through faith. Yet Paul himself finds no contradiction. Paul regards rewards for good deeds and punishments for evil deeds not only as a matter of divine justice and recompense, but also as constituting the *inherent* outcome of life lived according to the flesh or according to the Spirit of God, as we can see from Galatians 6:7-8.[127] The ultimate outcome ("harvest") of life lived towards sin is death, while the ultimate outcome ("harvest") of life lived towards the Spirit is eternal life. Put another way, the fruits of the Spirit have eternal life as their ultimate outcome (*telos*), while the works of the flesh have death as their ultimate outcome (Rom. 6:20-23). Thus the work (or fruit) produced by a person in his or her life, good or evil, stands in continuity with his or her final destiny, be that final death or eternal life. The recompense that each person receives for his or her deeds at the final judgment (2 Cor. 5:10) is precisely the enduring outcome of the life lived towards the flesh or towards the Spirit. Those who live by faith and in the Spirit can look forward to eternal life as the ultimate outcome of their lives (Rom. 6:22-23; Gal. 6:8). Those who live willfully towards the flesh, however, face the possibility of eternal loss as the ultimate outcome of their lives (Gal. 6:8).

---

[126] Some scholars describe God's declarative act of justification as "forensic justification" and the effects of such justification in the justified as "effective justification." See *Justification by Faith: Lutherans and Catholics in Dialogue VII*, 71 (§156). See further Karl Kertelge, *"Rechtfertigung" bei Paulus: Studien zur Struktur und zum Bedeutungsgehalt des paulinischen Rechtfertigungsbegriffs* (Münster: Aschendorff, 1967), 112-128 and 158-159; and his contribution, "Rechtfertigung aus Glauben und Gericht nach den Werken bei Paulus," *Lehrverurteilungen – kirchentrennend? II: Materialen zu den Lehrverurteilungen und zur Theologie der Rechtfertigung*, K. Lehmann, ed. (Freiburg: Herder/Göttingen: Vandenhoeck & Ruprecht, 1989), 173–190.

[127] Jerome D. Quinn, "The Scriptures on Merit," *Justification by Faith: Lutherans and Catholics in Dialogue VII*, 84, puts it this way: "A critical presupposition of the scriptural authors as they discuss recompense is their conviction of the unitary, integral character of human action. The purposeful, internal conception of an activity; the external implementation of that intent; and the effects produced—all are conceived of as a whole with an inner coherence and interdependence that does not permit one really to separate intention, activity, and effects.... In this problematic, retribution must somehow inhere in the activity itself."

102. The good works of the justified do not form, however, the foundation for final salvation. It is Christ alone who is the foundation for salvation. Thus elsewhere Paul can state that one who has done bad works (in this case, a Christian evangelist) will still be saved because he has Christ as his foundation (1 Cor. 3:10-15). Rewards and punishments are the enduring outcome of one's works, whether good or bad (1 Cor. 3:14-15). Paul can speak of such fruits of the Spirit as faith and love as enduring (1 Cor. 13:13), which suggests that the rewards for life lived towards the Spirit are, in a certain sense, inherent to the fruits of the Spirit themselves. It is in this sense that eternal life can be regarded as the ultimate harvest (outcome) of life lived towards the Spirit (Gal. 6:8). It may never be forgotten, however, that within this framework eternal life always remains God's gift (Rom. 6:23).

b. Doctrinal

1. Lutheran

103. Within the Lutheran Confessions, the Apology explains biblical texts on God rewarding good works (Rom. 2:6; John 5:29; Matt. 25:35) as referring only to works done in Christ, that is, by the justified.[128] This exclusiveness rests on what Article II of the Augsburg Confession says about original sin: All human beings are, from birth, "full of evil lust and inclination and cannot by nature possess true fear of God and true faith in God."[129] Without such faith, good works pleasing to God are impossible.[130]

104. Justification, the precondition of truly good works, comes "out of grace for Christ's sake through faith when we believe that Christ suffered for us and that for his sake our sin is forgiven and righteousness and eternal life are given to us."[131] Justification produces a "new obedience," for "it is also taught that such faith should yield good fruit and good works and that a person must do such good works as God has commanded for God's sake but not trust in them as if thereby to earn grace before God."[132] Thus, by the word of the gospel, faith in Christ, and the work of the Holy Spirit, a person becomes pleasing to God, relating rightly to God in trust and in works of the Spirit.

---

[128] *Book of Concord*, 171–172.

[129] Augsburg Confession, Article II, §2, *Book of Concord*, 38.

[130] Apology, Article IV, §36, *Book of Concord*, 126.

[131] Augsburg Confession, Article IV, §1-2, *Book of Concord*, 38 and 40.

[132] Augsburg Confession, Article VI, §1, *Book of Concord*, 40.

105. The role of good works in the Christian life and in the Christian's relation to God was a subject of discussion among Lutherans throughout the period in which the Confessions were written. From the earliest confessions (Luther's Catechisms[133]) through the last (the Formula of Concord[134]), the expectation was affirmed that God will reward good works (implying that God will judge our works). The most extensive discussion of the nature of such rewards occurs in the Apology's lengthy Article IV on justification.[135] The Apology states that good works, which can only be performed by those who are in Christ, "are truly meritorious, but not for the forgiveness of sins or justification. For they are not pleasing to [God] except in those who are justified on account of faith."[136] Since justification is a precondition of good works, good works cannot themselves merit justification.[137] While some works are rewarded in this life, most rewards will come only beyond death.[138] Melanchthon, the author of the Apology, is aware that the confessionally controversial

---

[133] "Those who keep God's will and commandment before their eyes, however, have the promise that they will be richly rewarded for all they contribute both to their natural and spiritual fathers, and for the honor they render them. Not that they shall have bread, clothing, and money for a year or two, but long life, sustenance, and peace, and they will be rich and blessed eternally [*ewig reich und selig sein*]." Luther's Large Catechism, I, §164, *Book of Concord*, 409.

[134] "For as it is God's will and express command that the faithful should do good works, which the Holy Spirit effects in the faithful, so God allows these works to please him for Christ's sake and promises a glorious reward for them in this life and in the life to come." Formula of Concord, Solid Declaration, Article IV, §38, *Book of Concord*, 580–581.

[135] This discussion is more extensive and detailed in the September 1531 octavo edition of the Apology that forms the basis for the Kolb and Wengert translation of the *Book of Concord* than the spring 1531 quarto edition used in the earlier Tappert translation. See *The Book of Concord: The Confessions of the Evangelical Lutheran Church*, trans. and ed. Theodore G. Tappert (Philadelphia: Fortress Press, 1959) and in *Die Bekenntnisschriften der evangelisch-lutherischen Kirchen*, 9th ed. (Göttingen: Vandenhoeck & Ruprecht, 1982). For arguments for the use of the later octavo edition, see the Editor's introduction to the Apology, *Book of Concord*, Kolb and Wengert, eds., 107-109, and Christian Peters, *Apologia Confessionis Augustanae: Untersuchungen zur Textgeschichte einer lutherischen Bekenntnisschrift (1530–1584)* (Calwer Theologische Monographien. Stuttgart: Calwer Verlag, 1997). The paragraph numbers cited for other parts of the Confessions do not exist for passages where the octavo edition departs from the quarto edition and so are missing for the passages cited in this paragraph.

[136] Apology, Article IV, *Book of Concord*, 171.

[137] Thomas Aquinas, *Summa theologiae*, I-II, q. 113, a. 8; a. 114, a. 5.

[138] "For God defers most rewards until he glorifies saints after this life, because he wishes them in this life to be strengthened through mortifying the old creature." Apology IV, *Book of Concord*, 171.

question is whether good works merit "eternal life." On the one hand, he is aware of the extensive New Testament references to rewards.[139] On the other, he is deeply suspicious of the conclusions that might be drawn from any assertion that eternal life is merited.[140] He thus argues:

> Scripture calls eternal life a reward, not because it is owed on account of works, but because it compensates for afflictions and works, even though it happens for a completely different reason. Just as an inheritance does not come to a son of a family because he performs the duties of a son, nevertheless, it is a reward and compensation for the duties he performs. Therefore, it is enough that the word "reward" is connected to eternal life because eternal life compensates for good works and afflictions.[141]

This careful statement shows that the Lutheran Confessions consider both justification by grace through faith and God's judgment upon our works as realities taught by Scripture and not in conflict with one another.

106. Later Lutheran theology continued to affirm both justification by grace through faith and a judgment of works. Recent Lutheran church teaching documents have insisted that the judgment of our works does not call into question our justification by grace through faith, but is rather a judgment of the reality of faith in our lives and actions.[142]

2. Catholic

107. In its *Decree on Justification*, the Council of Trent similarly taught that good works that are meritorious before God are possible only for those in Christ, for the justified. "For Jesus Christ himself continually imparts strength to those justified, as the head to the members and the vine to the branches, and this strength always precedes, accompanies and follows their good works, and without it they would be wholly unable to do anything meritorious and pleasing to God."[143] Such works done in

---

[139] Melanchthon cites 1 Corinthians 3:8; Romans 2:6; John 5:29; Matthew 25:35.

[140] "Indeed, if we grant to the opponents that works merit eternal life, the next thing you know they will fabricate absurdities: that works satisfy the law of God, that there is no need for God's mercy, that we are righteous (that is, accepted by God) on account of our works and not on account of Christ, that people are able to do more than the law. In this way, the entire teaching concerning the righteousness of faith will be buried." Apology IV, *Book of Concord*, 172.

[141] Apology, Article IV, *Book of Concord*, 171.

[142] *Evangelische Erwachsenenketechismus*, 886; *Unsere Hoffnung*, 87–88.

[143] Tanner, 2:678; Denzinger and Schönmetzer, 1546.

Christ will be judged and rewarded by God, "whose goodness towards all is so great that he desires his own gifts to be their merits."[144] The Council of Trent did teach, in distinction from the Lutheran Confessions, that "eternal life should be held out, both as a grace promised in his [God's] mercy through Jesus Christ to the children of God, and as a reward to be faithfully bestowed, on the promise of God himself, for their good works and merits."[145] The ecumenical question is the significance of the difference between the Apology's statement that eternal life is a reward in the sense of a recompense and the Council of Trent's statement that eternal life is a merited reward.[146] This dialogue would emphasize that for Trent,[147] as for the Lutheran Confessions, the judgment of works by God does not annul the affirmation that justification is a gift of grace.

3. Common Teaching in the "Joint Declaration on the Doctrine of Justification"

108.   As noted above, the Catholic Church and the churches of the Lutheran World Federation affirm together in the "Joint Declaration on the Doctrine of Justification" that we are accepted by God "not because of any merit on our part" and "receive the Holy Spirit, who renews our hearts while equipping and calling us to good works."[148] In the declaration's discussion of good works, Lutherans and Catholics confess together "that good works—a Christian life lived in faith, hope, and love—follow justification and are its fruits."[149] The respective Catholic and Lutheran paragraphs on good works link merit and reward to God's promise. "When Catholics affirm the 'meritorious' character of good works, they wish to say that, according to the biblical witness, a reward in heaven is promised to these works."[150] The Lutheran paragraph directly addresses the question of eternal life as a reward: "When they [Lutherans] view the good works of Christians as the fruits and signs of justification and not as one's own 'merits', they nevertheless also understand eternal

---

[144] Tanner, 2:678; Denzinger and Schönmetzer, 1548.

[145] Tanner, 2:678; Denzinger and Schönmetzer, 1545. Also Tanner, 2:681; Denzinger and Schönmetzer, 1582.

[146] For a discussion of this significance, see Michael Root, "Aquinas, Merit, and Reformation Theology after the 'Joint Declaration on the Doctrine of Justification,'" *Modern Theology* 20 (2004): 5–22.

[147] Decree on Justification, Ch. 5; Tanner, 2:672; Denzinger and Schönmetzer, 1525.

[148] JDDJ, ¶15.

[149] JDDJ, ¶37.

[150] JDDJ, ¶38.

life in accord with the New Testament as unmerited 'reward' in the sense of the fulfillment of God's promise to the believer."[151] The churches affirmed that these descriptions no longer come under the mutual condemnations of the sixteenth century.

4. Common Affirmations

109.   Catholics and Lutherans affirm together that God, who calls us into a life of communion with him, holds us accountable for our whole lives. The grace we have been given in Christ and the Spirit is not a "talent" to bury, but should become our empowerment for praising God in freedom and contributing to the good of our fellow creatures (cf. Matt. 25:1-14). We also cannot forget that God's gifts to us can be squandered. Each Christian must take seriously Paul's admonition, "Therefore let anyone who thinks that he stands take heed lest he fall" (1 Cor. 10:12, RSV).

110.   The truths that God will judge our lives, that what we have done in the dark will be brought to light, and that we will know as we are known, all affirm both the seriousness of how each of us lives and God's faithfulness to his human creatures. Both our traditions reject "security" in the face of divine judgment, while recalling that from those to whom much has been given, much will be required (cf. Luke 12:48).

111.   Both of our traditions, however, form us to live in joyful confidence and certainty of hope. We know that God's grace is sufficient. God's judgment is one aspect of the comprehensive establishment of God's justice, that is, the very justice that is an essential aspect of our hope. Judgment, as our encounter with God revealing the truth about the lives we have lived, is an important and necessary moment of our entrance into the joy of eternal life and thus should be an object of our hope as well.

112.   Foundational for our hope, however, is that our Judge will be none other than our Savior. **We can entrust the judgment of our lives to the one who died for our trespasses and rose for our justification (cf. Rom. 4:25).**

D. Hell and the Possibility of Eternal Loss

113.   If Scripture is rich in affirmations of eternal life as the hope of humanity and the goal of God's redemptive work, it is equally clear that the goal of eternal life can be missed as a result of human sinfulness. So, for example, the willful rejection of the Word of God is said to make one

---

[151] JDDJ, ¶39.

unworthy of eternal life (Acts 13:46). The opposite of the hope of eternal life we may call the possibility of eternal loss.

1. Biblical

114. Scripture is vivid in its imagery conveying the possibility of eternal loss. The New Testament uses the name Gehenna, usually translated as "hell," to denote a place (or state) of punishment for evil. In the Gospel of Mark, Jesus speaks of Gehenna as a place of "inextinguishable fire" where "their worm never dies" (Mark 9:44, 48). The imagery is drawn from Old Testament texts, such as Isaiah 66:24, that speak of the punishment of the wicked. Numerous other New Testament passages use the symbolism of fire to speak of the punishment that awaits evildoers (Matt. 3:12; 13:42, 50; 25:41; Heb. 10:27; 2 Pet. 3:7; Jude 7; Rev. 19:20; 20:10, 13-14; 21:8).

115. When we turn to the Pauline and Johannine literature, we find further admonitions regarding the possibility of eternal loss. For example, in Romans 2:6-8 Paul warns: God "will repay according to each one's deeds: to those who by patiently doing good seek for glory and honor and immortality, he will give eternal life; while for those who are self-seeking and who obey not the truth but wickedness, there will be wrath and fury." Paul speaks of "enemies of the cross of Christ" whose end is destruction (Phil. 3:18-19) and metaphorically of "objects of wrath that are made for destruction" (Rom. 9:22). The author of 2 Thessalonians 1:9 uses the term "eternal destruction" to speak of the punishment that awaits those who do not obey the gospel. Likewise, John 3:36 sets the one who believes in the Son and who has eternal life in contrast to the one who disobeys the Son, who will not see life; on him the wrath of God remains.

116. The frequent use of fire imagery in the New Testament in connection with the punishment of evildoers raises the question of its theological significance. Since God himself can be called the "consuming fire" (Heb. 12:29), imagery of the punishment of evildoers in fire may be understood to depict not simply the eternal torment that awaits the wicked (Luke 16:23-25, 28; Rev. 20:10), but also eternal confrontation with the judgment of God. If the hope of eternal life means hope for the recovery of unending communion with God, the possibility of hell and eternal loss is the possibility that a human can, through sin, become fully and finally lost to eternal communion with God.

2. Doctrinal

117. The reality of hell was simply assumed throughout much of Christian history. Theologians discussed hell, but there were few doctrinal controversies. The most significant exception was the debate over the heritage of Origen within Eastern Christianity. Origen taught that the punishment for sin, the fires of hell, aimed at rehabilitation and purification, which raised the question whether all persons, including the fallen angels, may at some time be purified and enter blessed glory.[152] Whether or not Origen himself ever systematically taught such an "apocatastasis," a redemption of all things, the idea suggested by his writings is advocated to varying degrees by such theologians as Gregory of Nyssa.[153]

118.   In the mid-sixth century, Origenist teachings about last things were condemned in a series of anathemas that originated with the Emperor Justinian. Explicitly condemned was anyone who taught that "the punishment of the demons and of impious men is temporary, and that it will have an end at some time, or that there will be a restoration (*apokatastasis*) of demons and impious men."[154] The condemnation of such *apokatastasis* was widely affirmed in both East and West and came to be accepted as binding dogma.

119.   As seen in the above discussion of judgment, medieval teaching in the West assumed the possibility that judgment could lead to the damnation of some persons. That hell is eternal for those within it was explicitly taught by the Fourth Lateran Council (1215).[155]

a. Lutheran

120.   The Lutheran Reformers accepted without debate the traditional teaching of hell and the possibility of damnation. The Augsburg Confession asserts in Article XVII that when Christ returns for judgment, along with giving eternal life to elect believers, he will "condemn the ungodly and the devils to hell and eternal punishment."[156] Further,

---

[152] On Origen's views, see Daley, *The Hope of the Early Church*, 56–60.

[153] On Nyssa, see Daley, *The Hope of the Early Church*, 85–87.

[154] Denzinger and Schönmetzer, 411. Just who authorized these condemnations seems unclear. Hünermann, in his introduction to this text in the 37th edition of Denzinger, states that they were "proclaimed" at the Provincial Synod of Constantinople in A.D. 543. Daley, in *The Hope of the Early Church*, believes that it "now seems certain" that they were adopted at the Ecumenical Council in Constantinople in A.D. 553 (190). Tanner, *Decrees*, does not include the anathemas in his edition of the conciliar decrees since he believes that "recent studies have shown that these anathemas cannot be attributed to this council" (pp. 105-106). What is certain is that the anathemas came to be accepted in East and West as authoritative. On their background, see Daley, *The Hope of the Early Church*, 188–190.

[155] Denzinger and Schönmetzer, 801.

[156] Article XVII, §3, *Book of Concord*, 50.

"Rejected, therefore [by the Lutheran estates] are the Anabaptists who teach that the devils and condemned human beings will not suffer eternal torture".[157] Luther held forth hell as a real possibility for unrepentant sinners. In the *Large Catechism* he admonishes parents who do not bring up their children in godliness: "You bring upon yourself sin and wrath, thus earning hell by the way you have reared your children."[158]

121. Post-Reformation Lutheran theologians agreed on the existence of hell, the nature of its punishments, and, with few exceptions, its duration for all eternity. The punishments are both bodily and mental, being felt in different degrees according to the gravity of the person's sins.[159]

122. More recently, the German Lutheran *Evangelischer Erwachsenenkatechismus* understands hell as the self-enclosure of the human person against God, the life of the person who, "since he will receive nothing, rather wishes to live on the basis of himself." In life, this closure against God is never final, but in death it becomes final. Hell is less a divine condemnation than a result of our own decision. To deny hell and affirm universalism would be incompatible with the teaching of Jesus and of the majority of the New Testament.[160]

b. Catholic

123. The Council of Trent spoke once of fear of hell as a motive for imperfect contrition, but offered no account of hell and the punishment of eternal loss.[161] The *Catechism of the Council of Trent*, however, made hell a part of its instruction on two articles of the Apostles' Creed. First, to clarify Christ's descent into hell, the *Catechism* from Trent states that what is properly called "hell" is not the temporary dwelling of the pre-Christian righteous, to which Christ descended, but is instead "that most loathsome and dark prison in which the souls of the damned are tormented with the unclean spirits in eternal and inextinguishable fire."[162]

124. Then, in its account of Christ's return to judge the living and the dead, the *Catechism* dwells on the sentence with which Christ the Judge, according to Matthew 25:41, will condemn the wicked who refused mercy to the needy. Their heaviest punishment comes from being told, "Depart from me," to suffer an eternal pain of loss in banishment from the sight of God. Being relegated to "eternal fire" indicates the sense of

---

[157] Article XVII, §4, *Book of Concord*, 50.

[158] Large Catechism, §176, *Book of Concord*, 410.

[159] See the selections in Schmid, *Doctrinal Theology*, 656–660.

[160] *Evangelischer Erwachsenenkatechismus*, 887.

[161] Tanner, 2:705; Denzinger and Schönmetzer, 1687.

[162] McHugh and Callan, 63.

pain that they will suffer without end. Then, the punishment of hell was "prepared for the devil and his angels," showing that the lost lack kindly companionship since they are forever with wicked demons.[163]

125. The documents of Vatican Council II do not use the word "hell," but the reality is treated in the *Dogmatic Constitution on the Church*, where it inculcates a spirituality of watchfulness, so as to be ready for acquittal by Christ the coming judge "and not be ordered, like the evil and lazy servants (see Matt. 25:26), to go down into the eternal fire (see Matt. 25:41), into the exterior darkness where 'there will be weeping and gnashing of teeth' (Matt. 22:13 and 25:30)."[164]

126. The *Catechism of the Catholic Church* treats hell in a section of the article of the Creed on life everlasting. From the consideration that union with God is incompatible with grave sins against God, our neighbor, or ourselves, it follows that hell is the condition of those who definitively exclude themselves from God and his mercy.

> "He who does not love remains in death. Anyone who hates his brother is a murderer, and you know that no murderer has eternal life abiding in him" [1 John 3:14-15]. Our Lord warns us that we shall be separated from him if we fail to meet the serious needs of the poor and the little ones who are his brethren [Matt. 25:31-46]. To die in mortal sin without repenting and accepting God's merciful love means remaining separated from him for ever by our own free choice. This state of definitive self-exclusion from communion with God and the blessed is called "hell."[165]

> The teaching of the Church affirms the existence of hell and its eternity. Immediately after death the souls of those who die in a state of mortal sin descend into hell, where they suffer the punishments of hell, "eternal fire." The chief punishment of hell is eternal separation from God, in whom alone man can possess the life and happiness for which he was created and for which he longs.[166]

In these recent texts, Lutherans and Catholics alike stress the possibility of hell as the result of a self-imprisoning of sinners in their own independent isolation. The seriousness of sin means that such a possibility cannot be excluded.

---

[163] McHugh and Callan, 85–86.

[164] *Lumen gentium,* 48; Tanner, 2:888.

[165] *Catechism of the Catholic Church*, no. 1033.

[166] *Catechism of the Catholic Church*, no. 1035.

3. Contemporary Discussion of the Possibility of Hope for the Salvation of Each and All

127.   While unqualified universalism—i.e., the affirmation that all persons will be redeemed—is rejected by the official teachings of the Catholic and Lutheran traditions, theologians continue to discuss the question of the breadth of Christian hope. Even if a firm belief that all will be saved does not accord with biblical and normative teaching, can the Christian nevertheless *hope* for the salvation of each individual and for the salvation of all? This question, vigorously discussed over the last century, can here be only briefly analyzed.

128.   Both Lutheran and Catholic traditions teach that God's saving will extends to all persons. In Catholic teaching, this assertion is made more than once by the Second Vatican Council.[167] The Council also affirmed that the possibility of salvation is offered to all, even those who have never heard the gospel.[168]

129.   Within the Lutheran tradition, debate about the universal saving will of God arose in debates over election. The *Formula of Concord* affirmed that God "wants no one to be lost but rather that everyone repent and believe on the Lord Christ [Rom. 11:32; 1 Tim. 2:4; cf. Ezek. 33:11; 18:23]."[169] When later Lutheran theology discussed the call to salvation that extends to all, it affirmed that this call was inherently efficacious, i.e., it was sufficient to save in every case. Sinful human rejection, not insufficiency of the gospel or of God's will to save, is responsible for those who may be lost.

130.   The impetus for a discussion of a hope for universal salvation among Catholics and Lutherans came from the work of the Reformed

---

[167] "[T]he Savior wishes all to be saved (see 1 Tim 2:4)," *Lumen gentium*, 16; ". . .the will of God, who 'desires all people to be saved and to come to the knowledge of the truth . . .'" (1 Tim 2:4)," *Ad gentes divinitus [Decree on the Church's Missionary Activity]*, 7 December 1965, 7.

[168] "For since Christ died for everyone, and all are in fact called to one and the same destiny, which is divine, we must hold that the Holy Spirit offers to all the possibility of being associated, in a way known to God, with this paschal mystery." *Gaudium et spes*, 22.

[169] Epitome XI, §10, *Book of Concord*, 518; cf. "[T]he promise of the gospel is *universalis*, that is, it pertains to all people (Luke 24)," Solid Declaration XI, §28, *Book of Concord*, 645. The topic was discussed by later Lutheran theology under the heading of the universality of the efficacious call of God to salvation. See examples in Schmidt, *Doctrinal Theology*, 445–446, 447–450. Quenstedt affirms that salvation reaches even "some Turks, Americans, and other barbarians," Schmidt, 450.

theologian Karl Barth and, in particular, his Christocentric understanding of election. If God's election of Jesus Christ is the foundation of God's saving will and if that saving will is supreme, how is eternal loss possible? On the basis of a comprehensive analysis of relevant biblical texts, Barth concludes that the possibility of final loss cannot be ruled out, but also that the final *reality* that some will be lost also cannot be affirmed.[170] "If we are certainly forbidden to count on this [the salvation of all] as though we had a claim on it, . . . we are surely commanded the more definitely to hope and pray for it as we may do already on this side of this final possibility, i.e., to hope and to pray cautiously and yet distinctly that, in spite of everything which may seem quite conclusively to proclaim the opposite, His compassion should not fail, and that in accordance with His mercy which is 'new every morning' He 'will not cast off forever' (Lam. 3:22f; 31)."[171]

131. Within Catholic theology, Barth's impetus was taken up most notably by Hans Urs von Balthasar.[172] Like Barth, he denies that the salvation of all can be affirmed, but he also insists that we are called to hope and pray with confidence for the salvation of each and all. He emphasizes the universal divine will to save,[173] the absence of New Testament teaching that any one in particular (other than the Devil) is lost,[174] and hope for others as an aspect of love for others.[175] While Balthasar's assertions have been vigorously criticized, they also have been widely influential.[176] In a General Audience address of July 28, 1999, John

---

[170] See Karl Barth, *Church Dogmatics* (Edinburgh: T. & T. Clark, 1956–1975), II/2:486–496.

[171] Karl Barth, *Church Dogmatics,* IV/3:486–487.

[172] See Hans Urs von Balthasar, *Theo-Drama: Theological Dramatic Theory: Vol. 5: The Last Act,* trans. Graham Harrison (San Francisco: Ignatius Press, 1998), 269-321; *Dare We Hope 'That All Men Be Saved?' with A Short Discourse on Hell,* trans. David Kipp and Lothar Krauth (San Francisco: Ignatius Press, 1988); "Some Points of Eschatology," *Explorations in Theology: I. The Word Made Flesh* (San Francisco: Ignatius Press, 1989), 255–277.

[173] *Dare We Hope,* 148–157.

[174] *Dare We Hope,* 29–46.

[175] *Dare We Hope,* 211–221.

[176] See the survey of recent discussion in Avery Dulles, "The Population of Hell," *First Things* 133 (May 2003): 36–41. For examples of recent Catholic theologians who speak similarly to Balthasar, see Dermot A. Lane, *Keeping Hope Alive: Stirrings in Christian Theology* (Eugene Oreg.: Wipf & Stock, n.d., reprint of 1996 Paulist Press edition), 162–167; Gisbert Greshake, *Leben—stärker als der Tod. Von der christlichen Hoffnung* (Freiburg: Herder, 2008), 202–226; Medard Kehl, *Dein Reich komme. Eschatologie als Rechenschaft über unsere Hoffnung* (Kevalaer: Topos, 2003), 297.

Paul II seems to take up Balthasar's perspective: "Eternal damnation remains a real possibility, but we are not granted, without special divine revelation, the knowledge of whether or which human beings are effectively involved in it."[177] The International Theological Commission's 1992 statement, "Some Current Questions of Eschatology," observed:

> God wants 'all . . . to be saved and to come to the knowledge of the truth' (1 Tim. 2:4). The church has always believed that such a universal salvific will on God's part has an ample efficacy. The Church has never once declared the damnation of a single person as a concrete fact. But, since hell is a genuine possibility for every person, it is not right . . . to treat salvation as a kind of quasi-automatic consequence.[178]

132.   Debate over this question has been less vehement in Lutheran circles, but the idea of a universal hope has been common. Already in the 1920s, Paul Althaus argued that one cannot exclude the possibility of the salvation of all. He declared, If I can hope for my own salvation, there is no one for whom I also cannot hope.[179] More recent Lutheran theologians have made similar claims, with varying degrees of emphasis.[180] The statement *Unsere Hoffnung auf das ewige Leben* of the German Union Evangelischer Kirchen strongly emphasizes such a universal hope, while also insisting that such hope must remain hope.[181]

---

[177] Online at *www.vatican.va/holy_father/john_paul_ii/audiences/1999/index.htm*, accessed Sept 10, 2010.

[178] International Theological Commission, "Some Current Questions in Eschatology (1992)," *Texts and Documents: 1986–2007*, Michael Sharkey and Thomas Weinandy, eds. (San Francisco: Ignatius Press, 2009), §10.3, 90.

[179] Paul Althaus, *Die letzten Dinge*, 212.

[180] For example, Wolfhart Pannenberg, "The Task of Christian Eschatology," *The Last Things: Biblical and Theological Perspectives on Eschatology*, Carl E. Braaten and Robert W. Jenson, eds. (Grand Rapids, Mich.: Eerdmans, 2002), 9–10; Robert W. Jenson, *Systematic Theology* (New York: Oxford University Press, 1997–1999), 2:364–365; Hans Schwarz, *Eschatology* (Grand Rapids, Mich.: Eerdmans, 2000), 346.

[181] Union Evangelischer Kirchen Theologischer Ausschuss, *Unsere Hoffnung auf das ewige Leben: Ein Votum der Union Evangelischer Kirchen in der EKD* (Neukirchen-Vluyn: Neukirchener Verlagshaus, 2006), 94–99.

4. Common Affirmations

133.   Our churches affirm the possibility of eternal loss, that human persons could be removed from the presence of God for all eternity. The possibility of loss is not to be ascribed to any will of God to damn some while redeeming others. God wishes the salvation of all. The possibility of loss points to the importance of a living faith in God. Those who refuse God's mercy can only live in the hell of their own self-enclosure. What is opposed to God cannot enter God's kingdom.

134.   Our churches also pray for all people. In accord with such prayer, this dialogue affirms the hope that no one will be lost from the community of the saints. We are confident in entrusting every person to the one Judge who died for their sins.[182]

E. Heaven and the Final Kingdom

135.   The ultimate hope of Christians is the triumph of God's will to bless creation through unity with Christ and the Spirit. The day will come when all things are subjected to Christ and God will be "all in all" (1 Cor. 15:28). Every tear will be wiped away; death shall be no more (Rev. 21:4). In the new heaven and new earth, the new Jerusalem that comes down from heaven, God will dwell with humanity (Rev. 21:3). There will be "no temple in the city, for its temple is the Lord God the Almighty and the Lamb" (Rev. 21:22).

136.   The advent of this final and definitive kingdom of God, its relation to history, the interpretation of the difficult biblical discussions of the "signs of the end," the nature of the resurrection, and other related topics have been matters of intensive theological discussion from the beginnings of the church,[183] but have played little role in Catholic-Lutheran disputes. Lutherans and Catholics have a common doctrinal heritage on these questions and have permitted a broad range of freedom for varying detailed theological views. The discussion below will not attempt to cover these issues in their range and depth, but only note points where our traditions have made firm definitions and especially note the final and perfect communion of the saints, which forms the end of our fellowship in this world and the background for our discussion of other topics.

---

[182] The representatives of The Lutheran Church–Missouri Synod in the dialogue not only affirmed "the possibility of eternal loss" for those "who refuse God's mercy," but also held that, contrary to God's expressed will that all be saved, Scripture teaches that there are those who do reject God's mercy.

[183] For a comprehensive ecumenical survey of the issues, see Jerry L. Walls, ed., *The Oxford Handbook of Eschatology* (New York: Oxford University Press, 2008).

1. Biblical

137. In various places New Testament authors use the term "heaven" or "heavenly" to refer to the "place" or state in which the faithful achieve eschatological perfection. In 1 Corinthians 15:47-49, Paul speaks of Christ as the one "from heaven" or as "the man of heaven" to whom Christians are destined to become conformed in the resurrection of the dead. Such conformity to Christ entails bearing the image of the heavenly Christ. Paul speaks elsewhere of the transformation, effected by Christ himself, that will enable such conformity (2 Cor. 3:18; Phil. 3:21). Since Christ is the image of God *par excellence* (2 Cor. 4:4) and the image of humanity to which the justified are destined to be conformed, this eschatological transformation suggests the recovery of humanity's original glory in the image of God (cf. Rom. 8:29-30; 2 Cor. 3:18; Phil. 3:21) and the consummation of human life in a new mode of existence which Paul calls the "spiritual body" (1 Cor. 15:44-45) that will be imperishable and immortal (1 Cor. 15:54).

138. Paul understands this transformation, which will reach completion only in the *eschaton*, to be under way even now, as Christians, through the Spirit of Christ, are already being transformed in the direction of their ultimate glory (2 Cor. 3:18). Thus the eschatological transformation will be the perfection of a change begun already in this life.

139. The author of Hebrews also writes of the perfection that is obtained in heaven. Perfection could not be obtained until Christ came and offered a perfect sacrifice for sin (Heb. 7:11, 19, 28; 10:1). Once this sacrifice was made, the righteous of all generations were made perfect (Heb. 10:14; 12:23). The righteous dead who have been so perfected dwell in heaven or in the heavenly Jerusalem (Heb. 12:22-23). This is the heavenly city that God has prepared for the faithful of all generations (Heb. 11:16), the heavenly rest prepared from the beginning of creation (Heb. 4:3-10). This promised rest in heaven is the goal of all of history. The faithful of all generations share in this promised rest together (Heb. 11:39-40; cf. 4:2).

140. The book of Revelation presents a vision of a new heaven and a new earth, and of a new Jerusalem, hidden in heaven and to be revealed at the end of time. This heavenly Jerusalem will be a place of purity, where sinners will not enter (Rev. 21:8, 27), but only those who have "washed their robes" in the blood of Christ (Rev. 22:14; cf. 7:14)—that is, those who have been purified through the forgiveness of sins in Christ. Those who enter the city will be able to eat of the tree of life (Rev. 22:2, 14; cf. 2:7); they will inherit eternal life and see God face to face (Rev. 22:4).

141. The New Testament foresees not only the transformation of humanity in the resurrection, but also the transformation of all of creation and its release from suffering (Matt. 19:28; Rom. 8:18-25). While at least one New Testament text speaks explicitly of a coming kingdom of God on earth (Rev. 20:4) and other texts hint at it (Matt. 19:28; 1 Cor. 6:2), it is not a main emphasis. The main emphasis in New Testament texts regarding the final kingdom of God or the kingdom of heaven does not fall on its location but on God's triumph over death and evil, God's gathering of the redeemed, and the communal nature of the kingdom, with the redeemed dwelling with God, with Christ, and with each other forever (Matt. 8:11-12; 13:43; 24:30; 25:34; 1 Cor. 15:24-28; 1 Thess. 4:16-17).

2. Doctrinal

142. Theological interest in the end of time, the resurrection, and the final reign of God waxed and waned in the church during the patristic and medieval periods. Very few matters, however, were doctrinally defined. An exception is the insistence that humanity will receive at the resurrection the same bodies they possessed in this life, although transformed. This identity between the earthly and risen body was taught by the Eleventh Regional Council of Toledo, Spain (675)[184] and then repeated by the Fourth Lateran Council (1215).[185] In both cases, the teaching opposed what were seen as overly spiritualized understandings of the resurrection that seemed to deny that the total person is the object of redemption. The precise nature of the identity of the earthly and resurrection bodies, however, was never defined.

a. Lutheran

143. Article XVII of the Augsburg Confession discusses "the Return of Christ for Judgment." Christ will return as judge, "to raise all the dead, [and] to give eternal life and joy to those who believe and are elect."[186] Condemned are those who teach that before the resurrection of the dead the godly will take possession of the kingdom of the world, while the ungodly are suppressed everywhere. The condemnation focused on opposing groups that believed that the end of the world was at hand and

---

[184] Denzinger and Schönmetzer, 540.

[185] Denzinger and Schönmetzer, 801.

[186] Augsburg Confession, Article XVII, §§1-3, *Book of Concord*, 50.

that the true saints were now to take control of this world by force and eliminate all evil.[187] This article was accepted by the Catholic response at the Diet of Augsburg[188] and these topics figured neither in further Catholic-Lutheran controversies nor in the intra-Lutheran arguments leading up to the 1577 *Formula of Concord*.

144.   Luther's catechisms speak of the end as the time when the Holy Spirit's work of sanctification begun in us at baptism is perfectly complete. In the presentation of the third article of the Creed, the Small Catechism stresses the gifts of the Spirit in this life and then ends: "On the Last Day the Holy Spirit will raise me and all the dead and will give to me and all believers in Christ eternal life."[189]

145.   The Large Catechism similarly stressed the constant work of the Spirit in this life: "The Holy Spirit will remain with the holy community or Christian people until the Last Day."[190] On the Last Day, that work is finished. "Then when his work has been finished and we abide in it, having died to the world and all misfortune, he will finally make us perfectly and eternally holy."[191]

146.   Later Lutheran theologians continued to teach that the eternal and supreme happiness of heaven consists in the person seeing God "face to face" and being filled with joy. This enjoyment of God will not be disturbed by "carnal attachments," for union with God will bring "complete rectitude of will and appetite." The blessed will be filled with love that results in adoration of God. Some theologians taught that the essential blessing of knowing and seeing God will be given to all the blessed without variation, but other aspects of heaven will be experienced in varied degrees of splendor and glory, according to different levels of capacity that were formed in this life.[192]

---

[187] Augsburg Confession, Article XVII, §5, *Book of Concord*, 50; Article Seventeen, *Confutation*, 116.

[188] *Confutation*, 116f; original in *Confutatio*, 117.

[189] Small Catechism, §6, *Book of Concord*, 356.

[190] Large Catechism, §53, *Book of Concord*, 438.

[191] Large Catechism, §62, *Book of Concord*, 439. Below, section D, 1 (on purgation), will treat this passage along with Luther's account of the Holy Spirit's work at the moment of the individual believer's death, namely, "then, when we pass from this life, in the blink of an eye, he will perfect our holiness and will eternally preserve us in it." Large Catechism, §59, *Book of Concord*, 439.

[192] See Schmidt, *Doctrinal Theology*, 669–671; Hutter, *Compend*, 228–232, 239–242, Hunnius, *Epitome*, 293–294.

147. Lutheran theology of the seventeenth and eighteenth centuries developed an idiosyncratic theology of the nature of the final kingdom of God. While individuals would rise with their bodies, the remainder of the world would not be transformed, but simply annihilated. Only the non-fallen angels and redeemed humanity would be taken into glory. This view, while widely taught, was never held to be a matter of doctrine and mostly disappeared.[193] The *Evangelischer Erwachsenenkatechismus* explicitly affirms that this world also is taken into God's kingdom: "This world is not an accidental arena of human action which can then disappear, but it should rather be transformed along with humanity."[194]

b. Catholic

148. The Council of Trent gave no developed account of heaven as the state of our eschatological perfection.[195] The reform-decree on the saints referred in passing to their condition as reigning with Christ and enjoying eternal happiness.[196]

149. *The Catechism of the Council of Trent,* on the article "life everlasting," explained that this is not only continued existence, but also "that perpetuity of happiness which is to satisfy the desires of the blessed."[197] The joy of the blessed in their heavenly homeland is utterly incomprehensible to us and so can only be approximated through a variety of biblical terms.[198]

150. Drawing on Chrysostom and Augustine, the *Catechism* describes the happiness of eternal life as both exemption from all evil, such as hunger and thirst, tears, sorrow, and death (Rev. 7:16 and 21:4) and

---

[193] For examples of such teaching, see Schmidt, *Doctrinal Theology,* 655–656; Hunnius, *Epitome,* 290. For an analysis of the teaching, see Konrad Stock, *Annihilatio Mundi: Johann Gerhards Eschatologie der Welt* (Munich: Chr. Kaiser Verlag, 1971).

[194] *Evangelische Erwachsenenkatechismus,* 891.

[195] See section a. (2), above. Before Trent the Council of Florence had defined that those dying without post-baptismal sins enter "straightway" into heaven and that all the lost do not suffer equal pains in hell (Tanner, 1:528; Denzinger and Schönmetzer, 1305–1306). Also Tanner, 681; Denzinger and Schönmetzer, 1582.

[196] Tanner, 2:774–775.

[197] McHugh and Callan, 132.

[198] McHugh and Callan, 134.

positive glories without measure. On the latter, tradition sanctions a basic division between essential beatitude and accessory happiness, which the Lutheran textbooks also taught. Essential beatitude consists in knowing God and Christ (John 17:3) in the vision of God (1 John 3:2), which makes people "partakers of the divine nature" (2 Pet. 1:4). Accessory happiness follows from the vision, in glory, honor, and peace (cf. Rom. 2:10).[199]

151. The Second Vatican Council emphasized the orientation of the church toward God's kingdom, of which it is the "seed and beginning."[200] Our worship on earth participates proleptically in the heavenly worship of God by the saints.[201] The *Constitution on the Church* offers this characterization of the church when it will be brought to the final perfection for which we long:

> For when Christ appears and the glorious resurrection of the dead takes place, the brightness of God will illuminate the heavenly city and the Lamb will be its light (see Rev. 21:23). Then the whole church of the saints in the supreme happiness of love will adore God and "the lamb who was slain" (Rev. 5:12), with one voice proclaiming: "To him who sits upon the throne and to the lamb be blessing and honor and glory and might for ever and ever" (Rev. 5:13).[202]

152. The main account of heaven in the *Catechism of the Catholic Church* comes in explaining the creedal article on life everlasting. The essential point about heaven is that "those who die in God's grace and friendship and are perfectly purified live forever with Christ. They are like God forever, for they 'see him as he is,' face to face . . . ," as indicated in 1 John 3:2 and in 1 Corinthians 13:12 and Revelation 22:4.[203]

153. A definition then follows in the *Catechism of the Catholic Church*: "This perfect life with the Most Holy Trinity—this communion of life and love with the Trinity, with the Virgin Mary, the angels, and all the blessed—is called "heaven." Heaven is the ultimate end and fulfillment of the deepest human longings, the state of supreme,

---

[199] McHugh and Callan, 135–140.

[200] *Lumen gentium*, 5; Tanner, 2:851.

[201] *Sacrosanctum concilium [Constitution on the Sacred Liturgy]*, 4 December 1963, 8; Tanner, 2:822–823.

[202] *Lumen gentium*, 51; Tanner, 2:891.

[203] *Catechism of the Catholic Church*, no. 1023.

definitive happiness."[204] This fulfillment centers on being with Christ and living in him, in which the redeemed find their own identity, for "the life of the blessed consists in the full and perfect possession of the fruits of the redemption accomplished by Christ. . . . Heaven is the blessed community of all who are perfectly incorporated into Christ."[205]

3. Common Affirmations

154.   Catholics and Lutherans confess together a common conviction that the triumph of God's grace will be consummated in a perfect communion of love, justice, and peace. All the redeemed will exist in harmony with God and with one another in a radically transformed world. This hope is significant for our ecumenical efforts. As is often said, our divisions do not reach to heaven.[206] We look forward to the day when all divisions among Christ's followers are erased before the throne of the Lamb.

F. Our Common Witness

155.   We began this chapter with an assertion of our common hope. The detailed elaboration of the witness of our two traditions that has followed provides a firm foundation for that assertion. Catholics and Lutherans are united in their hope for a future whose name is Jesus. This shared hope was asserted in an earlier round of this dialogue at a crucial juncture. In its important thesis statement on justification, Round VII of the dialogue affirmed: "Our entire hope of justification and salvation rests on Christ Jesus and on the gospel whereby the good news of God's merciful action in Christ is made known."[207] In our explorations of this hope, the dialogue has been encouraged to find how much we hold in common. This agreement is both at the level of foundations—in our common focus on God's act in Christ and the Spirit—and also at the level of many details.

---

[204] *Catechism of the Catholic Church*, no. 1024.

[205] *Catechism of the Catholic Church*, nos. 1025-1026.

[206] E.g., Walter Kasper, "Current Problems in Ecumenical Theology," *www.vatican.va/roman_curia/pontifical_councils/chrstuni/sub-index/index_card-kasper.htm*, accessed Sept. 12, 2010.

[207] *Justification by Faith: Lutherans and Catholics in Dialogue VII*, ¶¶4 and 157; 16, 72.

CHAPTER III

Traditional Disputes within the Context of Our Common Hope

156. Together, Catholics and Lutherans, as well as many other Christians, share a sure and certain hope of eternal life in fellowship with the Triune God. In the topics discussed—death, intermediate states, judgment, hell, and heaven—Lutherans and Catholics clearly have had only minimal disagreements. This shared framework forms the context for a consideration of the limited but historically significant disputes to be considered in this chapter: purgatory and prayers for the dead.[208] The importance and difficulty of these topics is bound up with the way they involve both conceptual issues (e.g., how we understand our communion with the departed or the transformation of the self between death and heavenly glory) and issues of practice (e.g., prayers and indulgences). Any ecumenical judgment on the weight of the differences between our traditions in these areas must consider both sets of issues.

A. Transformation Unto Glory: Purgation

157. If we die still deformed by sin, but will finally live before God fully transformed into what God intends for humanity, then some sort of change or transformation must occur between death and entry into eschatological glory. In this sense, the general topic of "purgation" is unavoidable. What is the nature of this transformation?

158. Lutherans and Catholics have given conflicting descriptions of this transformation from the earliest years of the Reformation. The

---

[208] The related topic of invocation of the saints, i.e., asking the departed saints, including Mary, to pray for us, was considered in detail in a previous round of this dialogue. See *The One Mediator, the Saints, and Mary: Lutherans and Catholics in Dialogue VIII*. That dialogue reached a carefully nuanced conclusion that, if the witness to the sole mediatorship of Christ is safeguarded, the invocation of the saints need not be church-dividing if the practice is neither condemned by Lutherans nor made mandatory by Catholics (¶¶ 97-98; 57–58).

questions for this dialogue concern the nature of the divergent answers and whether they represent a church-dividing difference, i.e., a difference that is incompatible with life together in full communion. We seek here to answer these questions.

1. Biblical Background

159.   No biblical text uses the word "purgatory," but various passages state or suggest that only the pure or holy will enter the presence of God. Jesus says, "Blessed are the pure in heart, for they will see God" (Matt. 5:8). The seer of Revelation says that nothing unclean will enter the heavenly Jerusalem (Rev. 21:27), but those who have washed their robes in the blood of Christ (cf. Rev. 7:14) will have the right to enter it (Rev. 22:14). They will see God's face (Rev. 22:4). At the final union of the church with Christ, the church is presented as a bride dressed in pure linen, symbolizing the righteous deeds of the saints (Rev. 19:8). The author of 1 John declares that "when [Jesus] is revealed, we will be like him, for we will see him as he is. And all who have this hope in him purify themselves, just as he is pure" (1 John 3:2-3). The author of Hebrews calls on his readers to pursue the holiness "without which no one will see the Lord" (Heb. 12:14)—holiness that results from purification in Christ (Heb. 9:13-14; 10:10).

160.   The most important texts that have been cited to provide biblical support for purgatory, however, are 2 Maccabees 12:39-45, 1 Corinthians 3:10-15, and Matthew 12:32. Because of hermeneutical or interpretive difficulties, they deserve more extensive discussion.[209]

161.   The first text, chronologically, is the deuterocanonical 2 Maccabees 12:39-45. Some Jewish soldiers under the command of Judas Maccabeus bury their fallen comrades. They discover under their tunics "sacred tokens of the idols of Jamnia," which means that these Jews were guilty of idolatry. The soldiers pray for their dead comrades, that their sin might be blotted out. Judas takes up a collection and presents a sin offering in Jerusalem. The author comments: "In doing this he acted very well and honorably, taking account of the resurrection. For if he were not expecting that those who had fallen would rise again, it would have been superfluous and foolish to pray for the dead. But if he was looking to the splendid reward that is laid up for those who fall asleep in godliness, it was a holy and pious thought. Therefore he made atonement for the dead,

---

[209] For an extensive discussion of biblical texts that have been used in connection with purgatory, see A. Michel, "Purgatoire," *Dictionnaire de Théologie Catholique,* vol.13/1 (Paris: Letouzy et Ané, 1936), cols. 1164–1179.

so that they might be delivered from their sin." Here we have undeniable reference to interventions by the living on behalf of the dead, specifically for purification and deliverance from sin. The significance of this text for the doctrinal status of belief in post-mortem purgation depends in part on the canonical authority of 2 Maccabees for our two traditions, a question that cannot be resolved here.[210]

162. The second text is 1 Corinthians 3:10-15, where the imagery of fire has been of particular importance in the history of interpretation.[211] In this text Paul is dealing with the problem that certain of the Corinthian Christians are aligning themselves with particular preachers (cf. 1 Cor. 3:4-5; see also 1:11-12), creating factions within the community. Paul points out that he and Apollos are merely servants of God, so that they are "not anything" (1 Cor. 3:7) in comparison to God, and there is no ground for Corinthian factionalism. Indeed, their work will be judged by God. Paul uses an architectural metaphor to make his point. Evangelists must exercise care in how they build upon the foundation of the church, which is Jesus Christ (1 Cor. 3:11), for the work of each evangelist will be tested on the day of judgment. If the evangelist's work has been of fine quality, symbolized by gold, silver, or precious stones—materials that will withstand a testing fire—the builder will receive a reward. If this work has been of poor quality, symbolized by wood, hay, and straw—materials that will be consumed in a testing fire—the reward will be lost, although the builder will be saved.

163. Several elements in this text are open to an interpretation that may go beyond their original context, and these are the elements that contributed to the use of this text in connection with purgatory. The fire,

---

[210] The German ecumenical working group (Jaeger-Stälin-Kreis) has recently treated the Old Testament canon. See *Verbindliches Zeugnis. I. Kanon-Schrift-Tradition*, W. Pannenberg and T. Schneider, eds. (Freiburg & Göttingen, 1992), 383–385, giving conclusions of the historical study. M. Hengel's book, *The Septuagint as Christian Scripture* (Edinburgh: T&T Clark, 2002) arose out of this discussion, as did no. 440 of the study document of the Lutheran-Roman Catholic Commission on Unity, *The Apostolicity of the Church* (2006), which tells why some Lutherans are seeing the Apocrypha (or deuterocanonical books) in a new light.

[211] Especially important interpretations were from Origen, *Contra Celsum* 5:15, English translation in Ante-Nicene Fathers, 4 (Peabody, Mass.; Hendrickson, 1995), 549; Augustine, *Enchiridion* 18:68-69, English translation in Augustine, *Christian Instruction*, Writings of St. Augustine, 4 (New York: Fathers of the Church, 1947), 427–428; and Gregory the Great, *Dialogues*, 4:41, Fathers of the Church, 39, 249. These citations indicate first the passage according to the internal divisions of the work (e.g., by book and then chapter). Then, second, by the volume and page number of the translation used herein.

which in this text functions as a testing fire, in later tradition came to be understood as a purgative fire. The words "each" (1 Cor. 3:10, 13) and "work" (3:13-15), which in the original context refer to each evangelist and the evangelistic work, came to be applied to each Christian and his or her deeds in general. The image of being saved "as through fire," which in the original context refers to the salvation of the evangelist, came to be applied to the salvation of individual Christians through a final, purifying fire.

164. The third text appears in Matthew 12:32, where Jesus says: "Whoever speaks a word against the Son of Man will be forgiven, but whoever speaks against the Holy Spirit will not be forgiven, either in this age or in the age to come (*oute en toutō tō aiōni oute en tō mellonti*)." That the sin against the Holy Spirit will not be forgiven in the age to come sometimes has been interpreted to mean that there are other sins that can be forgiven in the world to come, that is, in purgatory.[212] This argument may draw inferences that exceed the intention of the text.

165. The synoptic parallels read: "Truly I tell you, people will be forgiven for their sins and whatever blasphemies they utter; but whoever blasphemes against the Holy Spirit can never (*eis ton aiōna*) have forgiveness, but is guilty of an eternal (*aiōniou*) sin (Mark 3:28-29); "And everyone who speaks a word against the Son of Man will be forgiven; but whoever blasphemes against the Holy Spirit will not be forgiven" (Luke 12:10). The main point of Jesus' saying seems to be the difference between sins that can be forgiven and sins against the Holy Spirit, which cannot be forgiven. In the Markan version the reference to the eternal nature of such sin underlines the absolute impossibility of forgiveness. The Matthean reference to the age to come seems to serve the same function. At most the text of Matthew leaves open the question of the possibility of forgiveness of other sins in the age to come.

166. In reflecting on the foregoing discussion, we call attention to certain hermeneutical questions that arise in the use of biblical material to provide support for belief in purgatory. These include 1) the relationship between the original meaning of a text and meanings derived from a text over the course of the history of its interpretation (esp. 1 Cor. 3:10-15; Matt. 12:32); 2) the authority of deuterocanonical texts (2 Macc. 12:39-45); and 3) the degree to which imagery that serves one function in a metaphor may be taken to refer to a reality that is not explicitly expressed in the metaphor (1 Cor. 3:10-15). For example, can we assume without further argument that the testing fire of 1 Corinthians

---

[212] E.g., Augustine, *The City of God*, 21 (see paragraph 224 below).

3:13 is also a purging fire?[213] In any case, a theological evaluation of the doctrine of purgatory requires the integration of all of the biblical evidence into the whole of Christian anthropology and soteriology.

2. Development of Doctrine and Practice Related to Purgatory

167. Beliefs and practices related to a post-death purgation have a long and complex history.[214] As will be discussed in the next section of our text, Christians began praying for their dead at a very early date. By the beginning of the third century, Tertullian was writing of suffering after death that could be relieved by the intercession of the living,[215] and Clement of Alexandria was teaching about post-death punishments that serve to heal departed souls.[216] Tertullian speaks approvingly of a yearly offering to be made for the departed.[217]

168. Augustine, however, substantially contributed to the development of the doctrine of purgatory.[218] His *City of God*, especially its last three books (20-22) that address the final judgment, punishment, and heaven, became the source *par excellence* for later Western eschatology. In Book

---

[213] The last-named problem applies to another text that has sometimes been used in reference to or in the context of purgatory, namely, Matthew 5:21-26 (especially 5:25-26) (e.g., Cyprian, Ep. 55,20; incipiently already Tertullian, An. 35,3ff.). Matthew 5:21-26 reads: "Come to terms quickly with your accuser while you are on your way to court with him, or your accuser may hand you over to the judge, and the judge to the guard, and you will be thrown into prison. Truly I tell you, you will never get out until you have paid the last penny." On one level this text makes sense as wisdom on how to conduct oneself in this world. Commentators have noted, however, that Matthew 5:26 introduces eschatological overtones, suggestive of the last judgment (see, e.g., Ulrich Luz, *Das Evangelium nach Matthäus*, 3 vols., EKK 1 (Düsseldorf: Benziger/Neukirchen-Vluyn: Neukirchener Verlag, 2002), 1.260. The larger context of Matthew 5:21-26, which includes language of judgment (5:22), also has encouraged such a reading. One can understand, therefore, why this text came to be used in reference to purgatory. The sapiential nature of Matthew 5:25-26, however, makes direct application of the text to the question of purgatory hermeneutically problematic.

[214] The most important and comprehensive discussion of this history is Jacques Le Goff, *The Birth of Purgatory*, Arthur Goldhammer, ed. (Chicago: University of Chicago Press, 1984).

[215] Tertullian, *On the Resurrection of the Body*, 43.

[216] See Daley, *The Hope of the Early Church*, 46-47.

[217] *De corona militis*, III. See Le Goff, *Birth of Purgatory*, 47.

[218] Le Goff, *Birth of Purgatory*, 61-85.

21, he asks whether divine punishment beyond death is strictly retributive, the just consequence of earlier sin, or also purgative and remedial. A remedial punishment would clearly end if and when it brings about its intended improvement. Some punishments within this life are remedial. Augustine believes the same is true of some post-death punishment. "Not all who suffer temporal punishment after death are doomed to the eternal pains that follow the last judgment. For, as I have said, what is not forgiven in this life is pardoned in the life to come, in the case of those who are not to suffer eternal punishment."[219] In this regard, Augustine taught:

> Only those who die in Christ . . . suffer such remedial, non-eternal punishments: There are, of course, certain souls for whom the prayer either of the church or of some devout individuals is heard. These are the souls of those reborn in Christ whose lives in the body were not so evil that they are reckoned unworthy of mercy, but were not so good as to be found not needing such mercy. And so, even after the resurrection of the dead, there will be some who, after enduring the pains suffered by the spirits of the dead, will be granted mercy and so not be cast into everlasting fire. For it would never have been said rightly that some would be forgiven neither "in this world nor in the world to come" [Matt. 12:32], unless it were true that, even though they remain unpardoned on earth, some will be forgiven in the world to come.[220]

169. The fire Paul refers to in 1 Corinthians 3:11-15 is perhaps, Augustine thinks, the form of such remedial punishment:

> There is an interval between the death of the body and the last day that is set for damnation and remuneration after

---

[219] *The City*, 21, 13; Formula of Concord, §24, *Book of Concord*, 373. In the original, the text contrasts those who after the final judgment *veniunt in sempiternas poenas* with some *qui post mortem sustinent temporales [poenas]*. In the latter case, sins not remitted in this life *remitti in futuro saeculo* so that those who committed them escape eternal punishment (citing from Corpus Christianorum, Series Latina, 48, 779–780).

[220] *The City*, 21, 24; Fathers of the Church 24, 389 (translation modified in light of the original in Corpus Christianorum, Series Latina, 48, 790). At the end of Book 21, Augustine returns to the notion of a middling quality of earthly life, one that merits neither damnation nor beatitude, but that still qualifies one to be helped by others to receive mercy and salvation (*The City*, 21, 27; Fathers of the Church, 24, 411–413).

the resurrection of all bodies. In this interval of time the spirits of the dead may be supposed to suffer some kind of fire. This will not be felt by those who in their lives and loves on earth built no structure of wood, hay, and straw that will burn up, whereas others will feel this fire since they brought with them such structures. They may feel this only after death, or both then and here on earth, or only during life. The fire would be a transitory tribulation that burns away the venial worldliness not incurring damnation. I do not reject this idea, because perhaps it is true.[221]

170. Augustine suggests different forms that this fiery tribulation might well take, such as death itself, persecution, or the impact of the Antichrist. The crucial issue is how one has loved Christ and others. If Christ has had the first place, then imperfect human affections for others can be purged away.[222]

171. Post-mortem purgation by fire, a hypothetical possibility for Augustine, became a matter of certainty in Gregory the Great's *Dialogues*, Book 4, (early 590s), which was a widely influential account of faith and doctrine on life after death.[223] After Gregory suggested that some souls immediately pass to their merited recompense, Deacon Peter in the narrative asked about the level of doctrinal authority enjoyed by the notion of a cleansing fire after death, that is, "whether we have to believe it?" In response Gregory pointed to some biblical texts attesting to the finality of the condition one is in at the instant of death. Each person will meet the Judge just as he or she was at death. But "as one is at death" is not as simple as it might seem.

> Still, one must hold [*credendus est*] that there is to be a cleansing fire before judgment, in regard to certain minor

---

[221] *The City,* 21, 26; Fathers of the Church, 24, 402–403 (translation modified in light of the original in Corpus Christianorum, Series Latina, 48, 798–799).

[222] In his *Enchiridion,* Augustine states similarly: "That something similar may take place after this life is not impossible. The question, whether such is the case, is justified and may yield a solution or remain in doubt: that is, whether some of the faithful are saved by some kind of purgatorial fire (*per ignem quendam purgatorium*), and this sooner or later according as they have loved more or less the goods that perish." See *Faith Hope and Charity,* 18, 69; Ancient Christian Writers, 3, 70, slightly simplified and enhanced from the original, from Corpus Christianorum, Series Latina, 46, 87.

[223] On the importance of Gregory as "the last father of purgatory," see Le Goff, *Birth of Purgatory,* 88–95.

faults that may remain to be purged away. For Truth [Christ] says that "if anyone blasphemes against the Holy Spirit he shall not be forgiven either in this world or in the world to come" (Matt. 12:32). From this we learn that some sins can be forgiven in this world and some in the world to come. For, if forgiveness is refused for a particular sin, we conclude logically that it is granted for others. This must apply, as I said, to slight transgressions, such as persistent idle talking, immoderate laughter, or blame in the care of property. . . . All these faults are troublesome for the soul after death if they are not forgiven while one is alive.[224]

172.   Gregory added a later brief remark, however, that "generally . . . the very dread that grips a departing soul is sufficient to purify it of its minor faults."[225]

173.   The first centuries of the second millennium saw developments both in doctrine (e.g., the absorption of teachings about purgatory into the developing scholastic theology[226]) and practice (e.g., the introduction at Cluny in the eleventh century of the commemoration of all the dead on November 2[227]). The penitential system as it developed during this period formed the context within which purgatory was understood and addressed.

174.   Teachings about purgatory only became the object of dogmatic teaching, however, in the reunion discussions with the Orthodox at the Second Council of Lyons (1274) and the Council of Ferrara-Florence (1439). The Greeks, like the West, had the practice of offering alms, good works, and prayer, especially the Eucharist, for the dead. Nevertheless, they considered the Western development of a doctrine of purgatory an innovation when they first encountered it. They had no teaching of purgatory as a place or distinct state and were deeply suspicious of the image of purifying fire, which for them was associated with Origen's

---

[224] *Dialogues*, 4, 41; Fathers of the Church, 39, 248-249; Sources chrétiennes, 265, 130. Gregory goes on to treat briefly the testing of our workmanship, indicated in 1 Corinthians 3:12-15, with those attaining salvation, as by fire, even though they had built poorly on the foundation. Their wood, grass, and straw edifices may be taken to stand for venial sins, "which fire consumes easily."

[225] *Dialogues*, 4, 47; Fathers of the Church, 39, 259.

[226] See Chapter 8 of Le Goff, "The Scholastic Systemization," *Birth of Purgatory*, 237–288.

[227] Le Goff, *Birth of Purgatory*, 125.

teaching of a fire that would ultimately purify and redeem all humanity and even the devil.[228]

175. While the teaching adopted by both councils, in almost identical words, embodies the core of the Western teaching, it carefully sought to meet Orthodox concerns. The term "purgatory" as the name for a place or state was avoided and no mention was made of "fire." Of those "who are truly penitent and die in God's love before having satisfied by worthy fruits of penance for their sins of commission and omission," the Council of Florence said "their souls are cleansed after death by cleansing pains [*poenis purgatoriis*]."[229] In addition, "the suffrages of the living faithful avail them in giving relief from such pains, that is, sacrifices of Masses, prayers, almsgiving and other acts of devotion which have been customarily performed by some of the faithful for others of the faithful in accordance with the church's ordinances."[230] The conciliar teaching was thus 1) that post-death punishments cleanse the souls of those who have not completed adequate satisfaction, and 2) that the prayers of the living benefit those undergoing such punishment.

176. The Council of Trent was similarly reticent. The brief Decree on Purgatory teaches only "that purgatory [*purgatorium*] exists, and that the souls detained there [*ibi*] are helped by the prayers of the faithful and most of all by the acceptable sacrifice of the altar."[231] Bishops are instructed that, "in homilies to uninstructed people[,] the more difficult and subtle questions, which do nothing to sustain faith and give rise to little or no increase of devotion, should be excluded." They should avoid "uncertain speculation or what borders on falsehood" and "all that panders to curiosity and superstition."[232]

---

[228] On the discussions at Ferrara-Florence, see James Jorgenson, "The Debate Over the Patristic Texts on Purgatory at the Council of Ferrara-Florence, 1438," *St. Vladimir's Theological Quarterly* 30.4 (1986): 309–334; on Orthodox eschatology in general and purgatory in particular, see Andrew Louth, "Orthodox Eschatology," *The Oxford Handbook of Eschatology*, 233–247, esp. 242–243.

[229] Tanner, 1:527; Denzinger and Schönmetzer, 1304. The "Confession of Michael Paleologus" at the Second Council of Lyons, which functioned as the theological statement of agreed belief with the Orthodox, referred to "purging and purgatorial pains" [*poenis purgatoriis et catharteriis*], Denzinger and Schönmetzer, 856.

[230] Tanner, 1:527. The Confession of Michael Paleologus is identical.

[231] Tanner, 2:774; Denzinger and Schönmetzer, 1820. The question can be asked whether by the use of the noun "*purgatorium*" and the adverb "*ibi*" Trent goes beyond Florence in teaching purgatory as a place or state.

[232] Tanner, 2:774.

177. An important assumption of this teaching, mentioned in the teaching of the Council of Florence, is spelled out in a canon of Trent's earlier Decree on Justification: "If anyone says that after the reception of the grace of justification the guilt is so remitted and the debt of eternal punishment so blotted out to every repentant sinner, that no debt of temporal punishment remains to be discharged either in this world or in purgatory before the gates of heaven can be opened, let him be anathema."[233]

178. Trent's limited teaching was repeated in the *Catechism of the Council of Trent* and in the *Profession of Faith of the Council of Trent*, which asserted: "I steadfastly hold that a purgatory exists, and that the souls there detained are aided by the prayers of the faithful."[234]

3. Lutheran Criticism

179. The Lutheran Confessions are uniformly critical of the doctrine of purgatory. Their primary interest in the doctrine, however, is its relation to the proclamation of the gospel and its effect upon the article of justification. When the Confessions discuss purgatory, their concern is dominantly with the practices associated with purgatory: indulgences, Masses for the dead, and prayers for the dead. In response to these practices and in line with their understanding of the gospel, the Confessions, and the Lutheran Reformers more generally not only rejected these perceived abuses, but also indicated an alternative understanding of how the justified are perfected for glory by death and resurrection, without working out all the details.

180. For complex reasons rooted in the Saxon strategy at the 1530 Augsburg Diet of the Holy Roman Empire, the Augsburg Confession as presented at the Diet contained no reference to purgatory.[235] A sentence on satisfaction and purgatory was added to Article XII in the 1531 *editio princeps*.[236]

---

[233] Council of Trent, Sixth Session, 13 January 1547, can. 30. Translation from *The Canons and Decrees of the Council of Trent*, trans. H. J. Schroeder (Rockford, Ill.: TAN Books and Publishers, 1978).

[234] Denzinger and Schönmetzer, 998.

[235] Wilhelm Maurer, *Historical Commentary on the Augsburg Confession*, trans. H. George Anderson (Philadelphia: Fortress Press, 1986), 19, 28; Jared Wicks, "Abuses Under Indictment at the Diet of Augsburg 1530," *Luther's Reform: Studies on Conversion and the Church* (Mainz: Verlag Philipp von Zabern, 1992), 255. At the same time as the Diet, however, Luther wrote his most explicit and vehement rejection of the doctrine of purgatory. *Widerruf vom Fegefeuer*, Weimar Ausgabe, XXX/2, 360–390.

[236] *Book of Concord*, §10, 46.

181. The most explicit discussion of purgatory in the Lutheran Confessions comes in the 1537 Smalcald Articles, which addressed the Mass as sacrifice. Besides being itself a violation of the gospel, the Mass as sacrifice "has produced many noxious maggots and the excrement of various idolatries," the first of which is purgatory.[237] Purgatory, "with all its pomp, requiem Masses, and transactions, is to be regarded as an apparition of the devil for it obscures the chief article...."[238] Behind Luther's typically extreme language, however, a more nuanced understanding is elaborated. "Concerning the dead we have received neither command nor instruction. For these reasons, it may be best to abandon it [*derhalben man es mocht wohl lassen*], even if it were neither error nor idolatry."[239] In a revised version of the article, Luther added a discussion of the authority of Augustine claimed for the doctrine. "When they have given up their purgatorial 'Mass fairs' (something Augustine never dreamed of), then we will discuss with them whether St. Augustine's word, lacking support from Scripture, may be tolerated and whether the dead may be commemorated at the sacrament. It will not do to formulate articles of faith on the basis of the holy Fathers' works or words."[240] The existence of purgatory is not dogmatically denied. Rather, the declaration is made that: 1) the existence of purgatory is not taught by Scripture and thus cannot be binding doctrine, and 2) belief in purgatory is now hopelessly bound up with unacceptable practices. A belief that could be discussed in principle is concretely objectionable because of its associations.

182. These associations were not just with what could be called abuses, but with the developed penitential system and the idea that satisfactions were still owed for forgiven sins. That the justified must still suffer for their sins, even for forgiven sins, was not denied by the Reformers.[241] Such sufferings are not, however, rightly understood as satisfactions. "This whole theory [of satisfactions] is a recent fiction fabricated without the authority of the Scriptures or the ancient writers of the church. Not even Peter Lombard speaks this way about satisfactions."[242]

---

[237] Smalcald Articles, Second Article, §11, *Book of Concord*, 303.

[238] Smalcald Articles, Second Article, §12, *Book of Concord*, 303.

[239] Smalcald Articles, Second Article, §12, *Book of Concord*, 303.

[240] Smalcald Articles, Second Article, §§14f., *Book of Concord*, 304.

[241] "[T]he saints suffer punishments, which are the work of God. They suffer contrition or terrors, as well as other common troubles. So, too, some of them suffer specific penalties that have been imposed by God for the sake of example." Apology, Article XII, §156, *Book of Concord*, 214.

[242] Apology, Article XII, §119, *Book of Concord*, 207.

183. More decisively, the Lutheran Confessions argue that the proclamation of free forgiveness is obscured by an emphasis on satisfactions still owed after forgiveness. "Beneath these scandals and demonic teachings—too numerous to mention—the teaching of the righteousness by faith in Christ and Christ's benefits lies buried."[243] The criterion consistently applied is whether the gospel of free justification and forgiveness is communicated: "We should always understand whatever is cited about vengeance and punishments in such a way as not to overturn the free forgiveness of sins nor to obscure the merit of Christ and draw people away from trust in Christ to trust in works."[244]

184. For the Lutheran Confessions, the sufferings that follow forgiven sin are understood in relation to one of the most fundamental soteriological categories of the Reformation—namely, death and resurrection. Penance is a putting to death and a raising to life.[245] What had been understood in a juridical model of punishment and satisfaction is reconceived in the model of ongoing death and resurrection. "We grant that in repentance there is a punishment, but not as a payment. Rather there is in a formal sense a punishment in repentance because regeneration itself occurs through a continuous mortification of our old nature."[246]

185. In a reversal of stereotypes, the medieval forensic understanding of ongoing suffering as temporal punishments for past venial or forgiven mortal sins is replaced on the Reformation side by a transformational understanding of the afflictions of daily life as the ongoing slaying of the old person who continues to live within us. The penitential side of the Christian life is understood as the ongoing struggle with the old person within us, who must be slain daily. The Christian finally must be purged of this old self; this old self must be fully slain.

186. How and when is that purgation completed? The Lutheran Confessions present no extended argument in answer to that question, but assumed is the finality of bodily death and resurrection. The old self is finally purged in the death of the body and the new self is pure in its bodily resurrection. Thus, Luther says in the Large Catechism: "Because holiness has begun and is growing daily, we await the time when our flesh

---

[243] Apology, Article XII, §16, *Book of Concord*, 190.

[244] Apology, Article XII, §148, *Book of Concord*, 212–213. This passage was added by Melanchthon to the later octavo edition of the Apology.

[245] Apology, Article XII, §46, *Book of Concord*, 194.

[246] Apology, Article XII, §148, *Book of Concord*, 213.

will be put to death, will be buried with all its uncleanness, and will come forth gloriously and arise to complete and perfect holiness in a new, eternal life. Now, however, we remain only halfway pure and holy."[247] Death completes the process. Indeed, "when we pass from this life, in the blink of an eye he will perfect our holiness and will eternally preserve us in it."[248]

187.   Why assume that the old self is finally purged in death and not in a process that extends beyond death? The Lutheran Confessions give no systematic answer. At one point, Melanchthon finds a non-juridical purgation beyond death less objectionable.[249] More often, however, an implicit theology of the decisive character of death provides an explanation. This theology is not fully spelled out and has at least two variants.

188.   Frequently, the ongoing presence of the old self is tied to the ongoing life of the flesh, with which sin is bound up. For Melanchthon, "sin still remains present in the flesh."[250] Luther is more detailed in the Large Catechism. "Forgiveness is constantly needed, for although God's grace has been acquired by Christ, and holiness has been wrought by the Holy Spirit through God's Word in the unity of the Christian church, yet we are never without sin because we carry our flesh around our neck."[251] Even more explicitly: "Our flesh is in itself vile and inclined to evil, even when we have accepted God's Word and believe it."[252] Luther says that "we await the time when our flesh will be put to death."[253] "Flesh" here seems to encompass both the sheer fact of carnal embodiment and an aspect of the total person.

---

[247] Large Catechism, The Creed, §57, *Book of Concord*, 438.

[248] Large Catechism, The Creed, §59, *Book of Concord*, 439.

[249] In his discussion of penance in the Apology, Melanchthon notes that the Fathers understood penance as healing: "When they [the Fathers] referred to purgatory in this connection, they did not understand it as payment of satisfaction for eternal punishment but as the purification of imperfect souls." Apology, Article XII, §167, *Book of Concord*, 216.

[250] Apology, Article XII, §151, *Book of Concord*, 214.

[251] Large Catechism, The Creed, §54, *Book of Concord*, 438.

[252] Large Catechism, The Lord's Prayer,§ 63, *Book of Concord*, 448. In this context, it is important to remember the Lutheran comprehensive understanding of concupiscence (the pre-voluntary movement of aspects of the self in opposition to the self's right ordering) as sin.

[253] Large Catechism, The Creed, §57, *Book of Concord*, 438.

189. The Formula of Concord varies the argument, stating that original sin so pervades the self that: "The damage is such that only God alone can separate human nature and the corruption of this nature from each other. This separation will take place completely through death, at the resurrection, when the nature which we now have will rise and live eternally, without original sin."[254] The combined reality death-and-resurrection works the transformation. Luther's famous "blink of an eye" statement, quoted above, points in the same direction.[255]

190. In line with the emphasis on death and resurrection as the means of the self's post-justification transformation and purification, the Confessions assert a theological understanding of the decisive character of death as a turning point in that transformation, without doctrinally asserting any particular understanding of how death accomplishes that end.

191. The critique of the doctrine of purgatory within the Lutheran Confessions thus has three elements:

1) The doctrine of purgatory is not founded in Scripture and thus should not be binding teaching.

2) The concept of satisfaction with which the doctrine had been connected undercuts the sufficiency of the satisfaction of Christ and thus obscures the gospel.

3) God works the transformation of the self into sinless heavenly glory through death as a moment in death-and-resurrection-in-Christ.

4. Contemporary Discussions

a. Catholic

192. The recent discussions in Catholic theology of the nature of death and intermediate states has been accompanied by a discussion of the nature of purgatory. These discussions, culminating in official

---

[254] Formula of Concord, Epitome I, §10, *Book of Concord*, 489.

[255] On at least one occasion, Luther saw resurrection rather than death as the decisive moment of purgation: "Both spirit and flesh still dwell in man, and the flesh is still corrupt. We are not perfect saints, as we hope to be on the Last Day. Even though God begins to purify [*zureinigen*] us through death, so that we become dust and ashes, we must still await the final fire [*das letzte feuer*] to purge [*reinigen*] all that has not been removed by the corruption in the grave. Then we shall have neither spot nor blemish; but we shall be like the bright sun, yes, like the angels." *Luther's Works*, vol. 22, Jaroslav Pelikan, ed. (St. Louis: Concordia Publishing House, 1957), 262f; Weimar Ausgabe, vol. 46, 777.

statements, have at the very least altered the conditions of the Catholic-Lutheran disagreement. Four aspects of the Catholic discussion are particularly noteworthy.

1) A greater emphasis on the reparative and purifying nature of the punishments of purgatory.

193. In addition to maintaining juridical categories within divine justice applied to the remission of punishment, recent Catholic theology and teaching has emphasized the healing and reparative character of purgatorial suffering. Particularly important is the insistence that the purgatorial purification is "altogether different from the punishment of the damned."[256] These sufferings tend to be described as the pain attendant upon the purification that comes with assimilation into unimpeded communion with God. Thus, the International Theological Commission states: "Where there is a delay in reaching the possession of the beloved, there is sorrow, a sorrow that purifies."[257] Joseph Ratzinger, writing while still a professor, notes the language of purgatorial fire and asks, "Surely these terms must refer, not to something external to man, but to the man of little faith's heartfelt submission to the fire of the Lord which will draw him out of himself into that purity which befits those who are God's?"[258]

2) A greater emphasis on the Christological character of purgatory.

194. Various Catholic theologians have sought to understand the fire of purgatory as either the Holy Spirit[259] or Christ himself.[260] This idea has

---

[256] Sacred Congregation for the Doctrine of the Faith, "The Reality of Life After Death," *Recentiores episcoporum synodi*, 11 May 1979. English translation in Austin Flannery, ed., *Vatican II: More Postconciliar Documents* (Grand Rapids, Mich.: Eerdmans, 1982), 2:500–504. The Latin original is found in *Acta Apostolicae Sedis* 71 (1979), 939–943; English citation 502. See similarly, International Theological Commission, "Some Current Questions in Eschatology (1992)" in *Texts and Documents: 1986–2007*, Michael Sharkey and Thomas Weinandy, eds. (San Francisco: Ignatius Press, 2009), 84; *Catechism of the Catholic Church*, no. 1030.

[257] "Some Questions in Eschatology," *Texts and Documents: 1986–2007*, 84f. The text cites Catherine of Genoa's *Treatise on Purgatory,* English translation in Catherine of Genoa, *Purgation and Purgatory; The Spiritual Dialogue,* trans. Serge Hughes, The Classics of Western Spirituality (New York: Paulist Press, 1979).

[258] Ratzinger, *Eschatology*, 229f.

[259] John of the Cross, cited by the International Theological Commission, "Some Current Questions in Eschatology," *Texts and Documents: 1986–2007*, 85.

[260] Nicholas of Cusa, *De docta ignorantia*, III, 9, cited by Hans Urs von Balthasar. See also "Some Points of Eschatology" in *Explorations in Theology: I. The Word Made Flesh*, 265.

been appropriated by theologians, such as Joseph Ratzinger[261] and Hans Urs von Balthasar, who referred to "purgatorial fire" as "the sinner's encounter with Christ's 'eyes as a flame of fire' and 'feet . . . as a burning furnace' (Apoc. 1:14 = Dan. 10.6)."[262]

195.   Pope Benedict XVI, in his encyclical on hope, *Spe salvi*, describes this fire as Christ in a passage that deserves to be quoted at length:

> Some recent theologians are of the opinion that the fire which both burns and saves is Christ himself, the Judge and Saviour. The encounter with him is the decisive act of judgment. Before his gaze all falsehood melts away. This encounter with him, as it burns us, transforms and frees us, allowing us to become truly ourselves. All that we build during our lives can prove to be mere straw, pure bluster, and it collapses. Yet in the pain of this encounter, when the impurity and sickness of our lives become evident to us, there lies salvation. His gaze, the touch of his heart heals us through an undeniably painful transformation "as through fire". But it is a blessed pain, in which the holy power of his love sears through us like a flame, enabling us to become totally ourselves and thus totally of God. In this way the inter-relation between justice and grace also becomes clear: the way we live our lives is not immaterial, but our defilement does not stain us for ever if we have at least continued to reach out towards Christ, towards truth and towards love. Indeed, it has already been burned away through Christ's Passion. At the moment of judgment we experience and we absorb the overwhelming power of his love over all the evil in the world and in ourselves. The pain of love becomes our salvation and our joy.[263]

196.   This teaching makes clear that the Catholic doctrine of purgatory and the Lutheran teaching of the self being purified by death-and-resurrection intend to describe the same reality—namely, the process by which the self, distracted during this life by sin and the remnants of sin, is turned fully to Christ, purified of all that would hinder perfect communion with God, Christ, and the saints that will be the life of heaven. Juridical categories of satisfaction and debt, which helpfully emphasize our personal responsibility for sin, are not denied in this picture, but they are contextualized and integrated within a more

---

[261] Ratzinger, *Eschatology*, 231.

[262] Balthasar, *Explorations in Theology*, 265.

[263] *Spe salvi*, ¶47.

comprehensive picture of the power of God's love to transform the justified into persons fit for the kingdom.

197. As Ratzinger stated: "Purgatory is not, as Tertullian thought, some kind of supra-worldly concentration camp where man is forced to undergo punishment in a more or less arbitrary fashion. Rather is it the inwardly necessary process of transformation in which a person becomes capable of Christ, capable of God and thus capable of unity with the whole communion of saints."[264]

3) A greater integration of purgation with death and judgment.

198. The picture of purgatorial fire as Christ goes with an integration of purgatory with judgment itself. The encounter with Christ as Judge is the moment of purification.[265] Must this purification be interpreted as temporally extended in time? "Time" in this context must be understood analogously.[266] Pope Benedict XVI explains: "It is clear that we cannot calculate the 'duration' of this transforming burning in terms of the chronological measurements of this world. The transforming 'moment' of this encounter eludes earthly time-reckoning—it is the heart's time, it is the time of 'passage' to communion with God in the Body of Christ."[267] Karl Rahner, while granting that this purification is a process (i.e., every aspect of the person is perhaps not transformed simultaneously),[268] nevertheless sought to incorporate purification as a moment within the entire event of death as a closing of life and a confrontation with God.[269] If purification works within the person, cleansing the self in accord with the self's nature, then it perhaps must have a certain extension or "duration," but the temporal categories for understanding that extension must be applied with restraint, as was explicitly recommended by the

---

[264] Ratzinger, *Eschatology*, 230.

[265] Balthasar (op. cit.) is explicit on the need for such an integration.

[266] See e.g., Reginald Garrigou-Lagrange, *Life Everlasting and the Immensity of the Soul: A Theological Treatise on the Four Last Things: Death, Judgment, Heaven, Hell*, trans. Patrick Cummins (Rockford, Ill.: TAN Books, 1991), 90–93.

[267] *Spe salvi*, ¶47.

[268] Rahner, "The Life of the Dead," in *Theological Investigations, 4, More Recent Writings*, trans. Kevin Smyth (Baltimore: Helicon, and London: Darton, Longman & Todd, 1966), 353.

[269] For a discussion of Rahner on these matters, see Peter C. Phan, "Roman Catholic Theology," *The Oxford Handbook of Eschatology*, 223–224.

Congregation for Divine Worship and the Discipline of the Sacraments in its 2001 *Directory on Popular Piety and the Liturgy*.[270]

4) A specification of the ecumenically necessary.

199. Recent discussions of purgatory have stressed the bond of love that unites the living and the departed, a unity expressed in an unbroken community of prayer.[271] In *Spe salvi*, Benedict acknowledged that while the Orthodox do "not recognize the purifying and expiatory suffering of souls in the afterlife," they do share with the Catholic Church the practice of praying for the departed. In his earlier book on *Eschatology*, he had affirmed in relation to the Catholic-Orthodox disagreement on purgatory: "What is primary is the praxis of being able to pray, and being called upon to pray. The objective correlate of this praxis in the world to come need not, in some reunification of the churches, be determined of necessity in a strictly unitary fashion. . . ."[272]

200. While such a common basis in practice does not exist between Catholics and Lutherans, the openness to a variety of conceptualizations of the state of those who die in need of further purification is important.

b. Lutheran

201. During the nineteenth century, a few Lutheran theologians became open to the possibility of some sort of purification or continued sanctification that would continue in the person beyond death. K. F. A. Kahnis and Hans Martensen both objected that a total transformation at death did violence to the inherently developmental nature of the self. Such a transformation would be a violent "act of magic" [*Zauberschlag*], Kahnis argued.[273]

---

[270] Congregation for Divine Worship and the Discipline of the Sacraments, *Directory on Popular Piety and the Liturgy: Principles and Guidelines* (Vatican City, 2001). Online at *www.vatican.va/roman_curia/congregations/ ccdds/ index.htm*, accessed Sept. 2, 2010, ¶258.

[271] See *Spe salvi*, ¶48; International Theological Commission, *Some Questions Concerning Eschatology*, 80.

[272] Ratzinger, *Eschatology*, 233.

[273] Karl Friedrich August Kahnis, *System der lutherischen Dogmatik*, vol. 3 of *Die lutherische Dogmatik historisch-genetisch dargestellt* (Leipzig: Dörffling und Franke, 1868), 554. Kahnis linked this argument with wide-ranging speculations on the possibility of post-death conversion and the nature of spiritual bodies. For Martensen, see *Christian Dogmatics: A Compendium of the Doctrines of Christianity*, trans. William Urwick (Edinburgh: T. & T. Clark, 1892), 458–459. More recently, similar arguments that an immediate transformation is incompatible with an ongoing personal identity have been made by Protestant philosophers of religion, e.g. Jerry L. Walls, "Purgatory for Everyone," *First Things* 122 (April 2002): 26–30.

202. In the twentieth century, while many Lutherans continued to reject the idea of purgatory out of hand,[274] some prominent voices developed more nuanced positions. Paul Althaus contended that judgment will bring with it a painful recognition of the evil we have done. He saw such a painful recognition as an important part of our coming to fellowship with God.[275] In addition, sanctification is not complete at death.[276] Althaus rejects with some vehemence what he understands to be the Catholic understanding of purgatory, a continuation beyond death of a moralistically-conceived process of self-reformation. He insists that a transformation beyond death must be of a different sort, unlike sanctification in this life, in which God acts in a decisive way to transform the self.[277] While he identified this event with death, Alhaus also could connect it with judgment: "The pain of repentance into which God places us will then [*einmal*] illumine our sinful situation in life in all its aspects and corners. When God will give us that clarity, whether in the passage through death or with the entry into eternity, is hidden from us. . . . We can dare to confirm only the 'that,' not the 'when,' of such a revelation."[278]

203. Wolfhart Pannenberg, while critical of the concept of purgatory as a distinct, temporally-extended intermediate state, affirms purgation as an aspect of judgment. "The judgment that is put in Christ's hands is no longer destruction but a fire of purging and cleansing. . . . It involves the completing of penitence, but only as a moment in integration into the new life in fellowship with Jesus Christ. Thus the fire of judgment is purifying, not destructive fire." He develops this view in a discussion of the ideas of Joseph Ratzinger and concludes: "There is thus no more reason for the Reformation opposition."[279]

204. Recent Lutheran church documents have little to say about purgatory. The *Evangelischer Erwachsenenkatechismus* describes Catholic teaching and, while it does not explicitly reject the idea, its reticence about any temporally-extended intermediate state leaves little room for purgatory.[280] It does state, however, that divine judgment will

---

274 E.g., Werner Elert, *Der christliche Glaube: Grundlinien der lutherischen Dogmatik*, 6th ed. (Erlangen: Martin Luther Verlag, 1988), 527.

275 Paul Althaus, *Die letzten Dinge: Entwurf einer christlichen Eschatologie*, 3rd ed. (Gütersloh: C. Bertelsmann, 1926), 217.

276 Althaus, *Die letzten Dinge*, 225.

277 Althaus, *Die letzten Dinge*, 232.

278 Althaus, *Die letzten Dinge*, 237.

279 Wolfhart Pannenberg, *Systematic Theology*, trans. Geoffrey W. Bromiley (Grand Rapids, Mich.: Eerdmans, 1998), 3:619.

280 *Evangelischer Erwachsenenkatechismus*, 534.

bring with it a painful recognition of what were our motives and goals in this life.[281]

205.   More revealing is the statement from the Theological Committee of the Union Evangelischer Kirchen. In connection with the judgment of works, the statement cites 1 Corinthians 3: "Only the works that prove themselves to be 'evil' works, together with the traces they have left in the profile of our lives, will be 'burned' and pass away. Of the faithful persons *themselves*, however, who have done such works, it remains true: 'he himself will be saved, but only as through fire' (1 Cor. 3:15)."[282] This view is contrasted with what the committee takes to be the Catholic understanding of purgatory, in which purification occurs prior to judgment by Christ. Such a view is criticized as an "evasion of the comprehensive encounter with the gracious judge Jesus Christ."[283] It does conclude, however, with observation of a convergence between its own view and that of recent Catholic theology.[284]

5. Common Affirmations

206.   When misconceptions are stripped away and the continuing reflections of our churches are taken into account, the difference between our churches on the doctrine of purgatory is seen in a new light.

Agreements

207.   Catholics and Lutherans agree:

1. **During this life, the justified "are not exempt from a lifelong struggle against the contradiction to God within the selfish desires of the old Adam (see Gal. 5:16; Rom. 7:7-10)."[285]**

2. **This struggle is rightly described by a variety of categories: e.g., penitence, healing, daily dying and rising with Christ.**

3. **Borne in Christ, the painful aspects of this struggle are a participation in Christ's suffering and death. Catholic teachings call these pains temporal punishments; the**

---

[281]   *Evangelischer Erwachsenenkatechismus* 885.

[282]   *Unsere Hoffnung*, 88. Italics in original.

[283]   *Unsere Hoffnung*, 99.

[284]   *Unsere Hoffnung*, 99-100. The text cites the Catholic theologian Franz-Josef Nocke.

[285]   JDDJ, ¶28; cf. Trent, Denzinger and Schönmetzer, 1515 and 1690, and Large Catechism, Baptism, §§65-67, *Book of Concord*, 465.

Lutheran Confessions grant they, "in a formal sense," can be called punishments.[286]

4. This ongoing struggle does not indicate an insufficiency in Christ's saving work, but is an aspect of our being conformed to Christ and his saving work.[287]

5. The effects of sin in the justified are fully removed only as they die, undergo judgment, and encounter the purifying love of Christ. The justified are transformed from their condition at death to the condition with which they will be blessed in eternal glory. All, even martyrs and saints of the highest order, will find the encounter with the Risen Christ transformative in ways beyond human comprehension.

6. Christ transforms those who enter into eternal life. This change is a work of God's grace. It can be rightly understood as our final and perfect conformation to Christ (Phil 3:21). The fire of Christ's love burns away all that is incompatible with living in the direct presence of God. It is the complete death of the old person, leaving only the new person in Christ.

7. Scripture tells us little about the process of the transformation from this life to entrance into eternal life. Categories of space and time can be applied only analogously.

Distinctive Teachings

208. Catholics are committed to the doctrine of purgatory, i.e., to a process of purgation that occurs in or after death, and to the possibility that the living by their prayers can aid the departed undergoing this process. This aid will be discussed in the next section of this report, but here it should be noted that, for Catholic teaching, purgatory must be so understood as not to exclude this possibility.[288] As the survey of Catholic teaching on purgatory above shows, there is no binding Catholic doctrine on the spatial or temporal character of purgatory, on how many

---

[286] Apology XII, §148, *Book of Concord*, 213. This comment was added to the octavo edition of the Apology.

[287] JDDJ, ¶37.

[288] "The Church excludes every way of thinking or speaking that would render meaningless or unintelligible her prayers, her funeral rites and religious acts offered for the dead. All these are, in their substance, *loci theologici*." Sacred Congregation for the Doctrine of the Faith, "The Reality of Life After Death," ¶4. See also Neuner-Dupuis, *The Christian Faith*, 692.

Christians go through purgatory, or on the intensity or extent of their sufferings. While all the justified are transformed by eternal glory, Catholics admit the possibility that some people incur no further punishment after death.

209.   Lutherans teach that all the justified remain sinners unto death.[289] Sin and the effects of sin in those who die in Christ will be removed prior to entrance into eternal glory. In effect, they teach the reality of purgation, even if not as a distinct intermediate state. The rejection by the Lutheran Reformers of the doctrine of purgatory as they knew it focused on practices and abuses perceived as bound up with this teaching. They judged that the doctrine of purgatory obscured the gospel of free grace. The Lutheran Confessions explicitly express a willingness to discuss purgatory if the doctrine were separated from these practices and abuses, although at the same time expressing doubt about the biblical foundation of any such teaching.[290]

210.   The differences between Catholic and Lutheran teaching on purgatory thus focus on 1) how the living relate to those undergoing this purgation, and 2) the extent and explicit character of the binding teaching on purgation and purgatory. The more explicit the binding teaching, the greater the difficulty Lutherans have in seeing this teaching as biblical and thus binding. We have seen in this dialogue that explicit Catholic doctrine on purgatory is more limited than often recognized. As the Catholic attitude toward differences with the Orthodox indicates, these two differences are not entirely separable. Common practices toward the dead can provide an assurance that permits a diversity in formulation. The following discussion of prayer for the dead must thus be considered in assessing the ecumenical significance of Catholic-Lutheran understandings of purgatory.

Convergences

211.   Today, Lutheran and Catholic teaching integrates purgation with death, judgment, and the encounter with Christ. Recent Catholic and Lutheran understandings of purgation sound remarkably similar. While the word "purgatory" remains an ecumenically charged term, and for many Catholics and Lutherans signals a sharp division, our work in this round has shown that our churches' understandings of how the justified enter eternal glory are closer than expected.

---

[289] JDDJ, ¶29.

[290] Smalcald Articles, Part II, Second Article, §14, *Book of Concord*, 302.

212. In light of the analysis given above, this dialogue believes that the topic of purgation, in and of itself, need not divide our communions.[291]

B. Prayer for the Dead

213. Closely related to disputes on purgation and purgatory are beliefs and practices related to prayers for the dead. On the one hand, prayer for the dead became a common practice of the church during the patristic period and is a form of solidarity across the barrier of death overcome in Christ. On the other hand, many Lutherans came to see prayer for the dead as one aspect of a larger system of works offered to God which undercut reliance on the gospel of God's free grace. This dialogue will now explore whether the church-dividing character of our remaining differences over prayer for the dead may be overcome when prayer for the dead is placed in the context of 1) what is said above on purgation, 2) our agreement on justification, and 3) the understanding of communion developed in earlier rounds of this and other ecumenical dialogues.

1. Communion in Christ as the Context of Prayer for the Dead

214. Catholics and Lutherans share an understanding of the church as the communion of saints, the *communio sanctorum*.[292] For both Lutherans and Catholics, the Spirit unites the baptized into the body of Christ, the church (1 Cor. 12:13). The Second Vatican Council affirmed that God has willed "to make women and men holy and to save them, not as individuals without any bond between them, but rather to make them into a people who might acknowledge him and serve him in holiness."[293] In the Large Catechism, Luther speaks similarly writing that when the Holy Spirit redeems, "he first leads us into his holy community, placing us in the church's lap, where he preaches to us and brings us to Christ."[294]

---

[291] Questions of whether the process of purgation continues for some people after death and whether the living can aid them are discussed elsewhere in this text.

[292] A comprehensive discussion of the church as the communion of saints from a Catholic-Lutheran ecumenical perspective can be found in Bilateral Working Group of the German National Bishops' Conference and the Church Leadership of the United Evangelical Lutheran Church of Germany, *Communio Sanctorum: The Church as the Communion of Saints.*

[293] *Lumen gentium*, §9.

[294] Large Catechism, the Creed, §37, *Book of Concord*, 435–436.

215. In this communion, we are one with one another because we all share in Christ. "Our *koinonia* with God through Christ in the Holy Spirit constitutes our '*koinonia* with one another' (1 John 1:3, 7)."[295] This communion is not our achievement, but a gift of grace. As a gift of grace, we cannot take it for granted, but must regularly turn to God anew in prayer, asking that he continue to grant his Spirit of communion. In this sense, prayer is an embodiment of our justification by grace. [296]

216. Through the Spirit, "we are members one of another" (Eph. 4:25). This mutual membership then requires a sharing of one with another. "As Christ gives us nothing less than himself and the Spirit provides us with manifold gifts, so a mutual openness and a sharing of our spiritual and material gifts is a living out of our communion with one another."[297] In communion, we share our goods, our needs, and our concerns. Prayer, especially intercessory prayer for one another within the church, is a fundamental expression of communion.[298]

217. This intimate communion in the Spirit is not broken by death. As the Catholics and Lutherans in our dialogue stated in an earlier round: "The fellowship of those sanctified, the 'holy ones' or saints, includes believers both living and dead. There is thus a solidarity of the church throughout the world with the church triumphant."[299] This solidarity across the barrier of death is particularly evident in the Eucharist, which is always celebrated in unity with the hosts of heaven. In Catholic Eucharistic Prayer II, the celebrant introduces the Sanctus with the words: "And so we join the angels and the saints in proclaiming your glory as we say. . . ."[300] The Prefaces in *Evangelical Lutheran Worship* end with the declaration: "And so, with all the choirs of angels, with the church on

---

[295] Working Group on Ecclesiology, "Toward a Lutheran Understanding of Communion," in *The Church as Communion: Lutheran Contributions to Ecclesiology*, Heinrich Holze, ed., LWF Documentation (Geneva: Lutheran World Federation, 1997), 42:16.

[296] On this understanding of prayer, see further Regin Prenter, "The Evangelical Doctrine of Prayer," in *The Word and the Spirit: Essays on the Inspiration of the Scriptures* (Minneapolis: Augsburg Publishing House, 1965), 116–117.

[297] Working Group on Ecclesiology, "Toward a Lutheran Understanding of Communion," 42:21–22.

[298] John Zizioulas, *Being as Communion: Studies in Personhood and the Church* (Crestwood, N.Y.: St. Vladimir's Seminary Press, 1985), 257.

[299] *The One Mediator, the Saints, and Mary*, ¶103, 60.

[300] Eucharistic Prayer II, in *The Sacramentary of The Roman Missal* (Collegeville, Mich.: The Liturgical Press, 1985), 509.

earth and the hosts of heaven, we praise your name and join their unending hymn. . . ."[301] Particularly in praise and adoration of God at the Lord's table, the apparent division marked by death melts away. Lutherans and Catholics can together affirm what the Lutherans said in an earlier round of this dialogue that:

> [F]aith does not mean individualism, but rather a being born anew into the communion of believers, the body of Christ which is the church. As members of the church, believers participate by grace in the divine Trinitarian life—in a "mystical union" (*unio mystica*) that anticipates the full future glory of Christ "beheld with an unveiled face" (2 Cor. 3:18; cf. 5:1-10 and Rom. 8:20-30 in the context of 8:18-39).[302]

218. The ecumenically neuralgic question is whether this unity in prayer and adoration extends to a unity in intercessory prayer. Do the living in this world and those who live in Christ beyond death still share a communion of concern, expressed in intercessory prayer for one another? An earlier round of this dialogue addressed the question of the prayers for us by the saints in heaven and whether we can invoke such prayers. In a carefully nuanced statement, they recognized Catholic-Lutheran differences in belief and practice, but proposed that those differences need not be church-dividing.[303] What can now be said about the prayers of those living for those who have gone before us? Can the living lift up in prayer their concerns for their fellow members in the body of Christ who have already died?

2. Prayer for the Dead in Scripture and Tradition

a. Scripture

219. Prayers for the dead are not explicitly mentioned in the New Testament, although some interpreters believe that 2 Timothy 1:16-18

---

[301] These words conclude the preface for Sundays. See *Evangelical Lutheran Worship*, Leaders, 180. Prefaces for various celebrations sometimes mention particular saints with whom the congregation joins in praise. For example, the Preface for Easter mentions Mary Magdalene and Peter: "And so, with Mary Magdalene and Peter and all the witnesses of the resurrection, with earth and sea and all their creatures, and with angels and archangels, cherubim and seraphim, we praise your name and join their unending hymn. . . ." *Evangelical Lutheran Worship*, Leaders, 187.

[302] *The One Mediator, the Saints, and Mary*, ¶50, 41.

[303] *The One Mediator, the Saints, and Mary*, 49–62.

makes the most sense if Onesiphorus, for whom Paul prays, is dead.[304] Nor are there explicit references to or exhortations about prayers for the dead in the Hebrew canon of the Old Testament. The one explicit biblical reference to prayer for the dead comes in 2 Maccabees 12:42, as noted earlier.[305]

220. The absence of a command or exemplar in relation to prayer for the dead in either the New Testament or the Hebrew Old Testament is one of the primary Lutheran concerns about this practice.

b. Patristic and Medieval Developments

221. References to prayer for the dead appear already in the second century. Tertullian speaks of suffering after death that he believed to be relieved by the intercession of the living.[306] Such references are common in the writings of the Fathers. While specific questions of whom one might legitimately pray for were disputed, the general practice of prayer for the dead seems universally accepted. No author from the orthodox mainstream of the church, East or West, opposed prayer for the dead. In the mid-fourth century, Aerius, a presbyter of Pontus, is said to have denied the efficacy of prayer for the dead, for which (and other reasons) he was widely condemned.[307] The practice of such prayer assumed that prayer could have some effect on the state of the departed, but the practice was not bound up with any widely accepted and precisely developed set of beliefs about the exact situation of the departed or the manner in which prayer aids the dead.[308] Prayer for the dead predated any explicit theology elaborating its rationale.

---

[304] On this question, see Risto Saarinen, *The Pastoral Epistles with Philemon and Jude*, Brazos Theological Commentary on the Bible (Grand Rapids, Mich.: Brazos Press, 2008), 133–134.

[305] The canonical issue in relation to this text was more than simply formal. Martin Chemnitz argues that the prayer and sacrifice for the dead reported in 2 Maccabees reflect the degeneracy of faithful religious practice among Jews in the centuries just before Christ and thus texts from this period are rightly non-canonical. Martin Chemnitz, *Examination of the Council of Trent, Part III*, trans. Fred Kramer (St. Louis: Concordia Publishing House, 1986), 235.

[306] Tertullian, *On the Resurrection of the Body*, 43.

[307] Epiphanius, *Panarion*, in PG 42, cols. 513-516, in English in *The Panarion of St. Epiphanius, Bishop of Salamis: Selected Passages*, trans. Philip R. Amidon (Oxford: Oxford University Press, 1990), 327.

[308] For various patristic figures speaking on prayer for the dead, see Daley, *The Hope of the Early Church*, 74, 108, 111, 138, 166, 184, 200, 214.

222. As with the related idea of purgation, the writings of Augustine and Gregory the Great were widely read in the following centuries and became *loci classici* for the topic. In his *Confessions*, Book 9, Augustine refers to the request made by his mother Monica that "you should remember me at the altar of the Lord." Before Monica's burial, Augustine and others offered prayers "while the sacrifice of our redemption was offered for my mother." Once Augustine's grief for his mother quieted, he prayed that her sins, if there were any, be forgiven. "All that she wanted was that we should remember her at your altar, where she had been your servant day after day without fail."[309]

223. In *The Care to be Taken for the Dead* (421), Augustine cited approvingly Paulinus of Nola's indication of "the practice of the universal church to pray for their dead," and adds on his own that, even without the witness of 2 Maccabees, "the authority of the universal church which clearly favors this practice is of great weight, where in the prayers of the priest which are poured forth to the Lord God at his altar the commemoration for the dead has its place."[310]

224. Augustine raises a question that will be important for later debates: Who among the dead can benefit from such prayer? His answer is that such prayer only benefits "those who while they lived made preparation that they might be so aided."[311] In the *Enchiridion*, he explains that such persons

> . . . during their lives merited that these services should one day help them. For there is a manner of life neither so good as not to need such helps after death, nor so bad that they cannot be of benefit. But there are likewise those so devoted to good that they do not need these helps; and again, those so steeped in evil that when they depart this life these helps avail nothing. Evidently, then, it is in this life that the basis is laid on which a person deserves to have his condition in the afterlife alleviated or aggravated. . . . When, therefore, sacrifices either of the altar or of alms of any kind are of-

---

[309] Citing from *Confessions*, Book 9, chs. 11, 12, and 13, in the translation of R. S. Pine-Coffin (London: Penguin, 1961), 199, 201, and 204.

[310] *Care for the Dead*, 1, 1 and 3, citing from *Treatises on Marriage and Other Subjects*, 352-353. In a similar passage in an undated sermon, Augustine spoke of prayers and the eucharistic sacrifice offered for the departed who died in "the communion of the body and blood of Christ" as a "tradition received from the Fathers." Sermon 172, in *Sermons*, The Works of Saint Augustine, III/5 (New Rochelle, N.Y.: New City Press, 1992), 253.

[311] *Care for the Dead*, 18, 22, citing from *Treatises on Marriage and Other Subjects*, 383.

fered for all the baptized dead, they are for the very good thank offerings; for the not very bad propitiatory offerings; and, though for the very bad they have no significance as helps for the dead, they do bring consolation to the living.[312]

225.   As this quotation makes clear, in Augustine as in other writers of the period, prayers for the dead are seen in close conjunction with offering the Eucharist and good works for the dead. While we care for the dead in their burial, "we should be much more punctilious, more pressing, and more generous in seeing to those things which can help the spirits of the dead, such as offerings, prayers, and expenditure on good works and almsgiving."[313]

226.   Gregory the Great made clear that prayers benefit the dead only if they did not die burdened with mortal sin.[314] "Provided their guilty deeds are not beyond pardoning even after death, the holy offering of the saving Victim brings great benefits to souls after death. For this reason the souls of the dead sometime appear in order to ask this for themselves."[315] Gregory provides various accounts of such appearances.[316]

---

[312] *Faith Hope and Charity*, 29, 110; Ancient Christian Writers, 3, 103–104, modified from the original, given in Corpus Christianorum, Series Latina, 46, 108-09. He refers to this middling quality of life of those aided after death in *The City of God*, 21, 24 and 27. Luther knew this text of Augustine on aid to certain souls among the departed and referred to it in explaining indulgences applied to them, in his 1517 *Treatise on Indulgences* (see J. Wicks, *Luther's Reform*, 103–104). In *Care for the Dead*, Augustine says similarly: "But even though we do not know who these are, we ought none the less to do such works for all Christians, so that no one of them may be neglected for whom these aids can and ought to come. It is better that there be a superabundance of aids to help those for whom these works are neither a hindrance nor a help, than that there be a lack for those who are thus aided" (op cit.).

[313] Sermon 172, in *Sermons*, The Works of Saint Augustine, III/5 (New Rochelle, N.Y.: New City Press, 1992), 253.

[314] *Dialogues*, 4, 52; Fathers of the Church, 39, 263; Sources chrétiennes, 265, 176.

[315] *Dialogues*, 4, 57; Fathers of the Church, 39, 266; Sources chrétiennes, 265, 184.

[316] For example, Gregory recounts the story of the monk Justus of his own former monastery, who on his deathbed confessed in bitter contrition his offense against common life in hiding three gold pieces amid his effects. A month later the then Abbot Gregory had daily Masses offered for Justus, that is, "by helping as much as we can to gain his release" from purgatorial burning. On the thirtieth day of these Masses, Justus appeared to another monk to announce his release from bad straits and reception of the "communion" of heaven (*Dialogues*, 4, 57; Fathers of the Church, 39, 267–269; Sources chrétiennes, 265, 188–192). On the long-term outcome of these passages of Gregory on the release of souls from purgatory, see Cyril Vogel, "Deux conséquences de l'eschatologie grégorienne: la multiplication des messes privées et les moines-prêtres," in J. Fontaine *et al.*, eds., *Grégoire le Grand* (Paris: Éditions du CNRS, 1986), 266–276.

227. In the medieval and early modern period, prayers for the dead remained a significant part of Christian practice and found such liturgical expression as the institution of All Souls Day (November 2).[317] Two developments are important for the debates with Lutherans and others within the Reformation. First, as the concepts of merit and satisfaction were more precisely developed, prayer could come to be understood in relation to these concepts. Aquinas sees prayer as having a twofold efficacy, as impetration (i.e., an appeal to divine mercy) and as merit.[318] If the need for purgation is understood more juridically in relation to the need to complete satisfactions and less sanatively in relation to the need to heal the wounds due to sin, prayer for the dead also can be absorbed into the more juridical discourse of satisfactions. Second, the doctrinal statements on purgation and purgatory of the councils of Florence (1439) and Trent (1563), while reticent in many respects, both explicitly affirm that prayers and other suffrages applied to the dead are not only appropriate, but are so because by them those undergoing purgation are "relieved" (*releventur*; Florence) or "helped" (*iuvari*, Trent). While nothing is said about precisely *how* suffrages provide such assistance (e.g., by impetration or by satisfaction), *that* such suffrages in fact aid the dead becomes defined doctrine.

c. Reformation Critique

228. The Lutheran Confessions do not formally develop the topic of prayer for the dead; the Confessions, however, explicitly do not reject prayer for the dead in a reference to it in Article 24 of the Apology on Masses for the Dead. The Apology states: "We knew that the ancients spoke of prayer for the dead. We do not prohibit this. . . . Epiphanius testifies that Aerius believed that prayers for the dead were useless. This he rejects. We do not support Aerius either."[319] Not only are prayers for the dead not forbidden, but the Apology, in this instance, accepted the usefulness of such prayers without attempting to define precisely how they aid the dead.

229. The most important statement from Luther comes in his "Confession Concerning Christ's Supper" where he writes: "As for the dead, since Scripture gives us no information on the subject, I regard it as no sin to pray with free devotion in this or some similar fashion: 'Dear

---

[317] On the origin of All Souls Day, see J. Le Goff, *The Birth of Purgatory*, 125.

[318] Thomas Aquinas, *Summa Theologiae*, II-II, q. 83, a. 15.

[319] Apology, Article 24, §§94 and 96, *Book of Concord*, 275–276.

God, if this soul is in a condition accessible to mercy be thou gracious to it.' And when this has been done once or twice, let it suffice."[320]

230. These affirmations were noted in the debates of the time. In his response to Trent's statement on purgatory, Martin Chemnitz responds to Catholic apologists who argued that these statements from the Apology and Luther were inconsistent with a rejection of purgatory. Chemnitz argues that the doctrine of purgatory is not implied by these earlier statements. He does not repudiate what Melanchthon and Luther had affirmed.[321]

231. While in principle open to prayer for the dead, the Lutheran Reformation was opposed, even bitterly opposed, to the larger system of belief and practice within which prayer for the dead had come to be lodged. The decisive question for the Reformers was whether the concrete practice of prayer for the dead as it existed in their time supported or undercut the joyous proclamation of God's free grace. The complex network of beliefs and practices surrounding the relation of the living to the dead—purgatory, Masses offered for the dead, indulgences applied to the dead, and prayers for the dead—were seen by the Reformers as deeply antagonistic to that evangelical proclamation. That antagonism was seen to take at least two forms.

232. First, prayer for the dead was seen as at least potentially one form of a system in which salvation came to be purchased from God by good works. The context of the quotation given above from the Apology makes this connection clear:

> We know that the ancients spoke of prayer for the dead. We do not prohibit this, but we do reject the transfer, *ex opere operato*, of the Lord's Supper to the dead. . . . But we are contending with you for wickedly defending a heresy that clearly conflicts with the prophets, apostles, and holy Fathers, namely, that the Mass justifies *ex opere operato* and that it merits the remission of guilt and punishment even for the wicked [*iniustis*] to whom it is transferred, if they place no obstacle in the way.[322]

That the Apology groups together these issues is telling. While prayer for the dead is not prohibited, the worry is evident that such prayers will be seen not

---

[320] *Luther's Works*, vol. 37, Robert H. Fischer, ed. (Philadelphia: Muhlenberg Press, 1961), 369; Weimar Ausgabe, vol. 26, 508.

[321] Chemnitz, *Examination, III*, 259.

[322] Apology, Article 24, §§94 and 96, *Book of Concord*, 275–276.

as expressions of faithful dependence on divine grace, but as meritorious works, the benefit from which can be applied, in an impersonal, juridical fashion, to the dead. Luther's concern is similar; the quotation above from the "Confession Concerning Christ's Supper" immediately continues, "For vigils and requiem Masses and yearly celebrations of requiems are useless, and are merely the devil's annual fair."[323]

233. The second objection was closely connected to the first and can be seen in Luther's concern that one pray for the dead only "once or twice."[324] He feared that prayer for the dead, particularly extensively repeated prayers, manifested a lack of confidence in the sufficiency of the saving merits of Christ. In keeping with the statement quoted above from the "Confession Concerning Christ's Supper," Luther advised Bartholomäus von Starhemberg in a letter following the death of his wife to pray for her "once or twice." Extensive prayer "is a sign that we do not believe in God and with our faithless prayers we only anger him more."[325]

234. The primary Lutheran question in relation to prayer for the dead is whether such prayer is consistent with and supports the proclamation of God's free and justifying grace. The judgment of the Lutheran Reformers, expressed in the Confessions, is that while the general concept of prayer for the dead is acceptable, prayer for the dead had come to be associated with unevangelical beliefs and practices.

235. The Lutheran Reformers had three additional arguments against prayers for the dead, though these arguments are not explicitly made in the Lutheran Confessions. First, they regularly condemned the system of suffrages for the dead—prayers, Masses, and indulgences—as a corrupt money-making operation for the clergy.[326] Second, the absence of a biblical mandate for prayers for the dead was often stressed. Because Scripture does not prohibit such prayer, Luther, as noted in the quotation

---

[323] *Luther's Works,* 37:369.

[324] *Luther's Works,* 37:369.

[325] Weimar Ausgabe 18:6; quoted in Craig M. Koslofsky, *The Reformation of the Dead: Death and Ritual in Early Modern Germany, 1450–1700* (London: Macmillan, 2000), 84.

[326] "It is a long story, and long are the roundabout ways of the traffickings by which the Pope and the cardinals have acquired unlimited wealth. . . . Indeed, look at all the monasteries and temples that have been erected at no other costs than the money spent to buy offerings for the dead. For this purpose the whole world piled up its wealth to liberate souls from the tortures of purgatory." *Luther's Works,* vol. 7, Jaroslav Pelikan, ed.(St. Louis: Concordia Publishing House, 1965), 297. See also *Luther's Works,* vol. 44, James Atkinson, ed. (Philadelphia: Fortress Press, 1966), 180; Chemnitz, *Examination, III,* 302.

from the "Confession Concerning Christ's Supper," was unwilling simply to condemn it. As not biblically mandated, however, such prayer cannot be certain. Chemnitz concedes that the teachings of the Fathers on prayer for the dead is "not against Scripture," but adds that "the ancients acted dangerously when they did this without command and example of Scripture in the form of prayer for the dead." By doing so, they started down a road that finally led to "the purgatory of the papalists."[327]

236. Third, if the existence of purgatory has been denied and a particular judgment is said to occur in a definitive way immediately at death, then the question arises about what aid can be offered by our prayers. Luther comments on the prayer in the Mass that asks that "refreshment, light, and peace" be granted to those "who have gone before us with the sign of faith and repose in the sleep of peace." He notes that the priest "prays for those who repose in the sleep of peace and rest in Christ and have the sign of faith. If that is true, why should you pray for them? Are you not a madman and a fool?"[328]

237. As a result of this multiform critique, prayer for the dead mostly disappeared from Lutheran worship and piety. Chemnitz recommended prayer for an infant who dies unbaptized, but he remained deeply suspicious of prayer for the dead as a public practice.[329] A few sixteenth century Lutheran church orders preserved prayer for the dead,[330] but by the

---

[327] Chemnitz, *Examination, III*, 280.

[328] *Luther's Works*, vol. 36, Abdel Ross Wentz, ed. (Philadelphia: Muhlenberg Press, 1959), 322. See similarly *Luther's Works*, vol. 7, 296, 298.

[329] "[T]hose infants are to be brought and commended to Christ in prayers. And one should not doubt that those prayers are heard, for they are made in the name of Christ. John 16:23; Gen. 17:7; Matt. 19:14. Since, then, we cannot bring infants as yet unborn to Christ through Baptism, therefore we should do it through pious prayers. Parents are to be put in mind of this, and if perhaps such a case occur, they are to be encouraged with this comfort." Martin Chemnitz, *Ministry, Word, and Sacraments: An Enchiridion*, trans. and ed. Luther Poellot (St. Louis: Concordia Publishing House, 1981), 120.

[330] Württemberg (1536) states that the pastor, at the end of the funeral, should "commend the deceased to the gracious hand of God." Aemilius Ludwig Richter, *Die evangelischen Kirchenordnungen des sechszehnten Jahrhunderts*, vol. 1 (Leipzig: Ernst Julius Günther, 1871), 273; the Hanover church order (1536) states that "to remember the living and the dead at the table of the Lord is an old and fine usage, but one must act correctly and not as a sacrifice [*Opfer*] for their sins, but give thanks for the one sacrifice which we all enjoy in this life and after this life" (Richter, 275). A commendation prayer also is mandated in the Hesse church orders of 1566 and 1574. Emil Sehling et al. *Die evangelischen Kirchenordnungen des 16. Jahrhunderts* (Tübingen: Mohr Siebeck, 1965), VIII/1:336f, 450. The conclusion of Craig Koslofsky that prayer for the dead is "always forbidden" in sixteenth century Lutheran church orders is not correct; see Koslofsky, *Reformation of the Dead*, 106.

middle of the century "any hint of the practice was generally abandoned in the Lutheran churches."[331]

3. Contemporary Convergence

a. Liturgical Convergences

238. If Lutheran and Catholic liturgy and piety moved apart in their attitude to the dead during the sixteenth century, they have significantly converged over the last 100 years. Since the question in relation to prayer for the dead is precisely how the church prays, this liturgical convergence is of great significance.

239. Both Catholic and Lutheran funerals emphasize the continuing communion of the living and the dead. While Lutheran funeral rites in the past were generally modeled on the pre-Reformation Office for the Dead, recent rites have called for the celebration of the Eucharist. The Eucharist celebrates the communion that binds together those on the two sides of death. Prayers in both of our liturgies call to mind the overarching communion of saints. In the Catholic Church, the Opening Prayer at the Vigil for the Deceased, for example, addresses God saying, "But for those who believe in your love death is not the end, nor does it destroy the bonds that you forge in our lives."[332]

240. On the Catholic side, the critique that attitudes toward death had come to be dominated by a fear of judgment and purgatory finds little basis in contemporary Catholic funeral liturgies. Most significantly, the funeral liturgy focuses on the promise of resurrection rather than on the threat of divine judgment. The General Introduction to the Order of Christian Funerals identifies funeral liturgies with the gospel proclamation that "God has created each person for eternal life and that Jesus, the Son of God, by his death and resurrection, has broken the chains of sin and death that bound humanity."[333] By being baptized into Jesus' death, Christians went into the tomb with him and joined him in death, so that as Christ was raised from the dead by the Father's glory, we also live a new life. Imitating Christ in death, we shall imitate him in his resurrection (Rom. 6:3-5). The paradigm of the funeral rite is the

---

[331] Philip H. Pfatteicher, *Commentary on Lutheran Book of Worship: Lutheran Liturgy in Its Ecumenical Context* (Minneapolis: Augsburg Fortress, 1990), 476.

[332] *The Rites of the Catholic Church* (Collegeville, Minn.: Liturgical Press, 1990), 1:952.

[333] "General Introduction to the Order of Christian Funerals," §1, *The Rites of the Catholic Church*, 1:924.

baptismal rite with its symbolism of baptismal water (sprinkling the coffin), white garment (pall), candle (paschal candle). In the introductory rite, the priest says, "In the waters of baptism N. died with Christ and rose with him to new life. May *he/she* now share with him eternal glory."[334]

241. In this context, prayers for the dead become expressions of our confident entrusting of the departed to the care and mercy of God. Typical examples are:

> Remember our brothers and sisters who have gone to their rest in the hope of rising again; bring them and all the departed into the light of your presence.[335]

> Look with love on our dying *brother (sister)* and make *him (her)* one with your Son in his suffering and death that, sealed with the blood of Christ, *he (she)* may come before you free from sin.[336]

> Almighty God, our Father, we firmly believe that your Son died and rose to life. We pray for our *brother (sister) N.* who has died in Christ. Raise *him (her)* at the last day to share the glory of the risen Christ.[337]

The introduction to the rite states, "The Church intercedes on behalf of the deceased because of its confident belief that death is not the end nor does it break the bonds forged by life."[338]

242. On the Lutheran side, many Lutheran funeral liturgies, both in the United States and in Europe, have come to include commendations of the dead that are clearly a form of prayer for the dead:

> Into your hands, O merciful Savior, we commend your servant, _Name_. Acknowledge we humbly beseech you a sheep of your own fold, a lamb of your own flock, a sinner of your own redeeming. Receive *her/him* into the arms of your mercy, into the blessed rest of everlasting peace and into the glorious company of the saints in light.[339]

---

[334] Funeral Mass, §278, *The Rites of the Catholic Church*, 1019.

[335] Eucharistic Prayer II, "Commemoration of the Dead," *Roman Missal, The Sacramentary* (Collegeville, Minn.: Liturgical Press, 1985), 512.

[336] Mass of the Dying, Opening Prayer, *Roman Missal, The Sacramentary*, 829.

[337] Funeral Mass, Opening Prayer, *Roman Missal, The Sacramentary*, 861.

[338] General Introduction §4, "Order of Christian Funerals," *The Rites of the Catholic Church*, 925.

[339] *Evangelical Lutheran Worship*, Leaders, 671.

At the graveside, the presiding minister prays:

> In sure and certain hope of the resurrection to eternal life
> through our Lord Jesus Christ, we commend to almighty
> God our *sister/brother Name* , and commit *her/his* body to
> the ground; earth to earth, ashes to ashes, dust to dust. The
> Lord bless *her/him* and keep *her/him*. The Lord's face shine
> on *her/him* with grace and mercy. The Lord look upon *her/
> him* with favor and give *her/him* peace.[340]

> Keep our *sister/brother Name* , whose body we now lay to
> rest in the company of all your saints. And at the last O
> God, raise *her/him* up to share with all the faithful the end-
> less joy and peace won through the glorious resurrection of
> Christ our Lord. . . .[341]

243.   Similar prayers can be found in recent funeral liturgies of other
Lutheran churches. The funeral liturgy of the United Evangelical-
Lutheran Church in Germany includes similar commendation prayers
both for the liturgy in the church and at graveside, such as:

> May the angels lead you to heaven, the holy martyrs greet
> you and lead you into the holy city Jerusalem. May the choirs
> of angels receive you and through Christ who has died for
> you may you rejoice in eternal life.[342]

Swedish Lutheran liturgies also reflect these changes.[343]

244.   The inclusion of such prayers was not without controversy.
During the development in the United States of the 1978 *Lutheran Book
of Worship*, surveys found a strong majority in support of the proposed
funeral order, but objections were received to the commendation prayers
as untrue to Reformation principles. In response, the confessional
statement that prayers for the dead are not prohibited was cited, while

---

[340] *Evangelical Lutheran Worship*, Leaders, 673.

[341] *Evangelical Lutheran Worship*, Leaders, 672.

[342] Die Kirchenleitung der Vereinigten Evangelisch-Lutherischen Kirche
Deutschlands, *Agende fuer Evangelisch-Lutherische Kirchen und Gemeinden:
Band III: Die Amtshandlungen; Teil 5: Die Bestattung*, rev. ed. (Hanover:
Lutherisches Verlagshaus, 1996), 52, 54, 78.

[343] See the discussion already in the 1950s in Gustaf Aulén, *The Faith of the
Christian Church*, trans. Eric H. Wahlstrom (Philadelphia: Muhlenberg Press,
1960), 390.

distinctions were drawn between what was being proposed and the array of practices to which the Reformers objected.[344]

245.   Today, Catholic and Lutheran funerals alike emphasize a confident hope in the grace of God that gathers together the justified into the perfect communion that exists beyond death. Worship books of both traditions now call for funerals within the context of the Eucharist, celebrating our continued fellowship with the dead within the body of Christ. Catholic and many Lutheran funeral liturgies contain a prayerful commendation of the dead into the hands of a merciful and gracious God. While this convergence in practice does not extend to a common practice of prayer for the dead beyond funerals, it does indicate a growing unity in our practices in relation to those who have died in Christ.

b. Doctrinal Convergences

246.   These liturgical convergences are rooted in a convergence also in theology and doctrine. Three changes are most important.

247.   First, both of our traditions have seen a new emphasis on communion or *koinonia* as an overarching concept to understand the union of Christians with the Trinity and with each other.[345] Through Word and Sacrament, persons are taken into "the communion of the Holy Spirit" (2 Cor. 13:14), uniting them both with God and with one another. This focus has become central for reflection on the church. On the Catholic side, the 1985 Synod of Bishops, reflecting on the twentieth anniversary of the end of the Second Vatican Council, saw "communion"

---

[344] On such discussions, see Ralph W. Quere, *In the Context of Unity: A History of the Development of the Lutheran Book of Worship* (Minneapolis: Lutheran University Press, 2003), 108–110, 136, 172–173. The service books of The Lutheran Church–Missouri Synod (LCMS) do not include such commendation prayers. The inclusion of such prayers was one of the grounds for the LCMS not accepting the 1978 *Lutheran Book of Worship*. The committal prayer in the funeral liturgy in the LCMS *Lutheran Service Book* asks only that God "keep these remains to the day of the resurrection of all flesh." Commission on Worship of The Lutheran Church–Missouri Synod, *Lutheran Service Book: Altar Book* (St. Louis: Concordia Publishing House, 2006), 397. This difference between the LCMS and the ELCA, along with many other Lutheran churches within the Lutheran World Federation, means that the affirmations of this dialogue in relation to prayers for the dead cannot be embraced by the LCMS participants.

[345] For a survey of the significance of this concept, see this dialogue's earlier work in Randall Lee and Jeffrey Gros, eds. *The Church as Koinonia of Salvation: Its Structures and Ministries, Lutherans and Catholics in Dialogue X* (Washington, D.C.: United States Conference of Catholic Bishops, 2005), esp. ¶¶10-20.

as "the central and fundamental idea" of the council.[346] In 1990, the Lutheran World Federation redefined itself as a "communion of churches" and has since then engaged in extensive study of the meaning of communion.[347] A strength of the concept of communion is its capacity to be applied to a wide range of aspects of the church, from the institutional to the spiritual.

248. Because the foundation of the communion of Christians is their common life in Christ and the Spirit, this communion cannot be broken by death. Christ has overcome death. Both Catholics and Lutherans have affirmed this conclusion. For example, the General Introduction to the Catholic Order of Christian Funerals makes the point that "the Christian community affirms and expresses the union of the Church on earth with the Church in heaven in the one great communion of saints."[348] The German Lutheran *Evangelische Erwachsenenkatechismus* speaks similarly: "The communion of believers, the church, is not broken by death. As in life, so in death the Christian is dependent on the community. In prayer the congregation intercedes before God for the one who has fallen asleep. They ask for the forgiveness of his sin, acceptance by God, and eternal life. When in many congregations the dead are blessed at the graveside, that is a palpable expression of the connection beyond death."[349]

249. Within the framework of the communion of saints, prayer for one another and also for the dead can take on a different theological quality. It is an expression of solidarity in our common trust in the grace of God.[350] Expressions of connection with and care for the deceased, natural for a bereaved Christian, find their way into the communal prayers of the Christian assembly. Prayer for the dead arises primarily out

---

[346] The Final Report, "The Church under the Word of God, Celebrates the Mysteries of Christ for the Salvation of the World," II, C. 1 (*www.nytimes.com/ 1985/12/08/world/text-of-final-report-adopted-by-synod-of-bishops-in-rome.html,* accessed September 10, 2010).

[347] See, e.g., Heinrich Holze, ed., *The Church as Communion: Lutheran Contributions to Ecclesiology,* LWF Documentation (Geneva: Lutheran World Federation, 1997).

[348] General Introduction §6, "Order of Christian Funerals," *The Rites of the Catholic Church,* 925.

[349] *Evangelische Erwachsenenkatechismus,* 539.

[350] "All Christian prayer is prayer in fellowship—also that prayer which is prayed in the closet. For the place where those who pray meet is in Jesus' name." Regin Prenter, "The Evangelical Doctrine of Prayer," *The Word and the Spirit: Essays on the Inspiration of the Scriptures* (Minneapolis: Augsburg, 1965), 118.

of the bonds of grace that unite us in God and continue to unite us with our loved ones who have died. We confidently trust that God will continue to embrace our loved ones. Such prayer does not express anxiety, uncertainty, or the fear that our love for the deceased is greater than God's love for them. God's grace never, however, becomes a possession we can take for granted; we pray for it anew, for ourselves and others, each day.[351] Prayer is an expression of constant dependence on God and, on a different level, on one another in the church as each remembers the others in prayer.

250. Second, as already noted above, theology in the twentieth century re-emphasized the biblical and patristic centrality of the communal and universal "last things" which will consummate all history. A communal, public last judgment holds a prominent place among those last things (e.g., Matt. 25:31-46). As noted above, the precise relation between that last judgment and the judgment that occurs individually is difficult to define theologically. Individual judgment is not to be overturned by the last judgment, but the last judgment continues to hold the central place in the picture of judgment put forward by the New Testament and the early church. When prayer for the dead is seen in the context of this orientation to communal and universal eschatology, its contours again change. The church looks to the future and prays that all who die in faith may be raised on the last day. For example, the intercessions for Evening Prayer II of Week 1 in the Catholic *Liturgy of the Hours* conclude: "Grant to the dead the glory of resurrection, and give us a share in their happiness."[352] Recent Lutheran commendation prayers (noted above) also often have such an eschatological focus. Prayer is the appropriate Christian orientation toward God's promised future for the church past and present. Prayer in relation to the future is hope expressed in direct address to God.

---

[351] This outlook can be found in Martin Luther's 1519 sermon, "The Blessed Sacrament of the Holy and True Body of Christ, and the Brotherhoods," in which he affirms that "the blessing of this sacrament is fellowship and love, by which we are strengthened against death and all evil. This fellowship is twofold: on the one hand we partake of Christ and all saints; on the other hand we permit all Christians to be partakers of us, in whatever way they and we are able. Thus by means of this sacrament, all self-seeking love is rooted out and gives place to that which seeks the common good of all; and through the change wrought by love there is one bread, one drink, one body, one community." *Luther's Works*, vol. 35, E. Theodore Bachmann, ed. (Philadelphia: Muhlenberg Press, 1960), 67; Weimar Ausgabe, vol. 2, 754.

[352] *Shorter Christian Prayer: The Four-Week Psalter of the Liturgy of the Hours Containing Morning Prayer and Evening Prayer with Selections for the Entire Year* (New York: Catholic Book Publishing Co., 1988), 54.

251. Third, the consensus on "basic truths of the doctrine of justification" affirmed by our churches in the "Joint Declaration on the Doctrine of Justification" is of immediate relevance.[353] As shown above, the Lutheran Confessions did not object in principle to prayer for the dead. Their objections were to the form prayers for the dead took as part of a system of belief and practice which in their judgment repudiated God's free justification of the ungodly. The affirmation that Catholic teaching on justification as presented in the JDDJ does not fall under Lutheran condemnation places Catholic practices of prayers for the dead in a new context. They should be interpreted against the background of the Catholic affirmation that justification is "by grace alone, in faith in Christ's saving work and not because of any merit on our part."[354]

c. Remaining Differences

252. The liturgical and doctrinal convergences that have emerged in recent years between Catholic and Lutheran attitudes toward prayer for the dead have not removed all differences. Two differences are particularly significant—namely, the basis for prayers for the dead and prayer understood as satisfaction.

253. First, Lutherans and Catholics still disagree on the authoritative basis for the practice. Catholics view prayer for the dead as witnessed and approved in 2 Maccabees 12 and deeply embedded in the tradition of the church's piety from earliest days. Magisterial teaching at councils of Florence and Trent further affirm this practice, which has been repeated in recent teaching documents. Tradition and magisterial teaching do not play the same role for Lutherans as they do for Catholics, however, and the adoption of the Hebrew canon of the Old Testament means that 2 Maccabees lacks canonical authority for Lutherans. For Lutherans, the practice of prayer for the dead thus lacks an explicit authoritative mandate.

254. At the same time, Lutherans do not doctrinally deny what Catholic teaching affirms. The Apology explicitly does not reject the usefulness of such prayer.[355] Lutherans also have moved, in their funeral liturgies, toward the re-inclusion of prayers of commendation of the dead.[356] Therefore, this dialogue does not see that this difference in itself need hinder communion between us.

---

[353] Cf. JDDJ, ¶40.

[354] JDDJ, ¶15.

[355] Apology, Article 24, §96, *Book of Concord*, 276.

[356] Examples of such prayers are cited above in ¶242.

255.   The Lutheran understanding might be taken by some Lutherans to imply that prayer for the dead, while permissible, must be treated as adiaphoral, i.e., as not required. The presence of prayers for the dead in the funeral liturgies of *Lutheran Book of Worship* (1978) and *Evangelical Lutheran Worship* (2006), however, means that such prayers are widely used at such services. The actual use of such prayers supports a partially shared practice of prayer for the dead and sheds new light on remaining differences on purgatory.[357]

256.   Second, language of satisfaction remains problematic for Lutherans. Lutherans and Catholics agree that God commands us to pray and that prayer in obedience to that command is pleasing to God. They agree that such prayer is a good work of the justified.[358] They agree that good works will be rewarded by God in this world and the next, and in that sense can be called meritorious. They agree that prayer constitutes an aspect of penance.[359] They agree that prayer is efficacious; it can truly aid the person for whom one prays, although that aid does not operate automatically and is always under the will of God.

257.   The councils of Trent and Florence defined that the suffrages of the living (the Mass, prayers, alms) can aid the dead undergoing purgation. Neither council defined how such suffrages aid those undergoing purgation. As noted above, Catholic theology has understood prayer as an appeal to divine mercy, but also as a good work that can function as a satisfaction. The use of the concept of satisfaction to understand the efficacy of prayer for the dead, however, is not prominent in recent Catholic presentations of prayer for the dead. The *Catechism of the Catholic Church* mentions prayer as satisfaction neither in its discussion of purgatory,[360] nor in its extensive discussion of the nature of prayer.[361] Neither the letter of the Congregation of the Doctrine of the Faith on eschatology, the statement of the International Theological Commission on eschatology, nor Benedict XVI's encyclical on hope mentions prayer as satisfaction. Prayer for the dead is understood as a moment of the solidarity of the entire church before God's judgment and mercy.

---

[357] The Lutheran Church–Missouri Synod does not use prayers of commendation for the dead and therefore does not share this perspective.

[358] Regarding good works as the works of the justified, see the discussion above.

[359] JDDJ, ¶28.

[360] *Catechism of the Catholic Church*, nos. 1030–1032.

[361] *Catechism of the Catholic Church*, nos. 2558–2758.

258. When Catholics understand some prayer as satisfaction, Lutheran questions inevitably continue to arise about the potential role of our works in our acceptance by God. Only passing attention has been given in ecumenical dialogue to penance and satisfaction.[362] The topics of penance, satisfaction, and the pursuit of holiness by the justified need further ecumenical discussion among Catholics, Lutherans, and others.

4. A Note on Masses for the Dead and Indulgences

259. In addition to offering explicit prayers on behalf of the dead, additional means have traditionally been held by which the living might aid the dead, such as the offering of the Mass for the dead and the application of indulgences to the dead. These practices were contentious issues at the time of the Lutheran Reformation, and have been taken up in recent ecumenical discussions.[363] Both of these issues, however, extend beyond this dialogue's focus. We will address these issues only as they relate to *The Hope for Eternal Life*.

a. *Masses for the Dead*

260. Evidence of the practice of offering the Eucharist for the dead exists from the Patristic period. Tertullian alludes to the practice in *On Monogamy* 10, as does Augustine in the *Confessions* 9.12.32. The Council of Trent taught that the Mass is propitiatory, since Christ, who in the Mass is "contained and bloodlessly immolated" *(continetur et incruente immolatur)*, is the same who once for all offered himself

---

[362] Karl Lehmann and Wolfhart Pannenberg, eds., *The Condemnations of the Reformation Era: Do They Still Divide?* trans. Margaret Kohl (Minneapolis: Fortress Press, 1989), 56–66.

[363] On the sacrificial character of the Mass, the most important dialogues have been: [U.S. Catholic-Lutheran] "The Eucharist as Sacrifice," *Lutherans and Catholics in Dialogue, I-III*, Paul C. Empie and T. Austin Murphy, eds. (Minneapolis: Augsburg Publishing House, n.d.); Lutheran-Roman Catholic International Commission, "The Eucharist," *Growth in Agreement: Reports and Agreed Statements of Ecumenical Conversations on a World Level,* Harding Meyer and Lukas Vischer, eds. (New York: Paulist Press, 1984), 190-214; Anglican-Roman Catholic International Commission, "Final Report," *Growth in Agreement: Reports and Agreed Statements of Ecumenical Conversations on a World Level*, Harding Meyer and Lukas Vischer, eds., Faith and Order Paper 108 (New York; Geneva: Paulist Press; World Council of Churches, 1984), 68–77. An ecumenical consultation on indulgences including representatives of the Catholic Church, the Lutheran World Federation, and the World Alliance of Reformed Churches was held in Rome on February 9-10, 2001, but texts from the consultation have not been published.

bloodily on the altar of the cross *(in ara crucis semel seipsum cruente obtulit)*. It, therefore, concludes that the sacrifice of the Mass "is properly offered, according to the apostles' tradition, not only for the sins, punishments, satisfactions, and other necessities of the living faithful, but also for those who have died in Christ and are not yet fully purified.[364]

261. Trent saw no contradiction between the *epaphax* [once for all] character of the cross and the sacrificial character of the Mass. That the sacrifice of the cross is repeated, reiterated, or renewed in the eucharistic sacrifice is denied by Trent; rather, the same Christ is contained and immolated in a nonbloody way in the Mass. It is the same victim; the only difference is in the manner of the offering.[365] Unfortunately this left the unintended impression on the Reformers that there are two oblations, one bloody, the other unbloody.[366] Contemporary American, German, and international dialogues have consistently reached the conclusion that the sacrificial character of the eucharistic liturgy is not a church-dividing issue.[367]

262. With respect to the present dialogue, the question remains whether the eucharistic liturgy aids the dead. For Catholics, any prayer has the potential of aiding the dead. Thus, the eucharistic liturgy—

---

[364] "The Mass as Propitiatory Sacrifice," Session XXII, 17 September 1562, Chapter 2.

[365] Denzinger and Schönmetzer, 1730.

[366] See Jean Marie Tillard, "Sacrificial Terminology and the Eucharist," *One in Christ* 17 (1981): 318. On Luther's understanding of the eucharist and sacrifice, see the comprehensive study by Wolfgang Simon, *Die Messopfertheologie Martin Luthers: Voraussetzungen, Genese, Gestalt und Rezeption* (Tübingen: Mohr Siebeck, 2003).

[367] In the dialogues on the sacrifice of the Mass noted above, see the positive conclusions in the U.S. Catholic-Lutheran Dialogue statement, *The Eucharist as Sacrifice* (1967), 12–14; the international Catholic-Lutheran document, *The Eucharist*, ¶¶56–61, which speak only, however, of "growing convergence"; and the Anglican-Roman Catholic International Commission's Final Report, 68, claiming "agreement on essential matters" of the Eucharist; "nothing essential has been omitted." "Mass" is the common name for the Eucharistic liturgy of the Catholic Church and has been retained by some Lutherans as well. The word Mass comes from the Latin word used by the priest to dismiss the people at the end of a Eucharistic service, *"Ite, missa est."* Synonyms used in various traditions include Eucharist, Celebration of the Liturgy, Eucharistic celebration, Sacrifice of the Mass, Lord's Supper, and Divine Liturgy. The "Liturgy of the Eucharist" is the section of the Mass when the gifts are prepared and the Eucharistic Prayer proclaimed. The Eucharistic prayer is the prayer of thanksgiving and sanctification. Synonyms used in various traditions include *anaphora*, Great Thanksgiving, or Canon of the Mass.

understood as the prayer of Christ to which we are joined—is no exception. It is a unique form of prayer for the dead insofar as it is Christ's prayer and self-offering in which the Church participates.

263. Lutherans, emphasizing God's gift to us in the sacrament, have stressed the proclamatory nature of the eucharistic liturgy. With the advent of twentieth century Lutheran liturgical renewal in the U.S., this proclamation has been placed in the context of a Eucharistic prayer (*anaphora*/Great Thanksgiving), though the bare *verba* remain a liturgical option.[368] Thus, many Lutherans today do experience the eucharistic liturgy as, in part, prayer. Any continuing Lutheran-Catholic difference in this area is primarily a difference in how we understand the character of the eucharistic liturgy. More dialogue on this topic is needed.[369]

b. Indulgences Applied to the Dead

264. Debate between Lutherans and Catholics on the matter of indulgences has a complex history. Within the limitations of the present dialogue, the application of indulgences on behalf of the dead cannot be completely resolved. What can be noted here, however, has important pastoral implications for our communion with the dead.

265. Indulgences are not a required devotional practice, although they are an inherited element in the penitential discipline of the Church. Indulgences are a development unique to the Western church,[370] but they have never been a church-dividing issue between Catholics and

---

[368] See the *Service Book and Hymnal* (1958), *Lutheran Book of Worship* (1978), and *Evangelical Lutheran Worship* (2006) for examples of eucharistic prayers.

[369] On Luther's reformation of the Mass, with the elimination of a Eucharistic prayer, see Hans-Christoph Schmidt-Lauber, "The Lutheran Tradition in the German Lands," *The Oxford History of Christian Worship*, Geoffrey Wainwright and Karen B. Westerfield Tucker, eds. (Oxford: Oxford Univ. Press, 2006), 395–403. Luther "eliminated" not the genre of Eucharistic prayer, but specifically the Roman Canon that he believed could not be reformed. His *Formula Missae et Communionis* had the *Verba* preceded by the Preface and introduced by the word *Qui*. Cf. Frank Senn, *Christian Liturgy* (Minneapolis: Fortress Press, 1997), 277–278. The Swedish church's early (1531) use of an evangelical Eucharistic Prayer, written by Olavus Petri who studied at Wittenberg, is another indication that some Lutherans did, indeed, understand the Eucharist as encompassing prayer. Senn, 408–409.

[370] For a recent survey of the development of indulgences, see Robert W. Shaffern, *The Penitent's Treasury: Indulgences in Latin Christianity 1175–1375* (Scranton, Pa.: University of Scranton, 2007).

Orthodox.[371] Indulgences are to be understood in the context of shared mutual assistance among those who are joined by communion in Christ, which extends beyond this world to sharing of *bona spiritualia,* spiritual goods, with the departed.[372]

266.   The practice of indulgences depends on understanding sin as having a double consequence, as noted above in the discussion on purgation. Sin both breaks communion with God and the church, which requires reconciliation, and affects the person in ways that call for purification. Indulgences are a means of eliminating or mitigating the painful aspects of purification. The church appeals to the treasury of Christ's infinite merit, to which are joined the merits of the Virgin Mary and the saints. Indulgences are one of the means by which the church acts to administer this treasury for the sake of the justified believer's transformation in Christ.

267.   The twentieth century saw a significant ferment in the Catholic theology of indulgences.[373] Indulgences came to be understood less as a *quid pro quo* transaction and more as a prayer appealing to God's gracious mercy. John Paul II spoke of indulgences as prayer in *Incarnationis Mysterium,* a bull that instituted the Jubilee Year of 2000.[374] Indulgences disclose "the fullness of the Father's mercy, who offers everyone his love, expressed primarily in the forgiveness of sins" (no. 9). In a catechesis on September 29, 1999, John Paul II further stressed the notion of indulgence as prayer and treated the concept of a

---

[371] In his survey of Eastern-Western relations up through the fifteenth century, Henry Chadwick only mentions indulgences as a topic of discussion as one of a long list of Latin errors put forward by the Orthodox at a conference in 1234; see Henry Chadwick, *East and West: The Making of a Rift in the Church. From Apostolic Times until the Council of Florence* (Oxford: Oxford University Press, 2003), 241.

[372] Paul VI, *Indulgentiarum doctrina [Apostolic Constitution on the Revision of Indulgences],* 1 January 1967, no. 4-5, citing *Lumen gentium.* See *Vatican Council II: The Conciliar and Post Conciliar Documents,* Austin Flannery, ed., Vatican Collection (Northport, N.Y.: Costello, 1975), 1:65–67.

[373] Ferment in the historical study of indulgences is surveyed in chapter 1 of Shaffern, *The Penitent's Treasury.* The most important texts in the theological ferment are essays by Karl Rahner, "Remarks on the Theology of Indulgences," *Theological Investigations* (Baltimore: Helicon Press, 1963), 1:175–201; "A Brief Theological Study on Indulgence," *Theological Investigations* (London: Darton, Longman, & Todd, 1973), 10:150–165; "On the Official Teaching of the Church Today on the Subject of Indulgences," *Theological Investigations,* 10:166–198.

[374] The Bull is found in English in *Origins* 28, no. 26 (December 10, 1998): 445–452. The bull recommended to the faithful a variety of indulgences, many associated with pilgrimages to shrine churches, to those in prison, the shut-in, etc.

treasury of merit metaphorically. Far from being an automatic transfer, the distribution from the treasury "is instead the expression of the Church's full confidence of being heard by the Father—when in view of Christ's merits and, by his gift, those of Our Lady and the saints—she asks him to mitigate or cancel the painful aspect of punishment by fostering its medicinal aspect through other channels of grace."[375] This gift of intercession, the Pope said, can also benefit the faithful departed who receive its fruits in a manner appropriate to their condition.

268. Indulgences are not a purchase of God's mercy. Rather, God chooses to enlist the help of the church in restoring the order of justice and bringing about a healing of relationships that have been damaged by sin. Indulgences do not bring about Christ's justifying mercy, but rather presuppose justification. They also reinforce the bonds of ecclesial communion that allow for a dynamic communication of love among the faithful on earth and between the earthly fellowship and those undergoing purification so that they may be totally configured to Christ.

269. Careful theological interpretation and sound pastoral guidance are required so that the practice of indulgences is presented as an aspect of growth in Christ. An objectification or overly simple quantification of the aid made available to penitents and departed believers through the communion of saints should be avoided. The Apostolic Constitution on the Revision of Indulgences of Pope Paul VI eliminated in 1967 the frequently misunderstood specific number of days or years of penance attached to different partial indulgences.[376] To be effective, a rightful disposition and intention of the recipient must accompany these penitential practices. "It would be a mistake," John Paul II said, "to think that we can receive this gift by simply performing certain outward acts. On the contrary, they are required as the expression and support of our progress in conversion. They particularly show our faith in God's mercy. . . ."[377] Indulgences are meant to express *not* dependence on our works but a deeper dependence on the aid of Christ and, indeed, on the "whole Christ"—the head and members of the mystical body, the church.

270. As with Masses for the dead, indulgences appear in a different light when understood within the context of the solidarity of all the

---

[375] John Paul II, Catechesis of September 29, 1999, ¶4 (*www.vatican.va/holy_father/ john_paul_ii/audiences/1999/documents/hf_jp-ii_aud_29091999_en.html*, accessed September 3, 2010).

[376] Paul VI, *Indulgentiarum doctrina*, Vatican Council II: The Conciliar and Post Conciliar Documents, 62–69.

[377] John Paul II, Catechesis of September 29, 1999, ¶5.

justified with Christ and each other. Lutherans in this dialogue have come to see that the intent behind the contemporary practice of indulgences is an expression of an appeal to the mercy of Christ. Whether indulgences do or can adequately embody that intent remains a genuine question for Lutherans. Lutherans also ask whether indulgences are so open to abuse and misunderstanding that their evangelical intent is obscured. Nevertheless, since the practice of indulgences has not been seen as required for communion with the Catholic Church, Lutherans need not adopt these practices for the sake of such communion. Ecumenical rapprochement requires, however, that Lutherans not condemn Catholic teaching about the practice of indulgences as inherently contrary to the gospel.

271. This dialogue has not tried to settle the questions of the sacrificial character of the eucharistic liturgy or of indulgences in themselves, but is looking only at their application to the dead. As the relation of the Mass and indulgences to the dead is seen in the context of communion in the grace of Christ, many Catholic understandings and practices become clearer to Lutherans as expressions of dependence on Christ. Any final judgment by Lutherans on Masses for the dead and the application of indulgences to the dead is dependent upon judgments about the nature of the eucharistic liturgy and of Christian penance.

5. Common Affirmations

272. When misconceptions are stripped away and the continuing reflections of our churches are taken into account, the difference between our churches regarding prayer for the dead is seen in a new light.

Agreements

273. **Catholics and Lutherans agree that:**

1. **there is communion among the living and the dead across the divide of death;**

2. **Christians pray for one another and believe that such prayer is heard by God and aids those for whom we pray;**

3. **at the very least Scripture does not prohibit prayer for the dead;**

4. **prayerful commendation of the dead to God is salutary within a funeral liturgy;**

5. **insofar as the resurrection of the dead and the general final judgment are future events, it is appropriate to pray for God's**

mercy for each person, entrusting that one to God's mercy because such mercy is and remains God's gift;

6. even as a good work, prayer is an appeal to the divine mercy and not a purchase of spiritual goods.

274.   Thus, **we agree that prayer for the dead, considered within the framework of the communion of saints, need not be a church-dividing or communion-hindering issue for Lutherans and Catholics.**[378] This conclusion is shared by the German Lutheran-Catholic Dialogue. The members of that dialogue affirmed, and we join them in this affirmation, that we are "bound together in Christ beyond death with those who have already died to pray for them and to commend them in loving memory to the mercy of God."[379]

275.   Our agreements on purgation pointed to a needed agreement on prayer for the dead. We now can say together with the German dialogue that:

> . . . the communion in Christ into which human beings are called endures also into death and judgment. It becomes complete as, through the pain over failure in earthly life, persons come with their love to give perfect response to God. That this may take place, the communion of the faithful on earth may constantly pray on the basis of the all-sufficient sacrifice of Christ. This prayer is . . . a liturgical expression of their eschatological hope.[380]

---

[378] In response to the conclusion that the remaining differences between Lutherans and Catholics on indulgences, prayers for the dead, and purgation "need not be a church dividing or communion-hindering issue," the representatives of The Lutheran Church–Missouri Synod, at the end of this dialogue, issued the following statement: "The LCMS representatives to this round of discussions are grateful that the LCMS was invited to this dialogue on 'The Hope of Eternal Life.' Moreover, we rejoice in the unified expression of the Christian faith made visible in our common acceptance of the ecumenical creeds and in our common hope of eternal life only through the merits of Jesus Christ won for all sinners through the suffering, death, and resurrection of Jesus Christ. We believe that progress has been made in understanding and resolving the theological issues pertaining to prayers for the dead, indulgences, and purgatory. We nonetheless believe that further work remains to be done before it is possible to conclude that the remaining differences need not stand in the way of communion between our churches."

[379] Bilateral Working Group, *Communio Sanctorum*, ¶223.

[380] Bilateral Working Group, *Communio Sanctorum*, ¶228.

Challenges

276. Growth into fuller communion is not simply a matter of reconciling doctrine, but of pursuing a common life in Christ. Practices can be as important as statements of belief for such a common life. Problematic practices can both obscure our witness and harm ecumenical relations. Catholics and Lutherans each face challenges in our practices in relation to prayer for the dead.

277. Lutherans need to recognize that the thin veil that separates the living and the dead in the body of Christ has too often become a thick curtain in Lutheran piety. After the funeral, references to the dead in many contexts tend to disappear from prayer and worship. When this absence is combined with the doubts about intermediate states that became widespread in Lutheran theology in the twentieth century, the result is an isolation of the present generation from the "cloud of witnesses" that surrounds us (Heb. 12:1). An expanded calendar of commemorations to be celebrated liturgically in Lutheran congregations has helped to foster a sense of the communion of the church across time.[381] How else can Lutherans express solidarity with those who have gone before them? How can they express their ongoing concern for the needs of all, living and dead, for the grace of God? Can they find ways of praying for the dead that do not call forth images of purgatory foreign to the Lutheran tradition? How can All Saints' Day be shaped and celebrated to foster a living consciousness of the unity of the living and the dead in Christ? A more vigorous realization of the unity of church across time in Lutheran life would be both a contribution to Lutheran piety and an aid in greater ecumenical understanding and unity with Catholics.

278. The richness of Catholic practice in relation to the dead opens up a contrasting set of temptations. A lively sense of the presence of the saints can become credulous and superstitious. The *Directory on Popular Piety and the Liturgy* issued by the Congregation for Divine Worship included a discussion of prayers for the dead.[382] While commending suffrages for the dead, it also warned against practices that might make Christianity appear as a "religion of the dead," that might suggest divination, and that apply "spacio-temporal categories to the dead."[383] As

---

[381] See, e.g., *Evangelical Lutheran Worship*, Pew Edition, 15–17.

[382] Congregation for Divine Worship and the Discipline of the Sacraments, *Directory on Popular Piety and the Liturgy: Principles and Guidelines*; online at *www.vatican.va/roman_curia/congregations/ ccdds/index.htm*, accessed September 2, 2010.

[383] *Directory on Popular Piety and the Liturgy*, ¶258. *Directory on Popular Piety and the Liturgy*, ¶258.

inculturation of the faith advances in Asia and Africa, where a profound respect for ancestors is deeply embedded in culture, how can Catholic piety express such respect in a way that is true to Christian hope?[384] In a world of increased migration, with cultures from around the world existing in the same city, questions of the appropriate honoring of the dead can become more pressing. The challenge for Catholics is to maintain a focus on Christ as the basis of our unity with the faithful departed.

---

[384] See, e.g., the discussion of special prayers honoring the dead within the Mass in Congo and Vietnam in Peter C. Phan, "Suffrage for the Dead," *Directory on Popular Piety and the Liturgy: Principles and Guidelines: A Commentary*, Peter C. Phan, ed. (Collegeville, Minn.: Liturgical Press, 2005), 135–149.

CHAPTER IV

Conclusion

279. The world in which we live is one of limited hopes. The horizon of hope has become narrow and too often focused on individual concerns and the short-range future. Within such a world, the Christian faith confesses a larger hope. Since this hope is for nothing less than communion with God, it is the largest hope. All will become new in Christ Jesus.

280. The work of this dialogue has necessarily focused on our hope for eternal life from the perspective of Catholic-Lutheran ecumenical relations. Thus, we have explored many details of our two traditions. We hope, however, that our work can contribute not only to the ecumenical rapprochement of Lutherans and Catholics, but also to our common witness before the world to our hope of eternal life. Christians are called to be ready to "account for the hope that is in you, with gentleness and reverence" (1 Pet. 3:15). We offer our work to contribute to that accounting.

281. Our work is inspired by the example of the 1999 "Joint Declaration on the Doctrine of Justification." As we noted at the outset, the JDDJ sought to demonstrate that remaining differences between our churches on justification could co-exist within a single communion on the basis of a more fundamental and far-reaching framework of common convictions about justification. This document has pursued a similar method, although not written in the style of the JDDJ. Our discussions of purgatory and prayer for the dead in Chapter III must not be read in isolation from Chapter II, in which we develop our common convictions. Those common convictions form the necessary interpretive context for what we say about traditionally divisive topics.

282. In light of the "Last Things"—death, judgment, heaven, and hell—Lutherans and Catholics take up the same attitude of trust and dependence before God. Facing his own death, Martin Luther famously confessed in his last written note, "We are all beggars. That is true."[385]

---

[385] *Luther's Works*, vol. 54, Theodore G. Tappert, ed. (Philadelphia: Fortress Press, 1967), 476; Weimar Ausgabe, Tischreden, vol. 5, 318.

Similarly, Robert Bellarmine, S.J., one of the most important Catholic theologians of the late sixteenth and early seventeenth centuries, wrote in his will: "First, therefore, I desire with all my heart to have my soul commended into the hands of God, whom from my youth I have desired to serve. And I beseech Him, not as the valuer of merit, but as a giver of pardon, to admit me among his Saints and Elect."[386] Before God's judgment and God's grace, we stand as persons dependent on God's mercy and gifts. We hope not in ourselves but in God, who is surely faithful to his promises.

283.   At the end of our work, this dialogue looks forward to the day of rest when all division among Christ's followers will be overcome, when they gather together in the marriage feast of the Lamb. In that spirit, we can only say:

Marana Tha! Come, Lord Jesus!

---

[386] James Brodrick, *The Life and Work of Blessed Robert Francis Cardinal Bellarmine, S. J., 1542–1621* (London: New York, Longmans, Green, 1950), 2:441.

Appendixes

The following are cited at various points in the footnotes
of the Common Statement on the Hope of Eternal Life
on the preceding pages.

Participants and Protocol for Round XI

Co-chairs

The Rev. Lowell G. Almen
Evangelical Lutheran Church in America, Chicago, Ill.

The Most Rev. Richard J. Sklba
Auxiliary Bishop of Milwaukee, Catholic Church

Lutheran

The Rev. Dr. Theodore W. Asta, Ph.D.
New England Synod of the Evangelical Lutheran Church in America
Worcester, Mass.

The Rev. Dr. Stephen J. Hultgren, Ph.D.
Fordham University, Bronx, N.Y.

The Rev. Dr. Randall R. Lee, Th.D. (2005-2007)
Evangelical Lutheran Church in America

Dr. Lois E. Malcolm, Ph.D. (2005)
Luther Seminary, St. Paul, Minn.

The Rev. Donald J. McCoid (2007-2010)
Evangelical Lutheran Church in America, Chicago, Ill.

The Rev. Dr. Marcus J. Miller, D.Min.
Lutheran Theological Southern Seminary, Columbia, S.C.

The Rev. Dr. Samuel H. Nafzger, Th.D.
The Lutheran Church–Missouri Synod, St. Louis, Mo.

The Rev. Dr. Cheryl M. Peterson, Ph.D. (2006-2010)
Trinity Lutheran Seminary, Columbus, Ohio

The Rev. Dr. Winston D. Persaud, Ph.D.
Wartburg Theological Seminary, Dubuque, Iowa

The Rev. Dr. John H. P. Reumann, Ph.D. (+June 6, 2008)

Dr. Michael J. Root, Ph.D.
Lutheran Theological Southern Seminary, Columbia, S.C.

The Rev. Paul A. Schreck
Evangelical Lutheran Church in America, Chicago, Ill.

The Rev. Dr. Dean O. Wenthe, Ph.D.
Concordia Theological Seminary, Fort Wayne, Ind.

Catholic

The Rev. Dr. Joseph A. Fitzmyer, S.J., Ph.D.
Jesuit Community at Georgetown University, Washington, D.C.

Bro. Jeffrey Gros, F.S.C.
Memphis Theological Seminary, Memphis, Tenn.

The Rev. Dr. Arthur L. Kennedy, Ph.D. (2005)
United States Conference of Catholic Bishops, Washington, D.C.

The Rev. Dr. James Massa, Ph.D. (2006-2010)
United States Conference of Catholic Bishops, Washington, D.C.

Dr. Margaret O'Gara, Ph.D.
University of St. Michael's College, Toronto, Ontario

The Rev. Dr. George H. Tavard, A.A., S.T.D. (+Aug. 13, 2007)

Dr. Christian D. Washburn, Ph.D.
St. Paul Seminary School of Divinity, University of St. Thomas, St, Paul, Minn.

The Rev. Dr. W. Jared Wicks, S.J., Th.D.
John Carroll University, University Heights, Ohio

Dr. Susan K. Wood, S.C.L., Ph.D.
Marquette University, Milwaukee, Wis.

Protocol
for Round XI
(As approved in 2005)

The following protocol document was approved by the participating churches prior to the beginning of Round XI to guide the deliberations:

The U.S. Conference of Catholics Bishops (USCCB) has partnered with the Lutheran communities—The Lutheran Church–Missouri Synod (LCMS) and the Evangelical Lutheran Church in America (ELCA) and its predecessor bodies—in the first nine rounds of the dialogue since 1965. The texts from these dialogues have been a strong testimony to the Christian faith, to the commitment of these churches to the unity for which Christ prayed, and to the deepening of mutual trust and understanding.

With the 1999 signing of the "Joint Declaration on the Doctrine of Justification" (JDDJ) between the Catholic Church and member churches of the Lutheran World Federation, a new context has been created. This historical doctrinal agreement was possible, in part, because of the careful biblical, confessional, and theological documents produced in the United States dialogue.

Although The Lutheran Church–Missouri Synod is not a signatory of the Declaration, its participation in Round VII contributed to the theological foundation of the statement. The Lutheran Church–Missouri Synod, however, remains committed to dialogue and wishes to resolve theological differences respectfully, directly and through the process of dialogue. In Round X of the dialogue, *The Church as Koinonia of Salvation: Its Structures and Ministries*, a theologian designated by the LCMS participated as an observer with theologians designated from the USCCB and ELCA.

There is a commitment from all three sponsoring bodies that participation can continue based on the following agreed principles, approved by the sponsoring bodies of all three churches:

1) The desired goal of this dialogue is pulpit and altar fellowship/full communion, recognizing that all three sponsoring churches have different criteria for when it will be possible to recognize that goal as having been achieved.

2) The dialogue builds on the ten rounds of the U.S. dialogue and the nine rounds of the international dialogue, and presupposes the "Joint Declaration on the Doctrine of Justification," recognizing

that The Lutheran Church–Missouri Synod has not signed the JDDJ. The LCMS hopes that deepening agreement on such topics as the round's eschatological theme, *The Hope of Eternal Life*, can provide an opportunity for discussing the issues raised by both Catholics and Lutherans subsequent to the signing of the JDDJ (e.g., indulgences, communion of saints, and purgatory). Participants in the dialogue from all churches are accountable for the literature of the dialogue and its history, recognizing that one of the functions of the ongoing dialogue is to expand and deepen the consensus, and not merely to surface new obstacles, though these will undoubtedly emerge.

3) There will be no minority reports. Reservations or differences of point of view can be incorporated into the text or added as footnotes. This will be particularly important where the conclusions rely on agreements reached in the "Joint Declaration," which is foundational to all future theological work of the dialogue.

For the work of the dialogue, it is important that disagreements on these presuppositions be handled with the dialogue process itself, and that, in these matters, decisions not be made unilaterally, or interpretations given that do not take account of the commitments agreed to in this protocol after its approval by the three sponsoring bodies within the churches.

APPENDIX II

Meetings and Background Documents

Meeting I: December 1-4, 2005; Chicago

Joseph Fitzmyer, "Biblical View of Human Destiny"

Michael Root, "Lutheran Confessions on Hope for Eternal Life"

George Tavard, "The Council of Trent on Purgatory"

Jared Wicks, "Dialogue on Indulgences (2001)"

Susan Wood, "Hope of Life Everlasting: Themes from the Liturgy"

Meeting II: April 20-23, 2006; Phoenix

Theodore Asta, "Luther and Death, Judgment, and Resurrection"

Joseph Fitzmyer, "The Reception of 1 Corinthians 3 in the Church's Interpretation"

Stephen Hultgren, "'Interim States' in the New Testament"

Randall Lee, "Death, Judgment, and the Resurrection to Eternal Life in 20th Century Lutheran Theology"

Margaret O'Gara, "Eschatology in Roman Catholic Theology in the 20th Century"

Winston Persaud, "Review of *The Reformation of the Dead: Death and Ritual in Early Modern Germany, 1450-1700* (New York: St. Martin's Press, 2000)"

John Reumann, "Death and Judgment in the Bible"

Michael Root, "Eschatology in Lutheran Handbook Theology Prior to 1900"

Christian Washburn, "The Catholic Manualist Tradition and *De novissimis*: 1850-1950"

Susan Wood, "Is There Time and Space in Purgatory?"

Meeting III: October 12-15, 2006; Baltimore

Theodore Asta, "Funeral Liturgy in Evangelical Lutheran Worship"

Michael Root, "Satisfaction in the Council of Trent and the *Roman Catechism* (1566): An Attempt at Understanding With Reference to Purgatory"

George Tavard, "Purgatory and the Catholic Mystics"

Christian Washburn, "*Oratio pro defunctis*: From the Catacombs to Gregory the Great"

Jared Wicks, "Christ's Descent into Hell and Return to Judge the Living and the Dead: The Early Development of Two Creedal Articles"

Susan Wood, "Communal and Sacramental Dimensions of Eschatology"

Meeting IV: March 15-18, 2007; Columbia, S.C.

Winston Persaud, "A Lutheran Reflection on *The One Mediator, The Saints, and Mary* in Relation to the Question: How Do Lutherans Understand Prayer for Other People?"

Cheryl Peterson, "Communal Eschatology and the Communion of Saints: A Lutheran Perspective"

George Tavard, "The Intermediate State in Byzantine Orthodoxy"

Jared Wicks, "Christ's Descent into Hell and Return to Judge the Living and the Dead: Patristic Witnesses to Christ's Saving Descent to the Dead"

Jared Wicks, "Report on Cardinal J. Döpfner's Intervention on Indulgences at Vatican II, Nov. 11, 1965"

Meeting V: October 10-14, 2007; Washington, D.C.

Lowell Almen, "Lutheran Liturgical Reflection of the Unity of the Church Throughout Time and Eternity"

Joseph Fitzmyer, "Hell and the Possibility of the Loss of Eternal Life"

Stephen Hultgren, "Justification by Faith and Judgment by Works"

Margaret O'Gara, "Toward Convergence on the Eucharist Offered for the Dead"

Winston Persaud, "How Do Lutherans Understand Prayer for Others (Including the Dead)?"

John Reumann, "'Heaven' in Biblical Thought"

Michael Root, "Aquinas, Merit, and Reformation Theology after the 'Joint Declaration on the Doctrine of Justification'"

George Tavard, "Merit as an Ecumenical Problem"

Christian Washburn, "The Impetratory and Satisfactory Efficacy of Intercessory Prayer in Catholic Theology"

Plenary Drafting

Meeting VI: October 9-12, 2008; Washington, D.C.

Meeting VII: March 11-15, 2009; Washington, D.C.

Meeting VIII: October 14-18, 2009; Washington, D.C.

Meeting IX: March 10-14, 2010; Washington, D.C.

Meeting X: October 13-17, 2010; Washington, D.C.

Background Documents Distributed to Meeting Participants

Eugene Brand, "Burial Rites Compared: *Service Book and Hymnal* and *Lutheran Book of Worship*" (2005)

Walter Kasper, "Ten Theses on Indulgences" (2001)

Carl Peter, "Communion of Saints in the Final Days of the Council of Trent: *Apostolic Constitution Indulgentiarum Doctrina* (1992)

David S. Yeago, "Sanctification and Purification in Lutheran Theology" (2007)

Directory on Popular Piety and the Liturgy: *Principles and Guidelines,* Congregation for Divine Worship and the Discipline of the Sacraments (2001)

United States Conference of Catholic Bishops, "Popular Devotional Practices Basic Questions and Answers" (2003)

The Lutheran Church–Missouri Synod, Commission on Theology and Church Relations, "A Statement on Death, Resurrection and Immortality" (1969)

APPENDIX III

On the Interpretation of Biblical Texts

by Stephen J. Hultgren

As noted in paragraphs 25-26 of the common statement, the use of Scripture in ecumenical dialogue entails hermeneutical questions. This dialogue's presentation of biblical texts does not aim at settling these hermeneutical questions, but seeks instead to give the scriptural foundations of our churches' teachings on the hope of eternal life. Where these teachings differ, it is often over divergent readings of the meaning of particular texts or even over whether certain texts are authoritative or relevant to the doctrine at issue. Purgatory is one example on which Lutherans and Catholics have drawn different conclusions from biblical texts, such as 1 Corinthians 3:10-15 and Matthew 12:32.

Nonetheless, we believe that, for Lutherans and Catholics, the prospect has opened for common approaches to interpreting Scripture. In 1943 Pope Pius XII endorsed the historical-critical method as a tool for understanding the literal sense of biblical texts, and he encouraged Catholic exegetes to adopt methods that had been common among Lutheran biblical scholars for some time.[387] One should hold together the literal sense and the spiritual sense of texts, the latter being the sense intended by God, in accord with the rule of faith. Biblical typologies should be explored, but interpretation has to show great restraint in proposing figurative or allegorical readings.

The teaching of Pius XII was reaffirmed by the Second Vatican Council in its Dogmatic Constitution on Divine Revelation, *Dei*

---

[387] Pope Pius XII, *Divino afflante Spiritu [Inspired by the Divine Spirit]*, Encyclical on Promoting Biblical Studies, 30 September 1943, given along with other official documents in Dean P. Béchard, ed., *The Scripture Documents: An Anthology of Official Catholic Teachings* (Collegeville, Minn.: Liturgical Press, 2002). See especially §§15-22 of the encyclical, in Béchard, 125–130.

verbum,[388] by two dense paragraphs—first, on recovery of the literal sense by literary and historical analysis of texts in their original setting, and, second, on interpretation in the light of the Holy Spirit, this is, by a reading which takes account of the unity of Scripture, the living tradition of the Church, and the inner coherence of what God reveals.[389]

In 1993 the Pontifical Biblical Commission issued a lengthy document, *The Interpretation of the Bible in the Church*, which was emphatic on the need of careful investigation of the literal sense of texts, "making use of all the resources of literary and historical research."[390] At the same time the commission insisted that exegetes must never separate the literal sense from the spiritual sense, with the latter understood "as the meaning expressed by the biblical texts when read, under the influence of the Holy Spirit, in the context of the paschal mystery of Christ and of the new life which flows from it."[391]

This approach to Scripture, which holds together the literal sense and the spiritual sense of texts in a Christocentric way, comes remarkably close to the hermeneutical theory that underlay Martin Luther's reading of Scripture and that continued to be important in Lutheran Orthodoxy.[392] Similarly, the Pontifical Biblical Commission's insistence that texts should be read in harmony with the whole canon resonates with traditional Lutheran views,[393] even if Lutherans and Catholics disagree

---

[388] *Dei verbum [Dogmatic Constitution on Divine Revelation]*, 18 November 1965, §12.

[389] Béchard, 24–25. In its chapter on Scripture in the Church's life, *Dei verbum* underscored the importance of exegetical work for the enrichment of preaching and for the daily work of theology, the soul of which is "study of the sacred page" (§§23-24; Béchard, 29–30).

[390] The document is given in full in Béchard, 244–315, with 280 cited here.

[391] Béchard, 281–282. See also 295–296.

[392] See Gerhard Ebeling, "Die Anfänge von Luthers Hermeneutik," *Zeitschrift für Theologie und Kirche* 48 (1951): 172–230, trans. Richard B. Steele, Franz Posset, and Wilhelm Linss as "The Beginnings of Luther's Hermeneutics," in three successive issues of *Lutheran Quarterly* 7 (1993): 129–158, 315–338, and 451–468. Bengt Hägglund shows the importance in Lutheran Orthodoxy of the literal and spiritual senses united in Christ and the Holy Spirit, with reference to the rule of faith, in *Die Heilige Schrift und ihre Deutung in der Theologie Johann Gerhards. Eine Untersuchung über das altlutherische Schriftverständnis* (Lund: CWK Gleerup, 1951), 223–229, 233–234.

[393] *Interpretation of the Bible in the Church*, in Béchard, *Scripture Documents*, 260–262, 296. Hägglund gives an example of this principle in Lutheran Orthodoxy in *Die Heilige Schrift und ihre Deutung*, 179–184.

on the extent of the canon and the interpretive authority of tradition and the magisterium.[394] To be sure, common approaches do not overcome all differences between Lutheran and Catholic interpretation of Scripture, but they are bringing the two traditions towards agreement on authoritative meanings of biblical texts.

The fruits of the developing common approach to Scripture are reflected in this report. We use literary and historical methods to cast light on the literal meaning of texts in their original contexts. A Christocentric approach to Scripture that holds together literal and spiritual meanings has evident importance in the section on purgatory.[395]

---

[394] Lutheran-Catholic differences over the instances of ecclesial interpretation of Scripture have been treated and clarified, in a way showing certain convergences while still acknowledging important differences, in Round IX of the U.S. Lutheran-Catholic Dialogue. See *Scripture and Tradition: Lutherans and Catholics in Dialogue IX*, Harold C. Skillrud, J. Francis Stafford, and Daniel F. Martensen, eds. (Minneapolis: Augsburg, 1995), especially 26–33, 37–38, 40, and 45.

[395] See Chapter III, Section A of the common statement.

The Intermediate State: Patristic and Medieval Doctrinal Development and Recent Receptions

by Jared Wicks

This appendix treats the development of eschatological doctrine concerning the condition of those who die before the end-events of universal resurrection of the dead and general judgment. These are souls in the "intermediate state." On this issue, the Fathers of the Church, both Eastern and Western, left a great store of indications on this and the other eschatological topics, as amply attested by Brian Daley's broad survey.[396] Medieval theologians then selectively received and further developed understandings of life beyond death, with its rewards and punishments. A doctrinal turning-point for the Catholic Church came in the fourteenth century, with the teaching of Pope Benedict XII on salvation or loss immediately after the end of earthly life.

The treatment begins with (1) a patristic survey which will feature texts of Augustine and Gregory the Great, who had long-term influence in the Middle Ages and beyond. (2) Continuing, we will take up selected early and high medieval positions on the eschatology of departed souls, and then (3) present the outbreak of arguments over the intermediate state in 1331–1334, which led to Pope Benedict XII's dogmatic Constitution of early 1336, which remains a normative clarification of

---

[396] Brian Daley, *The Hope of the Early Church* (Cambridge: Cambridge University Press, 1991), which is the full length version of a more compact part of *Eschatologie, Schrift und Patristik*, in *Handbuch der Dogmengeschichte*, vol. 7a (Freiburg: Herder, 1986). Section 1 of this report depends in most sections on Daley's presentations.

Catholic teaching on death and what lies beyond. This will be a movement from widely varying conceptions of life in the spiritual realm beyond this world, through gradual clarifications, to precise dogmatic teaching issued to settle a dispute that engaged many in the 1330s.

1. Patristic Theologies of Life beyond Death, especially Augustine and Gregory the Great

Christian writers before Augustine left a large and varied legacy of exegetical interpretation and teaching about what follows death. At one extreme, the Syriacs, Aphrahat (died after 345) and Ephrem (d. 373), spoke of rewards and punishments beginning only with the resurrection, before which departed souls sleep in Sheol, where they sense only faintly the fate to be theirs after the resurrection and their judgment by Christ. Such souls are alive, but deprived, even though such sleep does refresh the righteous and bring discomfort to sinners.[397]

Arguing against the Gnostics' demeaning of the body as the soul's prison-house, Irenaeus (writing ca. 180) appealed to the churches' rule of truth as a sure warrant for the coming bodily resurrection of the dead.[398] But before this takes place, departed souls live on in an invisible place allotted to them by God, where they await the resurrection.[399] Irenaeus portrayed God's revelation through the Word and the Spirit in this world as now preparing believers for a mature final stage of seeing God and so sharing in unending life, according to the famous line, *Gloria Dei vivens homo, vita autem hominis visio Dei* ("God's glory is the living human, but true human life consists in seeing God.").[400] The Holy Spirit given in this life is the pledge (*arrabōn*) of an indescribable joy to come when the redeemed are raised bodily and come to see God face to face and so partake of immortality.[401]

---

[397] Daley, *The Hope of the Early Church*, 73–75. Departed souls, not being complete persons, are not capable of more. Later, the same conception of soul-sleep appeared in works of Hilary of Poitiers (d. 367), Theodore of Mopsuestia (d. 428), and Peter Chrysologus (d. ca. 450). See Daley, 95, 114, and 166.

[398] *Adversus Haereses*, I, 10,1; I, 22,1; III, 12,3; and III, 16, 6.

[399] *Adversus Haereses*, V, 31:2; Ante-Nicene Fathers, 1, 560–561; Sources chrétiennes, 153, 392–397.

[400] *Adversus Haereses*, IV, 20:7; Ante-Nicene Fathers, 1, 490; Sources chrétiennes, 100, 646–649.

[401] *Adversus Haereses*, V, 7:2–8:1; Ante-Nicene Fathers, 1, 533; Sources chrétiennes, 153, 90–97.

Tertullian (d. ca. 220) depicted the interim dwelling of souls as a vast subterranean vault, with regional differences of pain or refreshing consolation by which souls anticipate what will come after resurrection and judgment.[402] Hippolytus of Rome (d. ca. 235) spoke of souls being confined in the interim hospice and assigned to appropriate parts of it, that is, whether near the lake of fire or by a pleasant realm of light.[403]

Regarding an immediate reward of being with God immediately after death, First Clement (ca. 96) had spoken of present glory as the lot of the apostles and martyrs, while the letters of Ignatius of Antioch testified to the writer's hope that his imminent martyrdom will be a passage to be with God and Christ Risen.[404] For Tertullian, the martyrs go to glory, bypassing the interim hospice of souls.[405] Later, Gregory of Naziansus (d. ca. 390) spoke in funeral orations of good individuals, like the earlier martyrs, being in heavenly joy with the Lord while they await resurrection, and John Chrysostom (d. 407) taught that the righteous pass immediately upon death to Christ in God's City, where however their joy will only reach completion amid the whole company of the saved.[406] Regarding the lost, both Chrysostom and Jerome (d. 420) were convinced exponents of the immediate punishment of sinners after death, with the

---

[402] A. Stuiber, *Refrigerium interim* (Bonn: Hanstein, 1957), 51–61. This author emphatically contrasts belief in the immortality of souls and Christian hope of resurrection as sharp alternatives that admit no integration or synthesis, as does C. Tibiletti, in "Le anime dopo la morte: stato intermedio o visione di Dio?, *Augustinianum* 28 (1988), 631–659. Stuiber's book was trenchantly criticized for absolutizing its theory and neglecting iconographical details pointing to souls being refreshed and at peace in heaven, by L. De Bruyne, "Refrigerium interim," *Rivista di archeologia cristiana*, 34 (1958): 87–118. Also, the Fathers who spoke of the pre-resurrection place of expectation did not depict souls as annihilated or suspended in unconsciousness. At death, souls continue to have a degree of personal, conscious life, however incomplete before resurrection. This, for De Bruyne, suggests the possibility of combining of immortality with resurrection, instead of positing the two as alternatives excluding each other.

[403] Daley, *The Hope of the Early Church*, 30, 36, 37, and 85. This interim storehouse came back in some passages, not all, of Ambrose (d. 397) and in Theodoret of Cyrus (d. 466). See Daley, 100, 101, and 117.

[404] Daley, *The Hope of the Early Church*, 10, 11, and 13, adding from Ignatius that eucharistic communion with Christ is the "medicine of immortality" (Ephesians, 20, 2) and preparation for sharing Christ's resurrection (Smyrneans, 2, 1).

[405] Stuiber, *Refrigerium interim*, 74–81.

[406] Daley, *The Hope of the Early Church*, 103 and 109.

former holding different degrees of pain according to the extent of one's sins.[407]

Augustine on the State of Souls after Death and before Resurrection

Taking up the works of Augustine, we set out on the ocean of his biblical expositions, treatises, sermons, and letters, in which all the important eschatological topics are treated. Amid their variety, Augustine's works remain consistent in their emphasis on the radical difference between our present restless existence, amid distraction and "distention" in space and time, and the transformed, stable, and simple life, after the resurrection, of the saints' unending love and praise of God or of others' loss of his fulfilling nearness.[408]

In his famous letter to Proba on prayer (ca. 412), Augustine described the transformed life of heaven, the truly "happy life," that is the ultimate object of all our prayers in this life. This is the state in which,

> . . . immortal and incorruptible in body and spirit, we contemplate the delight of the Lord for all eternity. On account of this one thing, seek and properly ask for the rest. Whoever has this will have everything he wants, nor will he be able to want to have something there that will not be proper. There, of course, is found the fountain of life, for which we must thirst in prayer as long as we live in hope and do not as yet see what we hope for, under the protection of his wings before whom is all our desire, in order that we may be inebriated by the richness of his house and may drink of the torrent of his pleasure. For before him is the fountain of life, and in his light we shall see the light, when our desire will be satisfied with good things and there will remain nothing further that we seek amid groaning, but only what we possess amid rejoicing. [409]

---

[407] Daley, *The Hope of the Early Church*, 103 and 109. Jerome could also draw on Origen in spiritualizing punishment as the anguish of one's own guilty conscience and raising the question whether all these persons will be punished eternally.

[408] The characterization is from B. Daley's beginning of his 20-page treatment of Augustine in *Hope of the Early Church*, 131–132.

[409] Letter 130, no. 27, from The Works of Saint Augustine, II/2 (Hyde Park, N.Y.: New City, 2003), 197. Letters 147 and 148 treat heaven as that "seeing God" promised to the clean of heart, which will involve perceiving God with the "eyes of the heart" as he indwells and fills the person. The Works of Saint Augustine, II/2, especially 348 and 355–356.

Such are the utterly fulfilling delights of God's saints in heaven after body and spirit are joined in the resurrection. But what is the status and experience of souls before that final fulfillment?

In an early sermon on a feast commemorating certain martyrs, possibly in A.D. 401 or 402, Augustine noted that the end-events (arrival of the judge, resurrection of the dead, day of judgment) were still to come. This led both to pointers on preparing now for the judgment to come and to indications about the present and future conditions of the departed, including the martyrs, both in the interim "with Christ" and in their quite different post-resurrection state.

> We are all going to rise again, you see, each with their own cause. Just as you are now when you die and are committed to the prison, that is how you come before the judge. The urgent need is for you to put your case together now; since you cannot do it when you are locked up. So those who have good cases or causes are received into rest and quiet, while those who have bad cases or causes are received into pain and punishment. But they are going to suffer greater pains when they have risen again. In comparison with these, the pains that bad people who have died are now suffering are like the dreams of people who are being tortured in their sleep. . . .

> So while they have not yet received the fruits of their labors, the holy martyrs are already in bliss, since their souls are with Christ. But what may be in preparation for them in the resurrection—who could possibly find words to express this? "What eye has not seen, nor ear heard, nor has it come up in the heart of man what things that God has prepared for those who love him" (1 Cor. 2:9).[410]

Here, in a passage indicating clearly that the ultimate punishment and supreme reward will follow the coming resurrection, Augustine described the intermediate states of those who await the resurrection: rest and quite for those who left this life with "good cases" or pain and punishment for the others who brought "bad cases" before the judge.

---

[410] Sermon 328, nos. 5-6, from The Works of Saint Augustine, III/9, 178–179. A recent study of Augustine's sermons on martyrs' feast-days shows him portraying the real life that begins after death, the martyrs' death as a passage immediately to heaven, and how his hearers should direct their lives toward the eternal life now shared by the martyrs. Elena Martin, "*Timor mortis*: The Fear of Death in Augustine's Sermons on the Martyrs," in P. Clarke and T. Claydon, eds., *The Church, the Afterlife, and the Fate of the Soul* (Rochester, N.Y.: Boydell Press, 2009), 31–40.

Augustine made the same point in an early sermon on the memorial-day of the North African martyrs Perpetua and Felicity. He contrasted the martyrs' present interim consolation and joys with their future delights as whole persons after resurrection. "The rest enjoyed by souls without any bodies is one thing, and the glory and felicity of angels with heavenly bodies quite another and it is with them that the multitude of the faithful will be equated when they rise again."[411] Holy souls now separated from their bodies cannot be totally at peace, for they "look, with patient longing, for the resurrection of those bodies."[412]

Early in *The City of God* (begun 413, completed 425), Augustine said that the absence of the customary funeral ceremonies for those killed during the sack of Rome did not "cause any harm to those who already enjoy repose in the secret abodes of the just (*in occultis piorum sedibus*).[413] Later in the same work, near the end of the account of the angels, he spoke of the good angels as adhering to God, being in communion with him, and united to each other in the City of God now in heaven. The human part of the City, which he will describe more fully, is the whole race of mortal humans, destined one day to join the immortal angels, but which is now divided into two groups, namely, those "who at present are sojourning amid change on earth or, if dead, are resting in the hidden shelters and abodes of the souls of the departed" (*secretis animarum receptaculis sedibusque*).[414] Shortly after, he described the different experiences of the dead, both now and in the future, differentiating between the saints and the wicked.

> The separated souls of the saints are now in peace, while those of the wicked are in pain and will be so until the resur-

---

[411] Sermon 280, *Sermons* 5, in The Works of Saint Augustine, III/8 (1994), 74–75.

[412] *The City of God*, Book 13, ch. 20; cited from the Fathers of the Church Series, vol. 14 (New York: Fathers of the Church, 1952), 329. In his literal commentary on Genesis, Augustine spoke of the soul's natural orientation to governing and directing the body (*naturalis appetitus administrandi corpus*), by which the soul is prevented from totally turning itself to God—a condition holding both in this life and beyond. *Super genesi ad litteram*, XII, 35, 68; Corpus Scriptorum Ecclesiasticorum Latinorum, 28/1, 432.

[413] *The City of God*, 1, 13; Fathers of the Church 8, 41; Corpus Christianorum, Series Latina, 47 (Turnholt, 1955), 15.

[414] *The City of God*, 12, 9, adapting the translation of Fathers of the Church, 14, 262, inserting a Latin phrase from Corpus Christianorum, Series Latina, 48 (Turnholt, 1969), 364.

rection of their bodies, when the former will enter into life everlasting and the latter into a second and eternal death.[415]

Augustine spoke similarly in his treatise, *The Care to be Taken for the Dead*, written for Bishop Paulinus of Nola in 421, noting that even if funeral arrangements are omitted, this brings no misery "to those who are at rest in the hidden abodes of devout souls." Later in this work, he clarified that the souls now in these abodes are either in pain or peace, but they do not know events of our world or even the condition of their own graves and bodies. "How do they take part in the misery of the living, when either they are suffering their own evil desserts, if such they have merited, or they rest in peace?"[416]

Finally, in *The Enchiridion on Faith, Hope, and Charity*, written in A.D. 423–424 and frequently read and cited afterwards, Augustine spoke once more of the dwellings and conditions of souls during the intermediate states.

> During the time, however, which intervenes between man's death and the final resurrection, the souls remain in places specially reserved for them (*abditis receptaculis*), according as each is deserving of rest or tribulation for the disposition he has made of his life in the flesh.[417]

We conclude that some departed souls are, in Augustine's conception, presently in abodes of bliss, rest, peace, and consolation. Most importantly, they are "with Christ." This is the intermediate state of the souls of Christian martyrs, but also of the righteous patriarchs and prophets of old Israel, whose souls Christ released and took to be with himself, after he had descended to their place of waiting.[418] In this context, Augustine cited Jesus' account of the poor man and his going to "the bosom of Abraham." This widens further the community of saved souls,

---

[415] *The City of God*, 13, 8; Fathers of the Church, 14, 309. Later in this work, Augustine says it is certain that there is between bodily death and the last day an interval during which some souls suffer a fire of transitory tribulation (*City of God*, 21, 25; Fathers of the Church, 24, 402–403).

[416] *The Care to be Taken for the Dead*, chs. 3 and 13, citing from Fathers of the Church, 27 (1955), 357 and 375. Later in the treatise Augustine says he is sure *that* the martyrs help the living, but *how* they do this is a deep question which he has examined but not been able to solve (ch. 20, 379).

[417] The *Enchiridion*, translated as *Faith Hope and Charity*, 29, 109, by Louis A. Arand, Ancient Christian Writers, 3 (Westminster Md.: Newman Bookshop, 1947), 103, inserting a Latin phrase from the original in Corpus Christianorum, Series Latina, 46, 108.

[418] Letter 164, 3-6; The Works of Saint Augustine, II/3, 64–65.

because "the bosom of Abraham" was not "hell" where Jesus descended, but instead a state of "remarkable peace." The pre-Christian righteous souls embraced by Abraham were not even bereft of "the beatific presence of his [Christ's] divinity."[419]

Still, all these individuals, whether from the biblical past or from recent history, are separated souls. Although they now exist in peace, the resurrection is still to come, when their justification will be made perfect in an unspeakable way in their ultimate relation to God in the City of all the saved, angels and humans.[420]

Other Western Accounts of Departed Souls before Gregory the Great

Augustine's contemporary, Paulinus of Nola in Campania, wrote extensively on the coming resurrection of the dead, whether it be to light and glory with Christ or to damnation and pain. Before the resurrection, departed souls are fully conscious and are affected by their sense of the fate awaiting them after the resurrection. But some Paulinian passages also speak of individual innocent souls now resting in God while sinners are in the lower prison with Satan.[421]

The poet Orientius, bishop of Auch near Toulouse in the 430s, affirmed that souls begin their reward or punishment immediately after death. But God will reassemble our bodies at the resurrection, so that the guilty may suffer in the same bodies in which they sinned and the virtuous may be rewarded in the bodies in which they merited salvation.[422]

Peter Chrysologus, bishop of Ravenna (d. ca. 450), underscores Christian hope of the resurrection, while depicting the martyrs as now blessed with everlasting delights. But most souls are now in different pre-resurrection conditions and some of them who are now in penal detention can during the interim be released at the request of the church's prayers.[423]

---

[419] Letter 164, 7-8; The Works of Saint Augustine, II/3, 65–66.

[420] On justification perfected in resurrection at the end: *De trinitate*, 4, 3,5, cited by Daley, *Hope of the Early Church*, 136–137.

[421] Daley, *The Hope of the Early Church*, 159–160. Paulinus wrote extensively about his relation to St. Felix of Nola, the third-century confessor. At death Felix had been "born" into heaven, from where he was Paulinus' role model and intimate protector, and at whose tomb Paulinus built a basilica where well-to-do citizens of Nola sought to be buried. Peter Brown, *The Cult of the Saints: Its Rise and Function in Latin Christianity* (Chicago: University of Chicago Press, 1981), 53–60. When Prof. Brown gave these lectures at the University of Chicago in 1978, the series bore the popular title "Friends in High Places."

[422] Daley, *The Hope of the Early Church*, 160–161.

[423] Daley, *The Hope of the Early Church*, 165–166.

In the 490s, the presbyter Gennadius of Marseilles gave witness to developing Western doctrine on the souls of the dead, in his book listing the church's dogmas. Souls live on after departing from the body, with the souls of all the saints now being with Christ while awaiting bodily resurrection, when they will have complete and perpetual happiness with Christ. Similarly, now the souls of sinners are in hell.[424]

In the middle-third of the sixth century Caesarius of Arles showed that eschatological motivation had become a dominant theme. The ample volume of sermons which Caesarius had prepared for the clergy repeatedly urged an ethical-ascetic life upon the hearers as their preparation to meet Christ upon his return as Judge, according to Matthew 25:31-46. The sermons show no interest in the intermediate phase, but instead call for charity and almsgiving in order to avoid final exclusion from God and to gain instead entrance into the heavenly homeland as fellow-citizens with the angels.[425]

Intermediate States according to Gregory the Great

In the early 590s, 160 years after Augustine's death, Gregory the Great's *Dialogues*, Book 4, made a notable addition to patristic eschatology.[426] The context of Gregory's work was that of Rome struck

---

[424] *Liber de ecclesiasticis dogmatibus*, chs. 16, 18, and 79; *Patrologia Latina* 58, 984CD, 985A, 998C. On Gennadius, see *Theologische Realenzylopädie* 12 (1984), 376–379. Below, we will relate how Thomas Aquinas found Gennadius contributing to a firm tenet so doctrinally secure that contrary positions must be judged heretical.

[425] Daley, *Hope of the Early Church*, 136–137.

[426] The *Dialogues* were copied so frequently in the late antique and medieval West that scholars agree on the impossibility of working out a *stemma* of existing manuscriputs. The Greek translation by Pope Zacharias (Pope, 741–752) became popular in the East where the author was known as "Gregory of the Dialogues." Joan M. Petersen, *The* Dialogues *of Gregory the Great in the Late Antique Cultural Background* (Toronto: Pontifical Institute of Medieval Studies, 1984), 191. But Francis Clark argued for the *Dialogues* being a pseudonymous later compilation composed around 675, in *The Pseudo-Gregorian Dialogues* (Leiden: Brill, 1987), repeating his thesis in *The Gregorian Dialogues and the Origins of Benedictine Monasticism* (Leiden: Brill, 2003). But scholars of Gregory's texts are virtually unanimous in rejecting Clark's thesis. See, for example, R. A. Marcus, *Gregory the Great and His World* (Cambridge: Cambridge University Press, 1997), 15–16. Carole Straw relates the five main arguments given by Clark and indicates how scholars of Gregory have refuted them, in *Gregory the Great*, Authors of the Middle Ages, 12 (Aldershot Variorum, 1996), 54–55. The Bollandist, Robert Godding, offered a forceful rebuttal of Clark's second book in his "Tra due anniversari: Gregorio Magno alla luce degli studi recenti (1991–2003)," in *Gregorio Magno nel XVI centenario della morte* (Rome: Accademia nazionale dei Lincei, 2004), 89–106, at 99–102.

with a nine-month outbreak of the plague in 590, of Italy ravaged by Lombard invaders, and of conditions reported from afar that made obvious the decline of Roman order. These signaled for Gregory the impending crisis of a world drawing near to its end. Such surroundings could have made Gregory a somber prophet of doom, had not his Roman and Benedictine prudence prompted him to also insist how the church was rich in young members and caught up in missionary expansion, as to Britain. Still, he makes clear that death, judgment, and the retribution to come directly challenge each individual person.

Gregory wrote in this vein to Ethelbert, the King of the English, about the dire events of the times:

> If you recognize that some of these are occurring in your land, do not feel at all disturbed, because these signs of the end of the world are sent ahead, for the reason that we ought to be worried about our souls, and uncertain over the hour of our death. We should also be found well prepared with our good deeds for the coming Judge.[427]

At the end of Book 3 of the *Dialogues*, a rehearsal of ominous "signs of the times" gave Gregory the context for the pastoral message that the following Book 4 will inculcate.

> Our seeking after the things of heaven must, therefore, be all the more urgent, since we know that the things of earth are quickly slipping from our grasp. It would have been our duty to despise the world even if it had smiled on us, delighting our souls with prosperity. But now, struck as it is with countless scourges, worn out with adversity and daily lamenting its woes, what other message does it din into our ears but that we should cease loving it?[428]

---

[427] *Letters*, Book 11, no. 38, cited from *The Letters of Gregory the Great*, trans. John R.C. Martyn (Toronto: Pontifical Institute of Medieval Studies, 2004), 3:784. Gregory then closed the letter with this wish, "May almighty God complete in you the grace he has begun, and both extend your life here through the course of many years, and after a long time, receive you in the congregation of his heavenly homeland."

[428] Gregory the Great, *Dialogues*, Bk. 3, Ch. 34, no. 4; Fathers of the Church, 39 (1959), 187.

Book 4 then contains Gregory's teaching on death and the passing of the human immortal soul to the realm of eternity.[429] He offered first a narrative of souls going immediately upon death to heaven through ten accounts of visions that individuals had of such a passage at the moment of death or of heavenly personages, such as apostles, martyrs, angels, or Jesus himself, coming to take souls heavenward.[430]

Gregory's narratives call forth a request for theological and doctrinal clarification from his dialogue partner, Deacon Peter, who first asks whether the souls of the just are in fact received into heaven before being reunited with their bodies at the resurrection. To this Gregory answered, both on the fact, with an exception regarding some souls, and on the christological ground of the fact.

> We cannot affirm this of all the just, nor can we deny it either. For some just souls are delayed in certain dwellings (*quibusdam mansionibus*) outside heaven. The delay imposed on them would indicate that they are still lacking in perfect justice. Yet, nothing is clearer than that the souls of the perfectly just are received into the kingdom of heaven as soon as they leave the body. This is attested by Truth himself when he says, "Where the body lies there the eagles will gather" (Luke 17:37). For, wherever the Redeemer is bodily present, there the souls of the just are undoubtedly assembled. And St. Paul desires to have done with the present life, "and be with Christ" (Phil. 1:23). One

---

[429] Recent studies insist on the primacy of the didactic in Gregory's *Dialogues*, which use stories to make the reader attentive and ready to receive teaching, which in Book 4 covers the span of eschatological doctrine. C. Dagens, *Saint Grégoire le Grand. Culture et experience chrétiennes* (Paris: Études Augustiniennes, 1977), 345–420, on eschatology; G. Cremascoli, *Novissima hominis nei Dialogi di Gregorio Magno* (Bologna: Pàtron, 1979); and Sofia Boesch Gajano, *Gregorio Magno. Alle origini del Medioevo* (Rome: Viella, 2004), 231–252, on the interweaving of narratives and didactic expositions in the *Dialogues*.

[430] *Dialogues*, 4, 8-20; Fathers of the Church, 39, 200–214. After the recluse Romula received holy Viaticum, psalm singing choirs were seen at her bedside and "while these ceremonies for her departure were celebrated . . . , the soul of Romula was set free from the body to be conducted directly to heaven" (*Dialogues*, 4, 16; Fathers of the Church, 39, 210). In a contrasting story, devils come to take away the soul of a young blasphemer, "a sinner worthy of the fires of hell" (*Dialogues*, 4, 19; Fathers of the Church, 39, 213).

who doubts not that Christ is in heaven will not deny that
the soul of Paul is there, too.[431]

This claim that the souls of the just go to heaven as soon as they die
prompted Peter to ask Gregory about what this leaves for them to receive
as a reward on judgment day. To this Gregory answers with biblical
indications of the added *bodily* reward after final judgment. To what was
a christological grounding of "heaven now" in the previous answer,
Gregory adds from Rev 6 both an indication that final salvation has a
communal character and that judgment will lead to increased heavenly joy.

> They will indeed have an increase on the day of judgment,
> in that until then they enjoy only the bliss of the soul, but
> afterward they will also enjoy this in the body. The flesh
> in which they suffered pains and torments for the Lord
> will also share in their happiness. In regard to this double
> glory Scripture says, "They shall receive double in their
> land" (Isa. 61:7). About the time before the day of
> resurrection, it is written about the saints' souls, "A
> white robe was given to each of them, and they were
> bidden to rest a little while longer, until their number had
> been made up by their brethren and fellow-servants"
> (Rev. 6:11). Those, therefore, who now each receive a
> single robe are going to have a double robe at judgment.
> Just as they rejoice now only in their souls, they will then
> rejoice in the glory of their bodies as well.[432]

Later, Deacon Peter returns to the topic of reward immediately after
death to ask what can be said about when sinners receive their
recompense of punishment. Gregory then completes what he had said
earlier.

> If you believe from the witness of the divine word that the
> souls of the saints are in heaven, you also have to believe as
> well that the souls of the wicked are in hell. If retribution
> under eternal justice brings the just to glory, it must be that
> it also brings the wicked to punishment. Just as the elect

---

[431] *Dialogues*, 4, 26; Fathers of the Church, 39, 210. The translation is modified to
agree better with the original, given in Grégorire le Grand, *Dialogues*, A. de
Vogüe, ed., vol. 3, Sources chrétiennes, 265 (Paris: Cerf, 1980), 84.

[432] *Dialogues*, 4, 26; Fathers of the Church, 39, 218–219 (translation brought into
better agreement with Sources chrétiennes, 265, 84–86).

rejoice in bliss, it has to be believed that from the day of their death the reprobate burn in fire.[433]

Shortly after, Gregory brought out what was implicit in his position, namely, an anticipation of judgment, to determine the fate to which souls will pass. He told about a man who returned from death to life to relate his post-mortem vision of a river of foul waters giving off an unbearable stench. Across the river was a bridge and on the other side he saw grassy meadows dotted with fragrantly scented flowers amid which were light-filled dwellings. Gregory completed his doctrine of immediate recompense by having the man tell of "a final test," a personal *probatio*, administered on the bridge. "The unjust would slip off and fall into the dark, foul waters. The just, unhampered by sin, could walk over it, freely and without difficulty, to the beautiful meadows on the other side."[434]

Thus, Gregory the Great left what was for many in early medieval monastic life an engaging account of the end events, with texts exuding conviction about souls passing upon death to their reward or punishment.[435]

A Seventh-Century Eschatological Manual: Julian of Toledo

Julian of Toledo (644–690) assembled his doctrinal compilation, *Prognosticum futuri saeculi*, in three books on 1) death, 2) the souls of the dead before the resurrection of the body, and 3) Christ's second coming, the general resurrection and final judgment. This widely copied manual for the clergy became a principal transmitter of patristic

---

[433] *Dialogues*, 4, 29; Fathers of the Church, 39, 225 (translation modified to agree with Sources chrétiennes, 265, 98). Gregory completed his teaching on heaven and hell in a remark on the "many dwelling-places" of Jn 14:2, in which the plural indicates that souls in heaven are grouped to "allow them to enjoy the companionship of those with like merits (*propter meritorum consortium communiter laetantur*)." Similarly, in hell "the proud [are] burned with the proud, the avaricious with the avaricious, the dishonest with the dishonest." *Dialogues*, 4, 36; Fathers of the Church, 39, 236–237; Sources chrétiennes, 265, 122–124.

[434] *Dialogues*, 4, 37; Fathers of the Church, 39, 239; Sources chrétiennes, 265, 130.

[435] M. Idanza's research on the early manuscripts of Gregory's *Dialogues* shows that copies had spread by 680 not only to northern Italy, but as well to central Gaul, Visigoth Spain, and Britain. "Il tema della paternità gregoriana dei *Dialogi* e la tradizione manoscritta nei secoli VII e VIII," *Benedictina. Rivista di studi benedettini*, 42 (1995): 315–334.

eschatology to the early middle ages, especially by citing excerpts from the works of Augustine and Gregory the Great.[436]

In a series of short chapters in Book I, Julian gives reasons for believers not to fear death, because at death the soul will go to Christ to be in peace.[437] Book II passes on Gregory the Great's statement that the souls of the blessed go immediately to God in heaven, but it then also gives Augustine's text on the hidden abodes of the intermediate state in which souls have rest or distress.[438] Some short chapters relate the patristic indicators of post-mortem medicinal punishments, of different durations, applied to the less perfect, which from 1 Cor 3 can be taken as purifying fire.[439] Another text from Augustine says that after death the saints do not see God in the way that they will be able to see him after the resurrection, but later Julian cites Cyprian on the blessed seeing God and Christ immediately upon entry into heaven. On the latter text, Julian adds

---

[436] J. N. Hillgarth, "St. Julian of Toledo in the Middle Ages," *Journal of the Warburg and Courtauld Institutes* 21 (1968): 7–26, telling of the many manuscripts of the *Prognosticum* in monasteries and chapter libraries, in plain copies meant for reading and study. A recent essay contextualizes Julian's eschatological compilation in its setting: Jamie Wood, "Individual and Collective Salvation in Late Visigothic Spain," in Clarke & Claydon, *The Church, the Afterlife and the Fate of the Soul* (as in n. 410, above), 74–86. Candido Pozo, S.J., highlights the importance of Julian's *Prognosticum* for Catholic systematic eschatology in the Introduction to his widely used manual, *Theology of the Beyond*, trans. Mark A. Pilon (Staten Island: St. Paul, 2009; from the 4th Spanish edition of 2000), xxi-xxiii and 133. The new English translation, in the Ancient Christian Writers series, recapitulates and updates all aspects of recent scholarship on Julian in its ample introduction: Tommaso Stancati, O.P., trans. and ed., *Julian of Toledo: Prognosticum future saeculi. Foreknowledge of the World to Come*, ACW 63 (New York and Mahwah, N.J.: Newman Press, 2010), 1–364.

[437] *Prognosticum futuri saeculi*, I, 11-17; Corpus Christianorum Series Latina 115, 25–35; Ancient Christian Writers 63, 383–391, drawing on Augustine and Cyprian. Before these chapters, Julian said that when believers die the angels are at hand to bear their souls away to God, as they did for the poor man Lazarus in Jesus' parable (Luke 16:22). *Prognosticon*, I, 10; Corpus Christianorum Series Latina 115, 24–25; Ancient Christian Writers 63, 383.

[438] *Prognosticum*, II, 8-9; Corpus Christianorum Series Latina 115, 48–49; Ancient Christian Writers 63, 403, with excerpts first from Gregory, *Dialogues*, IV, and then Augustine, *Enchiridion*, ch. 109.

[439] *Prognosticum*, II, 10 and 19-23; Corpus Christianorum Series Latina 115, 49 and 55-60; Ancient Christian Writers 63, 404 and 408–412.

with emphasis that when they die those who have lived well will not be deprived of the vision but will enjoy it.[440]

Observations on the Ninth-Century West

The most recent scholarly survey of doctrinal development on the eschatological perfection of the saved in the vision of God includes a short section on John Scotus Eriugena (died ca. 877).[441] This Irish teacher in Carolingian France translated from Greek into Latin several works of Gregory of Nyssa, Maximus the Confessor, and Pseudo-Dionysius, and these influenced his constructive teaching in the direction of strong insistence on God's radical otherness, which is only overcome by God "coming out" in condescension to his creatures through various theophanies and in his Word made flesh.

Eriugena's treatment of divine theophanies and their extension into the life of heaven became for medieval scholastics the adversarial position against which they insisted that in heaven God no longer shows himself in images and likenesses but instead gives the blessed a vision of his own essence. But Eriugena's neo-platonic vision of intellectual creatures returning to God in the community united by Christ has also recently prompted a telling remark: the contrasting Latin theology of Eriugena's contemporaries and of many who follow has little sense of the universal dimension of salvation by and through Christ. Attention has shifted one-sidedly to the individual who will come to reward or punishment as meted out by the God of just judgment.[442]

2. Developments on Intermediate States in the West

Two twelfth-century writers on eschatology received the doctrine of the immediate state as formulated by Augustine and further elaborated by Gregory the Great, and passed this on in what became standard works for

---

[440] *Prognosticum*, II, 11 and 36; Corpus Christianorum Series Latina 115, 50 and 74; Ancient Christian Writers 63, 404, 405, and 423. During the intermediate phase, the soul's natural drive to "administer" the body will distract it from the supreme vision, but this will cease when it receives a spiritualized body. So Augustine, *Literal Commentary on Genesis*, 12, 35. But the text from Cyprian's *Exhortation to Martyrdom*, no. 13, describes death in a way that is decisive for Julian, that is, as closing one's eyes to this world and immediately opening them to see God and Christ.

[441] Christian Trottmann, *La vision béatifique. Des disputes scholastiques à sa définition par Benoît XII* (Rome: École Français, 1995), 74–83.

[442] Trottmann, *La vision béatifique*, 78.

the principal exponents of medieval scholastic theology. The first such work was Book II, Parts 16-18, which forms the last section of Hugh of St. Victor's *De sacramentis christianae fidei*, written in the 1130s.[443] Then in 1150–1158 Peter Lombard compiled his *Sentences*, in which the last part of Book IV treated the main questions of eschatology, drawing extensively on the Latin Fathers.[444] But in the same era, Bernard of Clairvaux (d. 1153) interpreted the interim state of souls differently, in works that grew out of monastic spirituality and Bernard's own biblical insights.

Hugh of St. Victor on Souls Passing at Death to their Recompense

Hugh of St. Victor's Christological section (*De sacramentis*, Book II, Part 1), in its analysis of the interval between Christ's death and resurrection, contains Hugh's affirmation that the soul is the properly personal element in a human being. Thus, souls of the deceased saints exist personally and are truly with Christ, as Paul desired to be (Phil 1:23), since departed souls are either being remunerated in glory or punished for sin.[445] According to the soul's merits, it receives the recompense first separated from the body without body, but afterwards united to the body in the body.[446]

Hugh's eschatology at the end of *De sacramentis* is both an update of the compilation by Julian of Toledo and a good organization of particular eschatological topics.[447] However, from Part 16, Ch. 6, to the

---

[443] The Latin text is in *Patrologia Latina* 176, cols. 173-618, and in a critical edition, Rainer Berndt, ed. (Münster: Aschendorff, 2008). An English translation made by Roy J. Deferrari (Cambridge, Mass.: Mediaeval Academy of America, 1951) is useful, even though it gives only general indications of the patristic texts that Hugh is citing. R. Berndt's edition indicates in detail the sources of Hugo's excerpted texts.

[444] *Sententiae in IV libris distinctis*, 3rd ed., 2 vols. (Grottaferrata: Editiones Collegii S. Bonaventurae ad Claras Aquas, 1971–1981). The English translation by Giulio Silano, coming out from the Pontifical Medieval Institute, Toronto, has not yet published Book IV.

[445] After death, souls will live, "quae vel gloriabuntur pro iustitia vel cruciabuntur pro culpa." *De sacramentis*, II, 1, 11; *Patrologia Latina* 176, 407CD; Berndt, ed., 326; Deferrari, 244–245.

[446] The soul, in the separation of death, "pro meritis praemium percipit primum separata a corpore sine corpore. Postea iuncta corpori in corpore" (*De sacramentis*, II, 1, 11; *Patrologia Latina* 176, 410B; Berndt, ed., 329; Deferrari, 247).

[447] Part 16 treats human death and what follows, in 15 short chapters. Part 17 is on the events of the Last Day especially the general resurrection, in 23 chapters. Part 18 presents the final states of the world, of the lost, and of the redeemed, in 17 chapters.

end of Part 18, Hugh simply gives under topical headings a generous offering of relevant citations from Augustine and Gregory without further argument or explanation on his own. Hugh begins Book II, Part 16, on the blessed dead who die in the Lord (Rev. 14:13), with his own explanation that they lived in God by faith, hope, and love, "afterwards however instead of faith and hope, by contemplation, with love remaining." Death is a defining moment, for "there is merit to the very point of death, but after death reward." With death, "the day of the Lord" begins when "one is in the power of the one to whom he or she has come to be remunerated."[448]

Hugh's own work early in Part 16 adds five more affirmations of an immediate passage at death to punishment or reward. Speculation abounds about how lost souls are punished, but "it is most truly proven by testimony on the authority of Sacred Scripture and Catholic faith that souls even now before the reception of bodies are tortured by corporeal and material fire."[449] Without knowing how God does this, faith is sure "that sinful souls who have not corrected blame in this life have punishment after this life," first without bodies but afterwards with bodies.[450] Wherever the infernal region may be, Christian thinking holds that the souls of deceased sinners go there straightway (*statim*) just as righteous humans who are purged of sin go without delay (*sine mora*) to heaven, where Christ in his humanity is in glory.[451]

Peter Lombard's Textbook Account of the Souls after Death

Peter Lombard's *Sentences*, in Book IV, Distinctions 43-50, gave to Western theology the topics and questions on eschatology that then

---

[448] *De sacramentis*, II, 16, 1-2; *Patrologia Latina* 176, 579A and 580D-581A; Berndt, ed., 548–549; Deferrari, 433–434.

[449] *De sacramentis*, II, 16, 3; *Patrologia Latina* 176, 584D; Berndt, ed., 554; Deferrari, 438 (corrected by inserting "now" for *etiam nunc* in the original).

[450] *De sacramentis*, II, 16, 3; *Patrologia Latina* 176, 585CD-586A; Berndt, ed., 555; Deferrari, 439.

[451] *De sacramentis*, II, 16, 4; *Patrologia Latina* 176, 586C; Berndt, ed., 556; Deferrari, 440. At the end of the chapter, Hugh repeats that at death the perfectly good pass *statim* to joys and the very evil descend *sine mora* to the torments of hell (*Patrologia Latina* 176, 587C; Berndt, ed., 557; Deferrari, 441). In chapter 5, he again distinguishes between the multitude of descriptions of *how* souls suffer after death and the simplicity of believing *that* they do so, which Augustine affirmed in *The City of God* and *Enchiridion*, on the abodes in which souls have rest or tribulation (*Patrologia Latina* 176, 589A-B; Berndt, ed., 559; Deferari, 443).

engaged major thinkers well into early modern times.[452] The major scholastic commentators on Lombard included Alexander of Hales, Albert the Great, Bonaventure, Thomas Aquinas, and Duns Scotus. Even after Thomas' *Summa theologiae* became widely used in the sixteenth century, Lombard's questions lived on, because the *Summa*'s eschatology, in the *Supplementum*, Questions 69-99, was created after Thomas' death out of excerpts from his early *Scriptum* on the *Sentences*.

The eschatological section of the *Sentences* is not a triumph of good order, for example, in treating the general resurrection before the intermediate state, but this did not prevent the *Sentences* from becoming the textbook of theology in Paris beginning with its adoption by Alexander of Hales in the 1220s.[453]

Lombard first mentions the intermediate state in an account of departed souls being tormented by corporeal fire. *That* this happens rests on Gregory the Great's *Dialogues* and on the rich man being in fiery agony in Luke 16:23-24. Lombard offers pointers to how this occurs, by citing Augustine on the human soul having a likeness to the body (*corporis similitudo*) and John Cassian on how the fate of the rich man shows that separated souls can still have feelings of longing, sadness, joy, and fear.[454]

Lombard speaks briefly but directly on the intermediate state when he cites Augustine's comments on John and his *Enchiridion* on souls going at death into dwellings (*receptacula*) of joy or torment, with the outcome in both cases becoming more intense after the resurrection.[455]

---

[452] Distinction 43 treats the general resurrection and last judgment (7 chapters). There follow Dist. 44 on the characteristics of risen bodies (8 chs.); Dist. 45 on the intermediate state of souls (1 ch.), suffrages for the dead (4 chs.), and saints in heaven as intercessors (1 ch.); Dist. 46 on pains of souls in hell (1 ch.), God's present judgments (1 ch.), and God's justice and mercy (3 chs.); Dist. 47 on the verdict of the Judge; Dist. 48 on the Judge's appearance (3 chs.), the place of judgment (1 ch.), and light and time afterwards (1 ch.); Dist. 49 on different dwellings in hell and especially in heaven (4 chs.); and Dist. 50 on the condition of the wicked in hell.

[453] The disorder, omissions, and disproportions in Lombard's account of eschatology were pointed out by Nicolaus Wicki in *Die Lehre von der himmlischen Seligkeit in der mittelalterlichen Scholastik von Petrus Lombardus bis Thomas von Aquin* (Fribourg: Universitätsverlag, 1954), 12–13.

[454] *Sententiae*, IV, 44, 7; vol. 2, 520–521, giving texts which Lombard found in Julian of Toledo's *Prognosticum*. Lombard cites Gregory the Great, *Dialogues*, IV, 29; Augustine, *Literal Commentary on Genesis*, XII, 13; and Cassian, *Collations*, I, 14.

[455] *Sententiae*, IV, 45, 1; vol. 2, 523, citing Augustine, *Tractates on John*, 49, 10, and *Enchiridion*, ch. 109.

The intermediate state is also implied in Lombard's account of the saints hearing our prayers and interceding for us before God. This is possible, first, because they bask in the light of God's face which they contemplate and by which they grasp as well what occurs elsewhere, insofar as this promotes their happiness and is helpful for us. Also, if the angels know our prayers and bring them to God (Tob. 3:35, 12:12), is it not most likely that the saints also do this, as those who contemplate God's face?[456]

Thus, Hugh of St. Victor and Peter Lombard, while they did not take up the intermediate state for detailed analysis, both delivered to later university theologians a clear teaching that departed souls, even before the general resurrection, exist in interim states of fiery punishment or heavenly reward.

Bernard of Clairvaux on the Final Stages of Salvation

Generally, Bernard depicts final salvation as the prolongation of contemplative union of the soul with God, but in a heavenly manner in no way possible in this life. Carefully avoiding any amalgam of Creator and creatures, he offered as images of ultimate heavenly union what happens when a drop of water is poured into wine and assumes the wine's color and taste, when molten iron becomes incandescent by fire, and when the air on a sunny day seems transformed into sunlight. These suggest how the final vision rests on communion of wills as God assimilates his creature to himself.[457]

But regarding *when* the elect come to see God, Bernard proposed a conception different from that conveyed by Hugh of St. Victor and Peter Lombard. Bernard recaptures the early patristic insistence on the resurrection as essential for final beatitude. At the end of his third sermon on All Saints, Bernard cited Revelation 6:9 and observed that the souls "under the altar" are not active in heavenly praise of God but instead are emitting prayers of petition. This calls for further pondering of the mysterious meaning of this altar that is now over the deceased holy ones.[458]

---

[456] *Sententiae*, IV, 45, 6; vol. 2, 527–529, citing Augustine, Letter 130, and *De trinitate*, Book 13.

[457] Bernard of Clairvaux, *On Loving God*, X, 28. See the translation in Cistercian Fathers Series, no. 13B (Kalamazoo: Cistercian Publications, 1995), 30. The reference came from Trottmann, *La vision béatifique*, 100.

[458] *Sancti Bernardi Opera*, J. Leclercq and H. Rochais, eds., vol. 5, *Sermones*, II (Rome: Editiones Cistercienses, 1968), 352–353.

Bernard's fourth All Saints' sermon then gives what he was given to understand through a prayerful review of the relevant biblical texts. This is his own insight, offered without contesting what others may hold on the topic.

Bernard explains the tradition that before Christ souls had no access to the heavenly kingdom, but were instead in detention, with the holy souls held in places of rest and consolation, while wicked souls suffered punishment. But at his death, Christ descended to lead the saints from their rest to an abode under God's altar until the full number of their brethren will reach completion (Rev. 6:11). Bernard takes "God's altar" to refer to Christ's own risen body in which the saints rest happily in union with the one whom, however, they know only in his servant-form. At the coming resurrection and judgment, however, all the saints will pass into the ultimate delight of knowing the Lord in his divine form, as he will lead them to perceive the Triune God, in a vision without which nothing ever satisfies the human spirit. This will be the knowing that is eternal life (John 17:3) and assimilation to God's likeness for seeing him as he is (1 John 3:2).[459]

In other texts, Bernard presented his idea, for spiritual clarification, by sketching a three-stage movement of humans to their final fulfillment. One imaginary scheme contrasts tents, a courtyard, and an ample palace. The righteous on earth live like soldiers in tents, which cover them, as by God's protecting grace, but the tents do not rest on a foundation, because the righteous are constantly moving on toward the Lord. After death, the souls of the blessed deceased live in a vast courtyard before the palace, where they have a secure foundation, but no roof before the resurrection. Finally, in the palace, their foundation is the stability of eternal beatitude and their roof is the consummate happiness of heaven.[460]

Bernard can say that the souls of the saints in the intermediate state, although they are separated from their bodies, "are completely engulfed in that immense ocean of eternal light and everlasting brightness."[461] But this is still not perfect peace, because they desire and hope to have their bodies once more, the bodies which when risen will share in the ascent of pure rapture into God. Bernard finds another three-stage image in a line of the Song of Solomon: "Eat, friends, drink, and be drunk with love" (5:1b). In the flesh and on earth, the faithful soul eats its bread, like Jesus

---

[459] *Opera*, 5, *Sermones*, II, 354–356.

[460] This is given by Trottmann, *La vision béatifique*, 105.

[461] *On Loving God*, XI, 30; Cistercian Fathers Series, 13B, 31.

doing the work of his Father (John 4:34). In post-mortem rest, the soul drinks the wine that makes it glow with love, but this is mixed with milk, that is, with the soul's natural affection for its body. However, resurrection brings a fullness of heavenly but sober intoxication by drinking wisdom's pure wine with Christ in his Father's house (Mark 14:25). Only in the third stage does the soul forget itself to pass entirely into God in whom it reigns amid divine delights.[462]

Thus, Bernard of Clairvaux left a legacy of texts on the intermediate state of the redeemed as not yet being the complete fulfillment that is the heavenly vision of God. These texts were at hand to ground a view which would contest the common position of major thirteenth-century theologians, who were teaching that souls reach eschatological fulfillment or punishment immediately upon death or upon completion of purgatorial purification. In 1331, Pope John XXII will draw on Bernard in his challenge to the scholastic consensus.

Mid-Thirteenth Century Accounts on the Saved Coming to See God

The middle years of the thirteenth century saw a remarkable increase of theological fascination with the final perfection of the blessed in seeing God face to face. The *Summa aurea* composed by the Parisian master William of Auxerre in 1222–1225 spoke of the beatific vision only once, in connection with the Apostle Paul being caught up to the third heaven, whereas some sixty years later Henry of Ghent treated the vision in eight of his fifteen *Quodlibeta*.[463]

The thirteenth-century masters who developed a systematic and deepened account of the beatific vision worked increasingly under the influence of Aristotelian philosophy, made newly accessible by translations into Latin. Aristotle gave Christian thinkers after 1200 what Peter Lombard and his contemporaries had lacked, namely, a detailed account of the human soul with its dynamic spiritual powers of intellection and volition. The scholastic masters were thus equipped to move beyond descriptions of the final happiness of the blessed (in vision, delight, enjoyment, love) to show how human souls are made capable of the actions constituting life in heaven. God is for the scholastics the operative cause of human beatitude, but new generations of theologians

---

[462] *On Loving God*, XI, 31–33; Cistercian Fathers Series, 13B, 32–35.

[463] H. F. Dondaine charted the development in "L'objet et le 'medium' de la vision béatifique chez les théologiens du XIIIᵉ siècle," *Recherches de théologie ancient et medievale*, 19 (1951): 60–99.

worked out accounts of where and how this divine work resonated in souls and elicited their personal activity on this supreme level of relating to God.

An important moment in the development on the beatific vision was the action taken in 1241 against a certain "Brother Stephen," who was Étienne de Venisy, O.P., who had been influenced by John Scotus Eriugena's revival of Greek patristic theses on God as being so transcendent that he is unknowable by created minds (cf. Jn 1:18a). So a spiritual theophany, out of the enlightened and enlightening realm of the heavenly hierarchy, must be given as the heavenly delight of the blessed.[464] The Bishop of Paris, William of Auvergne, himself a productive theologian, censured ten errors circulating in Stephen's writings, with the first being "that the divine essence will not be seen in itself, neither by humans nor by angels." In the censure, Bishop William acted in concert with and under advice of all the Masters of the University of Paris' Theological Faculty. By episcopal authority, those who deny a true vision of God as he is are excommunicated. They deviate from what the Bishop and Masters believe and affirm (*credimus et asserimus*), namely, "that God will be seen in his essence or substance by the angels and by all the saints, and he is now seen by glorified souls."[465]

This condemnation of 1241 confirmed that heavenly fulfillment is to see God face-to-face (1 Cor. 13:12) and to know him as he is (1 John 3:2). But different explanatory accounts were still possible and they did arise after 1241 in the works of Bonaventure, Albert the Great, and Thomas Aquinas. Bonaventure developed the will's role in beatitude as ecstatic, loving union with God. Albert contributed the notion of the *lumen gloriae*, as the infused grace proper to heaven that empowers the blessed and elevates their minds for seeing God as he is. Thomas showed the coherence of the total divine economy by his metaphysics of finality, according to which the human soul's natural desire for God will attain its supernatural fulfillment in the beatific vision.[466]

---

[464] Trottmann, *La vision béatifique*, 175–186.

[465] *Chartularium Universitatis Parisiensis*, eds. H. Denifle & E. Chatelain, vol. 1 (Paris: Delalain, 1891–1899; reprint Brussels: Culture et Civilization, 1964), 170–172.

[466] Trottmann, *La vision béatifique*, 197–208 (Bonaventure), 283–302 (Albert), 302–317 (Thomas). The author speaks of the shift in theological attention occasioned by the 1241 condemnation as being from the *quid* of vision, that is, what God gives the soul to see, to the *quomodo*, that is, how God works in the soul he has united to himself for the perfection of happiness. *La vision béatifique*, 15, 115.

Although the scholastic explanations differ among themselves on details, they all assume, in accord with the final phrase of the 1241 teaching, that the consummation of the vision is given after death and purgation to the souls of the blessed. To be sure, this point was not the central one of the 1241 censure. Still, "heaven-before-resurrection" is part of the doctrinal fabric of thirteenth-century theology

The Intermediate State in the Works of Thomas Aquinas

In 1252, in Paris, Thomas became a *baccalaureus* of the *Sentences* and began four years of lecturing on Lombard's text, which led to an ample and polished work, the *Scriptum super libros Sententiarum*, completed in Spring 1256. In four passages, Thomas treated souls in the intermediate state.

In the *Scriptum* Thomas handled two questions that could only arise on the assumption that at present departed souls are in fact in punishment or heavenly reward. First, *Sentences*, Dist. 44, Ch. 7, asks whether separated souls, being spiritual, can be punished by fire. Thomas gives a refined answer that the fire is real, but that its punishing effect is not by physical burning. Instead, the fire is the place in which the soul, while not physically touched, is still in some way (*quodammodo*) held and retained, which for the soul is injurious and tormenting.[467]

Then *Sentences*, Dist. 45, Ch. 6, gave Thomas the occasion to deal systematically with the prayers of the saints now in heaven, in three articles: 1) that the saints do know our prayers through their vision of God's essence; 2) that we should pray for them to intercede for us; and 3) that God does in some way hear all the saints' prayers for us.[468] The souls of those now in heaven, for Thomas, are not in a middle state awaiting what will be final.

In a third text, Augustine's notion of hidden dwellings (*abdita receptacula*) of souls before the general resurrection became a topic for Thomas to clarify. He explains that while separated souls neither inform bodies nor work upon them, still certain bodily places are assigned to

---

[467] *Scriptum suoer libros Sententiarum*, Dist. 44, Q. 3, Art. 3, Quaestiuncula 3; in the Parma *Opera omnia* (1852–1873) of Aquinas, vol. VII/2 (reprint, New York: Mursurgia, 1948), 1109–1110. Later, after Thomas died in 1274 before completing the *Summa theologiae*, his disciples made this text of 1256 part of the *Supplementum* to the *Summa*, as Q. 70, Art. 3.

[468] *Scriptum*, Dist. 45, Q. 3, Arts. 1-3; *Opera omnia*, VII/2, 1129b–1133a. These became ST *Supp.*, Q. 72, Arts. 1-3.

them by which they are, as it were (*quasi*), in place, which differs according to the souls' level of nearness to God by graced participation, which is to be in heaven, or their impediment to such participation, so that they are in "the contrary place."[469]

Fourth, Thomas faced the question of the intermediate state by constructing a sub-question on whether at death souls do in fact pass to heaven or hell. Four arguments go against such a passage, especially aspects of the Last Judgment. But in favor of immediate passage are 2 Corinthians 5:1 on having a heavenly dwelling; Philippians 1:23 on departing to be with Christ, as interpreted by Gregory the Great; and Luke 16:22-23 on the rich man going to torment in Hades.

Thomas explains that when one dies the intrinsic quality attained by the person, through his or her graced actions in this life, gives the soul a dynamic of movement, like a response to gravity, either to punishment or to reward (providing one is not delayed for purgation). This movement of holy souls, once beyond death and any needed purgation, is further elevated by God's created grace of the *lumen gloriae*, which disposes them for their reward of relating to God immediately in vision. The *lumen*, in fact, extends in eternity what, under sanctifying grace, had been the operative direction of the person in this life.[470]

At the end, Thomas stated that the soul's going to reward or punishment at death is a truth resting on authoritative biblical witness and the works of the Church Fathers. Hence, a contrary view has to be judged heretical, as Gregory the Great said and was affirmed in the book *De ecclesiasticis dogmatibus*.[471]

Later, Thomas composed in 1259–1265 the *Summa contra gentiles*, for his Dominican brethren who were contending with Muslims, Jews, and heretical Christians in Spain and North Africa. The last part of Book

---

[469] *Scriptum*, Dist. 45, Q. 1, Art. 1, Quaestiuncula 1; *Opera omnia*, VII/2, 1113ab and 1114ab. This became ST *Supp.*, Q. 69, Art. 1. In the next quaestiuncula, in answer to an objection, Thomas states that paradise and hell are among Augustine's hidden *receptacula*.

[470] On the *lumen gloriae* in Thomas: Trottmann, *La vision béatifique*, 312–320, who lists the terms Thomas uses regarding the *lumen* in his accounts of the vision. It is *elevatio, augmentum virtutis intellectivae, dispositio ultima supernaturalis ad formam*, and *illuminatio intellectualis*, as well as *similitudo divina, assimilatio divina, deiformatas*, and *participatio*. Trottmann, 317.

[471] *Scriptum*, Dist. 45, Q. 1, Art. 1, Quaestiuncula 2; *Opera omnia*, VII/2, 1113b–1114a and 1114b–1115a, with concluding references to Gregory, *Dialogues*, 4, 26 and Gennadius, *Liber*, Ch. 79. This sub-question became ST *Supp.*, Q. 69, Art. 2.

IV, Chapters 79-97, expounds eschatology, restating in Chapters 90-91 the last two positions from the *Scriptum* on the *Sentences*.[472]

Thus, the lost do suffer from bodily fire before the resurrection, since their souls are by divine power held there in bondage, albeit without being consumed (Chapter 90, nos. 2-4). Rational reflections (nos. 5-7) show that this is proper (*conveniens*), before Thomas clarifies (nos. 8-9) that while some descriptions of punishment in hell are figurative, such as the undying "worm" (Isa. 66:24) and "weeping and gnashing of teeth" (Matt. 8:12, 13: 50), the fire is different and must be understood realistically.

The immediacy of the separated souls' passage is first argued (Chapter 91, nos. 2-5) from the condition of such souls in relation to the reward of heaven or punishment of hell. After two numbers on purgatorial purification before heaven, nos. 8-10 give the biblical, especially Pauline, case for attainment immediately after death of the punishment or reward one is to have as the recompense of a wicked or good life.

Late in life (1269–1273), Thomas undertook his *Compendium of Theology*, which was to treat all doctrine under the theological virtues of faith, hope, and charity. But he had to break this work off a few months before his death. He did, however, complete the treatise on faith, including the articles of the creed, finishing with the Last Judgment. While treating Christ as final Judge given authority by the Father, Thomas wrote as follows about death and what follows for every individual:

> There is another judgment of God whereby, at the moment of death, everyone receives as regards his soul the recompense he has deserved. The just who have been dissolved in death remain with Christ, as Paul desired for himself; but sinners who have died are buried in hell.[473]

Thus, Thomas Aquinas taught the immediate passage through death and any needed purgation to the final recompense, for which he cited New Testament texts and supplied reasons based on the intrinsic dynamic of

---

[472] *Summa contra gentiles* (Rome: Marietti, 1934), 559–563, an edition based on vols. 12-15 of the stately Leonine edition. This smaller *Summa* came out in English in Doubleday Image Books in 1957, entitled *On the Truth of the Catholic Faith*, with the translation being republished in four volumes under its Latin title, by University of Notre Dame Press in 1975, with the nineteen eschatology chapters in 4, 297–349.

[473] *Compendium theologiae*, no. 242, in *Opuscula theologica*, vol. 1, *De re dogmatica et morali*, ed. Raymond A. Verardo (Turin-Rome, 1954), 122; cited from *Light of Faith: The Compendium of Theology* (Manchester, N.H., 1993), 318.

grace given in this life. By grace the personal actions and resultant state of the person tend spontaneously toward life in God. At death God supplies to the redeemed the grace of heaven, the *lumen gloriae*, making them able to enjoy seeing him as he is. Newman's dictum captures well this connection: Grace in this life is glory in exile; glory is grace at home.[474]

A Statement of Faith, 1267

While Thomas Aquinas was still alive, Pope Clement IV commissioned the preparation in 1267 of a Profession of Faith to serve as a basis of unity with the Greek Church. Emperor Michael VIII Palaeologus accepted this at the fourth session of the Second Council of Lyons on July 6, 1274, and the text went into the records as the faith of the Roman Church. After setting forth the fundamental trinitarian and Christological tenets, the Profession enunciates briefly a doctrine of purgatory and of the suffrages of the living. It then moves on to state that the baptized who die without having sinned and those cleansed in Purgatory "are received immediately (*mox*) into heaven," while those dying in mortal sin "go down immediately (*mox*) to hell." Nonetheless, the General Judgment of all those risen from the dead will follow, as the "Roman Church firmly believes and firmly asserts."[475]

Conclusions

This section has set forth the "high scholastic" doctrine of the intermediate state of souls before the end-events of resurrection and judgment. The leading university theologians of the twelfth and thirteenth centuries agreed in teaching that departed souls, before being reunited with their bodies, pass through the particular judgment into the final states. This would be for sinners the punishment of hell and for the justified, either immediately or after purgation, the supreme happiness of heaven.

Still, difficulties remained:

(1) If death and particular judgment combine as the gateway to the final eschatological state, theology has to explain what then

---

[474] Cited, without documentation, by Dermot Lane, *Keeping Hope Alive. Stirrings in Christian Theology* (Eugene, Oregon: Wipf and Stock, 2005), 126.

[475] Denzinger and Schönmetzer, 856–858, cited from J. Neuner & J. Dupuis, eds., *The Christian Faith in the Doctrinal Documents of the Catholic Church*, 7th ed. (Bangalore: Theological Publications in India; Staten Island: Alba House, 2001), 19–20 (nos. 26-27).

comes with the general resurrection and final judgment on all humanity, both of which have solid biblical and creedal bases.

(2) Since the separated soul remains related to the body that it no longer informs and animates, theology has also to explain how a soul, which by its nature is the *forma corporis*, can in this state enjoy a fulfillment given by God to it while outside the body.

However, parallel with university theology, there was the monastic tradition of teaching, in which the sermons of Bernard of Clairvaux were being copied and studied intently, especially every November 1 on All Saints' Day. Bernard highlighted the corporate dimension of salvation, by citing Revelation 6:11, on souls resting "until the number would be complete" of those destined to receive the final reward. Bernard's intermediate state would last until the communion of the saints reached completion and so pass to the vision of God and Christ in the communal definitive perfection of human beings.

Thus, on the doctrinal level, the 1241 Parisian episcopal intervention had defined the *essential content* of what the redeemed have or will have in heaven, namely, a vision in which they see God as he is. The Profession of Faith of 1267 attested to convictions on reward or punishment immediately on death, but this was for the Greek Church at the Council of Lyons, and not a teaching document aiming to bring clarity, beyond the scenario offered St. Bernard, to Catholic theology. But such a clarification came in the fourth decade of the fourteenth century.

3. Dogmatic Precision on the Intermediate Stage, as a Pope Corrects a Pope[476]

On All Saints' Day of 1331, in Avignon, the eighty-five year old Pope, John XXII, preached on the beatific vision the first of a series of sermons which, when news of them circulated, caused a short-lived but intense outbreak of theological argument over the condition of souls in the intermediate state. Pope John had copies of his sermons made for

---

[476] The controversy preceding the doctrinal settlement by Pope Benedict XII in 1336, has been studied with detailed attention to the range of theological positions, by Christian Trottmann in *La vision béatifique* (as in note 141, above). Trottmann gives a concise summary on pp. 413–416, before his wide-ranging account in six subsequent chapters, pp. 417–811. Trottmann also surveys the controversy more concisely in C. Trottmann and Arnaud Dumouch, *Benoît XII. La Vision béatifique* (Avignon: Docteur angélique, 2009), 9–115.

circulation, some of which went out with requests for evaluations of the positions that he was advancing.[477]

Pope John XXII's Arguments for Delay of the Final Human Recompense

On November 1, 1331, John XXII led his hearers to consider the reward of glory that the departed saints receive for their works. Drawing on the sermon of St. Bernard, also for All Saints, the Pope explained that now, until the Last Judgment, the reward of the saints is to be "under the altar" (Rev. 6:9), in a place of protection, rest, and consolation given by the humanity of Christ. In this state, the souls are freed from the tears and fears of battle in this world and the outcome of their salvation is certain, since they can no longer commit sin. But union with Christ's humanity is not their final condition but remains intermediate, for only after the resurrection of their bodies, with the full assembly of the body of Christ, will they contemplate the divinity of Christ, along with the Father and the Holy Spirit, thus fulfilling John 17:3 on "eternal life" as knowing the true God and Jesus Christ sent on mission.[478]

John argued briefly that because the separated soul is imperfect until it again informs its body, it cannot receive perfect joy. This will come at the word of the Judge, "Enter into the joy of the Lord" (Matt. 25:21-23), a joy which will be the Lord's own rest, once he has consigned the wicked to punishment and the righteous to glory. It will be our rest as well, if we act well by uniting our wills to the divine will. But now, those under the altar cry out for judgment and justice (Rev. 6:9-10), whereas after the

---

[477] The sermon texts circulated in Avignon and beyond (Naples, Munich, Paris). When theologians sent in their responses and comments, they cited the Pope's arguments precisely. It cannot be excluded that John intended to shift theological discussion from highly technical speculation about *how* and *with what intensity* God works in the souls which see and enjoy him in heaven to more basic biblical and patristic arguments, by raising the question about *when* full heavenly happiness begins. C. Trottmann says that this in fact happened, as John XXII's sermons had the effect of "re-centering" theological reflection on the vision. *La vision béatifique*, 7.

[478] The sermon, the first of John XXII's six sermons on the delayed vision, is given by Marc Dykmans, *Les sermons de Jean XXII sur la vision béatifique* (Rome: Gregorian University Press, 1973), 85–99, esp. 93–99. Dykmans' introduction shows that John XXII was proposing an innovation. Over a century before, William of Auxerre spoke of stupid people who hold a delay of the vision for the elect, which is heretical. Dykmans shows that William's own position on an immediate passage to the vision by the redeemed and purified was not only the common position of theologians whose works John XXII could have easily consulted, but it was also taught in documents he issued before 1331 (Dykmans, 14, 19–22, 35–37).

Judgment the redeemed will only praise God for ever and ever for the glory he has given them.[479]

John XXII preached a second sermon on the departed souls on Gaudete Sunday of Advent 1331, from which an extensive written text circulated. The day's gospel led to treating the second coming of Christ, when he will give glory to his elect. This glory consists in the vision of the divine essence, which Augustine explained as the finally satisfying object of all our love and desires. This will not be the soul's delight alone, but of the whole human composite being, and so it must follow the general resurrection.

Pope John took pains to show that the vision is not yet the reward of innocent departed souls, as he worked out arguments which began with the parables on payment (Matt. 20:1-20, 25:14-30), went on through texts from St. Paul, and then advanced twelve passages of St. Augustine. So, at the end Christ will say, "Come, blessed of my Father, take possession of (*percipite*) the kingdom . . ." (Matt. 25:34). "But how would he say this if they had taken possession of it before?" John XXII wanted to retain the full significance of the final judgment, at which the community of the redeemed will be complete. He closed with a remark that he was open to correction by someone who knows the matter better. But for his part, he sees it as he has explained and he will hold this until someone shows him either a contrary determination of the church or Scripture texts of greater clarity than those he has advanced.[480]

When Pope John preached on the vigil of Epiphany 1332, he noted that some are claiming that on the intermediate state he is preaching a novelty that should not circulate. He argues from the Judge's condemnation of the wicked (Matt. 25:41) that the devil and his angels must not yet be in the eternal fire, for if they were, they would not now be tempting us. Also 1 Corinthians 15:24 has Christ handing over the kingdom to the Father only at the end, after Christ returns victorious over all his enemies. At the end John challenges anyone with a better view to speak out, but he will only change his view of the question if someone shows him that the church has decided the question in the sense opposed to him.[481]

---

[479] Dykmans, *Les sermons de Jean XXII*, 97–99.

[480] Dykmans, *Les sermons de Jean XXII*, 100–139, citing 138–139.

[481] Dykmans, *Les sermons de Jean XXII*, 144–148. C. Trottmann examines positively the hypothesis that church-political considerations swayed John XXII, for his view extends to the final judgment the sovereign power of Christ in his human nature, in which the successor of Peter and Christ's earthly vicar would participate on earth until the last day. *La vision béatifique*, 450–453.

On Annunciation Day in 1332 or 1333, John XXII repeated his notion of the saints as now resting while they await their final assembling and admission to the vision of God after the Last Judgment. He added that he was not issuing binding teaching, but would gladly change his position if he saw biblical texts or a determination of the church in the contrary sense.[482] From John's sermon on Ascension Day 1334, a fragment is extant, which contains a brief reference to the whole human person being adopted by God, and so the soul alone will not have the children's inheritance of the kingdom. This will come only when the children are "further clothed" (2 Cor. 5:4).

On December 4, 1334, John XXII died near the age of 90 after an 18-year pontificate. The day before, he made a notarized retraction of what he had been advancing in his sermons on the delay of the vision until the end-events of Christ's return, the general resurrection, and the Last Judgment.[483]

Critics of John XXII's Thesis on Delay of the Final Recompense

The reasons for Pope John's death-bed change are not documented, but it came after his position was pelted by a rainstorm of critical responses during the months after he began preaching on the delayed vision in late 1331.[484] The news of his position energized the ecclesiastical and theological community to produce arguments and conclusions, some of which agreed with John XXII, but most of which held against him that redeemed and purified souls enter the heavenly vision of God before the Last Judgment.

---

[482] Dykmans, *Les sermons de Jean XXII*, 153–159, with this clarification: "Non enim dixi nec dico hoc aliquid determinando, ... Et ubi ostenderetur auctoritas scripturae vel determinatio ecclesiae contraria, libenter dicerem oppositum" (156).

[483] John's retraction was published in March 1335 by his successor, Pope Benedict XII, and was given in O. Rinaldi's continuation of Baronius' *Annales ecclesiastici*, A. Theiner, ed. (Bois-le-Duc: L. Guerin, 1872), 25:15–16. It came into wider circulation by inclusion in Denzinger and Schönmetzer, 990–991.

[484] Anneliese Maier surveyed the interventions for and against John's positions in "Schriften, Daten und Personen aus dem Visio-Streit unter Johann XXII," in *Ausgehendes Mittelalter*, 3 vols. (Rome: Edizioni di storia e letteratura, 1964–1967), 3:543–590. Dykmans also offers a chronicle of the controversy from John XXII's first sermon to his successor's dogmatic pronouncement of January 1336. *Les sermons de Jean XXII*, 165–197.

In Munich William of Ockham completed in Spring 1332 his "Work of Ninety Days," against John XXII's positions on Christ's poverty and Franciscan practices. Ockham inserted in the final chapter a short passage accusing John XXII of preaching a doctrine contrary to what Catholics of all classes hold as a truth "promulgated" in the church, namely, that the souls of the wicked are new being punished along with the demons in hell while the Virgin, the Apostles, the martyrs, and other saints are now in heaven where they see God.[485] Ockham returned to the subject in his "Compendium of the Errors of Pope John XXII," in a chapter singling out four errors from John's sermons on the departed souls, giving against each a short rebuttal drawn from Scripture and the *Dialogues* of Gregory the Great.[486] After the Pope's death, Ockham argued at length that his end-of-life retraction was so phrased as to undercut its validity and that John died a heretic because of his notorious errors, especially those on the beatific vision.[487]

Late in 1332 or early in the following year, John received the first three chapters of a treatise, *De visione beata*, composed by Robert of Anjou, King of Naples, in refutation of the Pope's sermons.[488] A Dominican Master in Paris held a *Quodlibet* disputation before thirty colleagues, marshalling arguments against John's position in December 1332.[489] On January 3, 1333, Thomas Waleys, O.P., preached in the Dominican

---

[485] *Opus nonaginta dierum*, in Ockham, *Opera politica*, J. G. Sikes, H. S. Offler et al., eds. (Manchester: Manchester University Press, 1940–1997), 2, 852.

[486] *Compendium errorum Ioannis Papae XXII*, ch. 7, in *Opera politica*, 4, 56–61.

[487] *Tractatus contra Ioannem*, in *Opera politica*, 3, 29–156. C. Trottmann presented Ockham's attacks in *La vision béatifique*, 470–495, concluding that the treatises contain no substantial theological argument against John XXII, but are single-mindedly intent on proving that the Pope is a heretic who should be condemned at a future council and, for the present, has no jurisdiction for measures against the Franciscan radicals.

[488] *La vision bierheureuse. Traité envoyé au pape Jean XXII*, ed. Marc Dykmans (Rome: Gregorian University Press, 1970), presented analytically by C. Trottmann, *La vision béatifique*, 695–713. King Robert argues in Ch. I from *rationes convenientiae* for entry into the vision before judgment, moves on in Ch. II to nine texts from St. Thomas (whom John had canonized in 1323) in this sense, and gives in Ch. III no fewer than 73 patristic interpretations of Scripture against John, adding as a 74th text John's 1317 bull of canonization of St. Louis of Toulouse which speaks of the saint having the joy of contemplating God whose face is being revealed to him in heaven.

[489] C. Trottmann, *La vision béatifique*, 646–648.

church of Avignon against what he held to be John's manifest error.[490] The scholastic doctor, Durandus of Saint Porçain, O.P., now Bishop of Mende, responded to a request from the Pope and sent John a treatise against his views in mid-1333.[491] The opponents argued that God would act unjustly in depriving souls of the blessed recompense they have merited in this life. The urged the *hodie mecum* promised to the repentant thief (Lk 24:43) and Jesus' prayer that his own may see his glory in loving vision (Jn 17:24), but they also admitted that the beatitude of the saved will increase in the assembly of the whole body of Christ at the end.

Late in 1333, in Paris, the Franciscan Master General, Gurial Ot (*Geraldus Odonis*) held a disputation concluding to a vision of the Deity given before judgment, but then, after judgment there begins the *visio aeterna*, which is different.[492] Early in 1334, 29 masters of theology in Paris submitted the results of a consultation called by the French King, who sent their conclusions to the Pope in the form of a complaint that preachers were spreading views, including the Pope's own, which no Parisian theologian has held and which were disturbing the realm. The Pope should issue a definition against these ideas and in favor of the saints now seeing God, which is a conviction that has nourished the devotion of the whole Christian people.[493] In March 1334, John XXII wrote the King and Queen that he had himself submitted the issue to cardinals, other prelates, and doctors of theology residing in Avignon for their diligent study.

---

[490] Waleys had to answer to the Inquisition for his intervention. His sermon is given in T. Kaeppeli, *Le procès de Thomas Waleys, o. p. Études et documents* (Rome: Institutum Historicum FF. Praedicatori, 1936), 93–108. On Waleys' arguments: Trottmann, *La vision béatifique*, 586–592. Also Simon Tugwell, "Waleys, Thomas (*fl.* 1318–1349)," *Oxford Dictionary of National Biography*, (Oxford University Press, 2004) online at *www.oxforddnb.com/view/article/28554*, accessed August 5, 2009.

[491] Text in Baronius-Raynaldus, *Annales ecclesiastici*, 24, 530–534, presented by Trottmann, *La vision béatifique*. 592–601. Durandus argues from Christ's descent to the dead to bring righteous souls to the vision of God, from Jesus' words to the good thief on paradise "today," from Phil. 1:23, from the heavenly dwelling of 2 Cor. 5:1-2, from the white robe of Rev. 6:11, from the readiness of souls after purgation for the vision, from the church's hymns on apostles and martyrs now in beatitude, and from Gregory the Great's first answer to Deacon Peter on souls being in heaven.

[492] Treated by A. Maier, "Die pariser Disputation des Geraldus Odonis über die visio beatifica Dei," in *Ausgehendes Mittelalter*, 3, 319–372, and by C. Trottmann, *La vision béatifique*, 718–722.

[493] C. Trottmann, *La vision béatifique*, 723–733.

The Argument Develops over John XXII's Thesis on Delay of the Final Recompense

John XXII did not remain alone in the views presented in his sermons. The curial cardinal Annibal de Ceccano presided at a consultation of theologians in Avignon and from this came his review of biblical and patristic texts on the intermediate state, from which he rebutted Ockham, Durandus, and other critics of the Pope's idea that the redeemed enjoyed the beatific vision only after the general resurrection and last judgment.[494]

But the critical voices were many, voicing and writing at times substantial arguments against John XXII's view, for example, in the long anonymous treatise, *De visione beata*, by an unknown author, written in Avignon against Annibal de Ceccano.[495] Also the Cistercian Cardinal, Jacques Fournier, composed against Pope John a lengthy text favoring the vision being given after death and any needed purification of the souls of the redeemed.[496] This latter work grew in significance on December 20,

---

[494] Annibal's untitled work is given in M. Dykmans, ed., *Pour et contre Jean XXII en 1333. Deux traits avignonnais sur la vision béatifique* (Vatican City: Vatican Library, 1975), 61–166, and is treated analytically by C. Trottmann in *La vision béatifique*, 502–522. Annibal goes through 38 biblical texts cited in the controversy, to show in each case that the text does not prove the granting of the vision before resurrection and final judgment. For example, the "paradise" promised the good thief (Lk 23:43) can well have several meanings other than the beatific vision. On 2 Cor 5:1-2, the standard Gloss takes this being "clothed" as referring to the resurrection. Phil 1:23 tells for John, as Paul's hope to be "with Christ" in his humanity during the intermediate phase. Other texts cited against the Pope refer to the vision and final beatitude given to the reconstituted human supposit of soul and risen body, not to the separated soul.

[495] M. Dykmans, *Pour et contre Jean XXII en 1333*, 169–396, giving parts of the text refuting Ceccano, which C. Trottmann presents in *La vision béatifique*, 602–616. The text argues from early councils and papal decrees (e.g., canonizations), from the text at the Second Council of Lyons for the Greek emperor, from the decision of the University of Paris in 1241, from the efficacy of Christ's saving passion and resurrection, from the efficacy of baptism, and from 107 biblical texts which revered church fathers have taken in a sense contrary to the view of Pope John XXII.

[496] C. Trottmann presents Fournier's treatise, of which he is preparing a publication from manuscript, in *La vision béatifique*, 747–795, giving ample citations in notes.

1334, when Cardinal Fournier was elected to succeed John XXII, taking the name of Benedict XII.[497]

Binding Papal Doctrine Issued by Pope Benedict XII

Immediately after his election, Benedict XII ordered the mendicant orders to abstain from public preaching and disputing on the question of the beatific vision. In July 1335 the Pope left Avignon for vacation, taking with him a group of cardinals and sixteen theologians to study the disputed doctrine. The latter worked until the end of the year, chaired by Pierre de La Palu, O.P., and then gave the Pope their conclusions.[498] From this study Benedict XII included key passages in his Constitution of January 29, 1336, *Benedictus Deus*, by which the Pope brought an end to the wide-ranging debate stirred up by his predecessor.

The Constitution defines a doctrine to remain in force forever concerning both the souls of the saints from the time before Christ's passion and those of the baptized since then, provided the latter either died without need of purification or have been purified.

> All these souls, immediately (*mox*) after death, and in the case of those in need of purification, after the purification mentioned above, since the ascension of our Lord and Savior Jesus Christ into heaven, already before they take up their bodies again and before the general judgment, have been, are, and will be with Christ in heaven, in the heavenly kingdom and paradise, joined to the company of the holy angels.[499]

---

[497] M. Dykmans contrasts the work of the Neapolitan King Robert of Anjou, whose work arose while he governed a realm, with the much longer and detailed text of Cardinal Fournier, who had behind him his monastic formation as a Cistercian, studies in Paris, service in judging heresy as bishop of dioceses infested with Cathars and Albigenses, and the composition of theological refutations of Joachim of Fiori, Meister Eckhart, and the Franciscan dissidents around Michael of Cesena. *Pour et contre Jean XXII en 1333*, 29*-30*. C. Trottmann speaks of Fournier-Benedict as *l'homme providentiel* who was singularly prepared to resolve the doctrinal crisis unleashed by John XXIII, *La vision béatifique*, 415–416 and 745.

[498] Published in Kaeppeli, *Le procès de Thomas Waleys, o. p. Études et documents*, 85–87. Analysis in Trottmann, *La vision béatifique*, 795–801. Nineteen theologians respond to the Pope's twelve questions. One answer and one question refer to a book, which in all likelihood was the Pope's work written before his election.

[499] This and the following paragraphs are cited from J. Neuner and J. Dupuis, eds., *The Christian Faith in the Doctrinal Documents of the Catholic Church*, nos. 2305-2307, pp. 1018–1019, which translates Denzinger and Schönmetzer, 1000–1002.

Continuing, the Constitution declares, with theological refinement selectively taken over from consensus views of leading scholastic doctors, what is the essential happiness of these redeemed souls in heaven:

> Since the passion and death of the Lord Jesus Christ, these souls have seen and see the divine essence with an intuitive vision and even face to face, without the mediation of any creature by way of object of vision; rather the divine essence immediately manifests itself to them, plainly, clearly, and openly, and in this vision they enjoy the divine essence. Moreover, by this vision and enjoyment the souls of those who have already died are truly blessed (*beatae*) and have eternal life and rest.

After adding that the enjoyment of this vision will also be given to the souls of those who will die in the future span of time before the general judgment, Pope Benedict clarifies the relation of the vision to our relation to God in this life, adding a word on its perennial duration.

> Such a vision and enjoyment of the divine essence do away with the acts of faith and hope in these souls, inasmuch as faith and hope are properly theological virtues. And after such intuitive and face-to-face vision and enjoyment has or will have begun for these souls, the same vision and enjoyment has continued and will continue without any interruption and without end until the last judgment and from then on forever.[500]

To complete its doctrine, the Constitution then speaks on hell and the future general judgment: "Moreover we define that according to the general disposition of God, the souls of those who die in actual mortal sin go down into hell immediately (*mox*) after death and there suffer the pain of hell." Nevertheless, on the day of judgment all will appear with their bodies "before the judgment seat of Christ" to give an account of

---

[500] While the Constitution affirms the continuity of the vision before and after the final judgment, it does not take over Pope Benedict's personal position on a notable intensification of heavenly happiness after resurrection and the judgment. In mentioning "theological virtues," the text uses scholastic terminology, but faith and hope are termed "acts" and the virtues are not called "infused habits." This gives the teaching a degree of affinity with patristic and early medieval theology, from eras before the widespread adoption, ca. 1200, of Aristotelian views of the soul, the soul's endowments, and its action which result in habits. C. Trottmann underscores that the Constitution does not adopt the Thomistic notion of the *lumen gloriae* in an attempt to give a complete account of the "how" of the beatific vision. *La vision béatifique*, 808.

their personal deeds, "so that each one may receive good or evil, according to what one has done in the body" (2 Cor. 5:10).[501]

Catholic Reception of Pope Benedict's Constitution of 1336

With the papal teaching of 1336, the Catholic Church came to dogmatically based clarity on death as the portal to the person's recompense from God, either the pain of loss and punishment in hell or the reward of heaven, whether immediately or after needed purgation. Heaven is the relationship in which God manifests himself "plainly, clearly, and openly" in personal immediacy to souls who have come into his presence, with Christ and the holy angels.

Pope Benedict XII's teaching ended the dispute begun by John XXII and laid down binding teaching. The doctrine of *Benedictus Deus* echoed in university theological teaching and undergirded late medieval popular preaching and instruction. The sense of the definitive character of death and the particular judgment became so deeply rooted in ordinary Catholic attitudes that the *Catechism of the Council of Trent* (1566) took pains to offer arguments of fittingness to support faith in the creedal article of the general judgment in the midst of the end-time events.[502]

For centuries the text of Pope Benedict's Constitution was found only in large tomes of ecclesiastical documents.[503] Even the *Catechism of the Council of Trent* does not cite or refer to *Benedictus Deus*. But the text became widely accessible to theology professors and their mainly seminarian students in the mid-nineteenth century, when the teachings of the conciliar and papal magisterium were coming to loom large in Catholic dogmatic theology.[504] To provide professors and students with

---

[501] C. Trottmann's final analysis of the Constitution *Benedictus Deus* admits that it gives an individualistic account of heavenly glory. However, the treatise composed by J. Fournier before his election to the papacy did draw on patristic texts to express a stronger sense of the final community of the saved. *La vision béatifique*, 811.

[502] *Cathechism of the Council of Trent for Parish Priests*, trans. John A. McHugh, O.P., and Charles J. Callan, O.P. (New York: Joseph F. Wagner, Inc., 1923), 82–83.

[503] Examples are the *Annales ecclesiastici* begun by Cardinal Baronio in the 1580s, which gives *Benedictus Deus* in vol. 25, 50–51, published in the 1650s. Charles du Plessis d'Argentré gave it in his *Collectio judiciorum de novis erroribus*, vol. 1/ I (Paris, 1728), 321b–322a. The text was also given in the *Nova et amplissima collectio* of Council texts begun by J. D. Mansi in 1759, in vol. 25 (1769), 985–987.

[504] See J. Wicks, "Manualistic Theology," in R. Latourelle and R. Fisichella, eds., *Dictionary of Fundamental Theology* (New York: Crossroad, 1994), 1102–1105.

the documents, Heinrich Denzinger of Würzburg compiled in the early 1850s his influential handbook of creeds, definitions, and declarations.[505] From Denzinger's first edition down through all the revised and expanded editions, the text of Benedict's Constitution has had its place, with its importance underscored in the systematic index.[506]

With the development of systematic manuals of Catholic dogmatic theology, the theses on the human person's final state of the vision of God or of eternal loss were regularly presented by citation of or reference to the Denzinger edition of Benedict XII's intervention of 1336, taking his text as *ex cathedra* teaching that the intermediate state before the end events does entail final beatitude or loss.[507] Benedict XII's Constitution remains a stable and authoritative point of reference in Catholic teaching,

---

[505] *Enchiridion Symbolorum, Definitionum et Declarationum de rebus fidei et moribus*, 1st ed. (Würzburg: Stahle Verlag, 1854). After Denzinger died in 1883, further editions of his manual of magisterial documentation came out from Herder of Freiburg, with Jesuit editors (Umberg, Bannwart, K. Rahner, Schönmetzer). Peter Hünnermann of Tübingen oversaw a 34th edition in 1991, which for the first time gave the introductions to each text in the vernacular and the texts both in the original (Greek, Latin) and in German translation on facing pages. From the beginning, the *Enchiridion* gave its texts in chronological order, with successive enumeration of the sections, but it offered as well a detailed systematic index organized according to the areas of dogmatic and moral theology. Complete translations came out in Spanish (Barcelona: Herder, 1955) and English as *The Sources of Catholic Dogma*, trans. Roy J. Deferrari (St. Louis-London: Herder, 1957). Joseph Schumacher studied the origin, development, and significance of Denzinger's collection for modern Catholic theology, giving, amid much else, the known press-runs, e.g. 14th ed. (1922) 10,530 copies; 28th ed. (1952) 6000 copies; 31st ed. (1957, with three reprints) ca. 30,000 copies. *Der "Denzinger". Geschichte und Bedeutung eines Buches in der Praxis der neueren Theologie* (Freiburg: Herder, 1974), relating the number of printed copies on pp. 233–235.

[506] *Enchiridion Symbolorum*, 33rd ed. (Barcelona, Freiburg, et al.: Herder, 1965), 296–297, nos. 1000-1002, with references in bold in the eschatology section of the systematic index, 923–924.

[507] Representative of the manuals is the 4 vol. work of Spanish Jesuit theologians, *Sacrae theologiae summa* (Madrid: Biblioteca de autores cristianos), in which vol. 4 (3rd ed., 1956) gives a 200-page exposition by José Sagües of eschatology in thesis form. Benedict XII's constitution is cited to show the defined status of key doctrines, such as the immediate passage upon death to final recompense (870–871), beatitude as the intuitive vision of the divine essence (908), and the eternity of heavenly beatitude (921) and of the pains of hell (954). The designation *ex cathedra* is from A. Schönmetzer's introduction to "Benedictus Deus," *Enchiridion Symbolorum*, 33rd ed., 296.

as is evident in the *Catechism of the Catholic Church*,[508] nos. 1022 (particular judgment, referencing *Benedictus Deus* in note 595), 1023 (heaven and the beatific vision[509]), and 1035 (on hell).[510]

The recent manual of Catholic eschatology by Candido Pozo receives *Benedictus Deus* of Pope Benedict XII as decisive on key points of binding Catholic teaching, which continued at the Councils of Florence, Trent, and Vatican II.[511]

The Constitution of Benedict XII in Recent Historical and Systematic Eschatology

The historians of doctrine and theologians of eschatology have recently treated Benedict XII's Constitution of 1336 in several different ways. This essay will close with a sampling of the variety of scholarly opinion.

The Protestant historian of the early church, Reinhard Staats, strikes a critical note at the end of his survey of "resurrection of the dead" in *Theologische Realenzyklopädie*. Staats observes that when Pope Benedict raised to the level of Catholic dogma the conscious vision of God by redeemed separated souls this signaled the superimposition of Augustine's psychological doctrine of the soul's immortality upon the earlier Christian doctrine of resurrection. Thereby Western thought has been left unable to grasp the early and enduring confessional tenet of the resurrection of the dead.[512]

---

[508] *Catechism of the Catholic Church*, 2nd ed. (Washington, D.C.: USCCB Publishing Services, 2000).

[509] Here the *Catechism of the Catholic Church* cites 15 lines of Benedict XII's Constitution.

[510] Benedict XII's Constitution is recalled again in the *Catechism of the Catholic Church* in note 617 via Denzinger and Schönmetzer, 1002). Vatican II did not cite *Benedictus Deus* on the beatific vision of God by the saints, but stated concisely in *Lumen gentium*, 49, the essential point of this doctrine by citing eight words from the "Decree for the Greeks" of the Council of Florence.

[511] C. Pozo, *Theology of the Beyond*, 241–242 (*Benedictus Deus* defines the survival of a conscious human element between death and the Parousia.), 267 (It affirms beatitude and loss in the intermediate state.), 346–348 (The Constitution is the principal magisterial document on the nature of eternal life.), 355, note 10 (It does not exclude the eternal mediation of the vision by Christ Risen.), 394 (It defines the immediate passage of the wicked to hell.), 432 (It clarifies *ex cathedra* that full recompense is given in the intermediate stage.), and 455 (It teaches purgatorial purification before the vision.).

[512] R. Staats, "Auferstehung, I. Auferstehung der Toten, 4. Alte Kirche," *Theologische Realenzyklopädie*, 4 (1979), 467–477.

The Italian historian Carlo Tibiletti also sees an unfortunate turn in the 1336 doctrinal constitution, since for him it put an end to the original Christian "intermediate state" of the departed who await the day of their resurrection and re-composition of their human totality for entry as whole persons into the ultimate happiness of final union with God. What took the upper hand, for Tibiletti, was the neoplatonic-gnostic view of the soul liberated for a fulfillment outside its bodily prison.[513]

Another contributor to *Theologische Realenzyklopädie*, the medievalist Robert E. Lerner, states in the entry on medieval eschatology that Pope John XXII's sermons on a delayed final recompense were in fact sharply opposed to convictions universally held at the time. Thus Pope Benedict's Constitution made explicit and confirmed as doctrine what was held in faith by the Christian people of his day.[514]

The Jesuit theologian of Frankfurt, Medard Kehl, presents the 1336 Constitution of Pope Benedict XII in the context of his account of the individual person within the event by which the Kingdom of God comes to complete fulfillment.[515] Convictions about the soul's immortality, going back to Cyprian and Augustine, came to be explained more precisely in the teaching of Thomas Aquinas on the soul as *forma corporis*. The soul after death is thus not an independent reality, for it is by nature oriented to present, express, and realize itself in bodily form. Before the resurrection the soul has a peculiar existence, as it is creatively supported by God's love until resurrection. In 1336 Pope Benedict confirmed the faith-conviction concerning the soul's beatitude or loss as it subsists non-corporeally. Kehl qualifies Benedict's teaching as a dogmatically decisive moment. But

---

[513] C. Tibiletti, "Le anime dopo la morte: stato intermedio o visione di Dio? (dalla Patristica al secolo XIV)," *Augustinianum* 28 (1988): 631–659. At the end of his essay, Tibiletti finds hope for restoration of balance in the 1979 Letter on Questions of Eschatology, from the Congregation for the Doctrine of the Faith, which makes no mention of *Benedictus Deus*, but instead emphasizes the dogma of final resurrection and the difference between the condition of individuals after death and in the phase that will open with the glorious final manifestation of Christ.

[514] R. E. Lerner, "Eschatologie, VI. Mittelalter," *Theologische Realenzyklopädie*, 10 (1982), 305–310, at 305–306. Lerner understands Benedict XII's teaching as confirming what had developed among the later Fathers and the major medieval theologians as they went beyond the early church's emphasis on Christ's Parousia in which he will mete out recompenses at the final judgment.

[515] M. Kehl, *Dein Reich komme. Eschatologie als Rechenschaft über unsere Hoffnung* (Kevelaer: Topos, 2003); reprint of *Eschatologie* (Würzburg: Echter, 1986), Part III/2, "Der Einzelne im Vollendungsgeschehen des Reiches Gottes," 252–298.

for M. Kehl the Constitution of 1336 leaves one baffled over the final element of its definition, that is, "and that nevertheless (*et quod nihilominus*)" all will appear with their bodies before Christ for an accounting of their bodily lives and to be recompensed for their conduct (2 Cor. 5:10). The Pope affirms the truth of resurrection, but simply tacks it on, without any further integrating explanation, to his definition of beatitude or loss for souls before the final events.[516]

Movement beyond the difficulty signaled by M. Kehl has, in recent Catholic theology, advanced by developing christological theses. Karl Rahner pointed out the direction of enrichment in the final pages of his 1953 essay, "The Eternal Significance of the Humanity of Jesus for Our Relationship with God."[517] The created human nature of Christ, now in glory, remains

> . . . the indispensable and permanent gateway through which everything must pass if it is to find the perfection of its eternal validity before God. . . . One always sees the Father only through Jesus. Just as *im*mediately as this, for the directness of the vision of God is not a denial of the mediatorship of Christ as man. . . . [I]t remains eternally true to say that no one knows the Father except the Son and those to whom he wishes to reveal it; he who sees him, sees the Father. . . . [T]he Word—by the fact that he is man and in so far as he is this— is the necessary and permanent mediator of salvation, not merely at some time in the past but now and for all eternity.[518]

---

[516] Kehl, *Dein Reich komme*, 270–272, on the Constitution and its *theologische Ratlosigkeit* concerning the resurrection. Wolfart Pannenberg speaks of Benedict's teaching on the immediacy of the vision as making more severe the problem of holding together convictions (1) on life fulfilled after death in fellowship with Christ and (2) the consummation of humanity and the cosmos at the end of history. *Systematic Theology*, 3 (Grand Rapids: Eerdmans & Edinburgh: T & T Clark, 1998), 546 and 577. Also, Josef Finkenzeller of the Munich Catholic Faculty, offers a *placet iuxta modum* on the Constitution of 1336. While it expressed deeply held faith-convictions rooted in early Christian certainties about the martyrs, it still neglected concerns of the Orthodox and tended to overshadow, rather than clarify, essential biblical and creedal convictions about the end-events of humanity and creation. "Eschatologie," in Wolfgang Beinert, ed., *Glaubenszugänge, Lehrbuch der Katholischen Dogmatik*, 3 vols. (Paderborn: Schöningh, 1995), 3:527–671, at 585–586.

[517] *Theological Investigations* (Baltimore: Helicon, 1967), 3:35–46, esp. 43–46. The article appeared originally in the spirituality quarterly *Geist und Leben* 26 (1953): 279–288.

[518] Rahner, "The Eternal Significance of the Humanity of Jesus," 43–45.

Rahner's proposal then stimulated Juan Alfaro of the Gregorian to work out in 1958 the Johannine basis of Christ's ongoing mediation of knowledge of God and to extend this consideration, in the light of St. Thomas's account of the constitution of the Word Incarnate, to the activity of the risen and glorified Christ. United with Christ glorified and knowing his glory, the redeemed come to see the Triune God, through, with, and in Christ, in immediate and beatifying vision.[519]

The French Jesuit Gustave Martelet took up Rahner's point in his 1975 account of eschatology. He asserts that while death ends the relation we now have to the world, at the same time it opens each person to encountering the glory and sovereign Lordship of Christ Risen. In death one does not pass into nothingness but to the Lord who died and rose to be the Lord of both the dead that the living (Rom. 14:7-9). The passage involves existential stages of purification and judgment, but in the interval before Christ's parousia for all humanity and all creation, his redeemed members come to live in the shadow of his glory.[520] A firm dogmatic truth teaches that this involves an immediate vision of God which gives complete beatitude, but the immediacy in no way excludes the glorified humanity of Christ in his mediation of this vision, this is, his own vision, in which he gives his saints to share. Here, Matthew 11:27 remains eternally valid.[521]

In the interim before his parousia, the Risen Christ has not yet transformed the world or our bodies. The cosmos has still to be integrated into the glory of Christ, which will take place, as the Creed affirms, with his manifestation as Lord to all humans. Amid the apocalyptic images of the end-events, Martelet focuses sharply on Who is coming rather than on what will happen to creation. The coming Last

---

[519] J. Alfaro, "Cristo Glorioso, Revelador del Padre," *Gregorianum* 39 (1958): 222–270. Alfaro makes it explicit on 270, in note 75, that Rahner's brief suggestions motivated him to work out his more detailed theoretical account.

[520] G. Martelet, *L'Au-delà retrouvée. Christologie des fins dernières* (Paris: Desclée, 1975), 133–150.

[521] Martelet, *L'Au-delà retrouvée*, 159–162, referencing Rahner's 1953 article in its French translation of 1964. In treating the beatific vision, Martelet recalls the images of the heavenly banquet and the wedding feast, which denote fulfilled human hungers and yearnings, communal sharing with others, and Christ's loving union with his bride and body. But John 17:3 tells of what is essential: "And this is eternal life, that they may know you, the only true God, and Jesus Christ whom you have sent." Dermot Lane also turns to the mediating role of Christ in eschatology as a needed way to avoid distortions flowing from the definition by Benedict XII on the beatific vision. *Keeping Hope Alive. Stirrings in Christian Theology* (Eugene, Ore.: Wipf and Stock, 2005), 139–140.

Adam (1 Cor 15:45), in a way beyond our imagining, will banish corruption and death and lead creation, including our bodies, to share in the freedom of the redeemed (Rom. 8:21). This freedom, however, they now have in the mode of glorious communion with God in Christ Risen and in his Spirit. At the end, the whole universe will pass under Christ's liberating and life-giving dominion. Still, the central reality of the final reign and kingdom will be for us not the resurrection of the body, but our filial communion with God in face-to-face vision.[522]

Benedictus Deus received a positive reading and fresh interpretation from Joseph Ratzinger in his last work as chair-holder in dogmatic theology at Regensburg. The constitution signaled the presence of a new stage of teaching beyond earlier Christian conceptions featuring bodily resurrection. In the fourteenth century, John XXII fell back into an "archaizing conception" when he proposed that souls of the redeemed are "under the altar" of Christ's humanity until our Lord hands over the kingdom to the Father (1 Cor. 15:24). Although texts can be cited for this conception, including some from Bernard of Clairvaux, it has not yet sufficiently "christologized" the realm beyond death.

For Ratzinger, Pope Benedict XII's dogmatic teaching of 1336 draws upon a deeper Christological truth and connects it with the relation of the justified person with Christ. By his ascension and glorification Christ brought it about "that now . . . there is no longer a closed heaven. Christ is in heaven: that is, God has opened himself to man, and man, as he passes through the gate of death as one justified, as someone who belongs to Christ and has been redeemed by him, enters into the openness of God."[523]

Today christological reflection informs an important part of Catholic theology on the central point of eschatology made certain by Pope Benedict XII. Along this line, beginning from Rahner and developed by Alfaro, Martelet, and Ratzinger, C. Pozo makes the point as he re-states christologically an idea of von Balthasar inspired by the famous line of Augustine, "Ipse [Deus] post istam vitam sit locus noster."[524]

---

[522] Martelet, *L'Au-delà retrouvée*, 173–175.

[523] J. Ratzinger, *Eschatology. Death and Eternal Life* (Washington, D.C.: Catholic University of America Press, 1988), 136–138, citing p. 138; originally published, Regensburg: Pustet, 1977. Note that the author errs on p. 137 in speaking of John XXII's successor as a Franciscan academic theologian. Benedict XII was a Cistercian who had served as bishop in areas infested with Albigensian and Catharist heresies.

[524] *Expositions of the Psalms*, Ps. 30, Sermon 3, no. 8 ("May he . . . be himself our place after this life.").

Christ is the final realty of the creature. As attained, He is heaven; as lost, hell; as examining, judge; as purifying, purgatory. Christ is that "where" the finite dies and by whom it rises for Him, in Him. The "states" which constitute the world beyond are defined by diverse relations to Christ. . . Christ must be the center of all reflection on eschatology.[525]

---

[525] C. Pozo, *Theology of the Beyond*, 60.

Background papers

Here are two examples of the background papers
that are listed in Appendix II. The papers were prepared
for review and discussion by the U.S. Catholic-Lutheran Dialogue
in the development of the report of Round XI.

Communal and Sacramental Dimensions of Eschatology

by Susan K. Wood

Any consideration of Christian eschatology must take into account its communal dimension, for eschatology is not just about one's particular judgment and an individual's eternal fate as saved or damned. Nor is it solely about an individual resurrection. Eschatology also concerns the form or general character of last things. This is where the communal dimension of eschatology finds its place. The form of the eschaton is none other than the communion of the whole Mystical Body of Jesus Christ in which the faithful achieve full union with Christ in whom God reconciles all things to himself (Col. 1:19-20).[526] The form of salvation is communion—communion with Christ and, in Christ, with all those also in union with Christ. Thus human destiny is a communal destiny, not an individualistic one.

This communal destiny repairs an original unity that has been fragmented by sin. Henri de Lubac observes "the unity of the Mystical Body of Christ, a supernatural unity, supposes a previous natural unity, the unity of the human race."[527] He cites a number of early writers such as Origen, Gregory Nazianzen, Gregory of Nyssa, Cyril of Alexandria, Maximus, Hilary, and others who envisioned redemption as affecting the whole of the human race, as re-uniting it and knitting it together as one. The unity of the mystical body in Christ is the redeemed counterpart of the unity of the human race in Adam. This unity seems evident, for if God

---

[526] *Lumen gentium [Dogmatic Constitution on the Church]*, 21 November 1964, 50; cited hereinafter as *Lumen gentium* with section numbers.

[527] Henri de Lubac, *Catholicism*, trans. Lancelot C. Sheppard (New York: A Mentor-Omega Book, The New American Library, 1964), 17. This is the English translation of *Catholicisme,* 4th ed, 1947.

made humanity in his divine image, then that humanity is one since all share the same image.[528] Monotheism implies that we are all children of the one Father and therefore related to one another.[529] Maximus the Confessor considered original sin as a separation, a breaking up, an individualization of this unity.[530] Certainly Genesis depicts the fruits of the original sin as fraternal enmity. Christ unites human nature to himself in the Incarnation and assumes all of human nature into his redemptive act.

Although such ideas are supported both by a Platonic notion of original unity shattered into individuation by a fall and by the Stoic conception of universal being, de Lubac observes that the starting point for these reflections are less philosophical than biblical. True, the Fathers made use of the philosophies of their time, but the reflection on original unity really developed out of a reflection on redeemed unity. Crucial for this understanding were such biblical texts as John 11:51-52 where Caiphas prophesies "Jesus was about to die for the nation, and not for the nation only, but to gather into one the dispersed children of God." The great priestly prayer of Christ that all may be one, the Johannine image of the vine and the branches, and the Pauline metaphor of the body all point to an unity achieved in Christ.

While one could develop a Christian account of the social destiny of humankind in any number of ways, including the testimony of the church Fathers and an exegesis of biblical texts, I will support this thesis here by an analysis of the third article of the Apostles' Creed by way of sacramental theology and an examination of Chapters II and VII of *Lumen gentium*.

The Apostles' Creed and *Communio Sanctorum*

The origins and development of the Apostles' Creed remain somewhat obscure, and it has evolved to its current form over time.[531] Since an early form was most probably used as a summary of Christian doctrine for baptismal candidates in Rome, it is also known as *The Roman Symbol*. Initially, the third article was very brief. The phrase

---

[528] de Lubac, *Catholicism*, 18.

[529] de Lubac, *Catholicism*, 19.

[530] de Lubac, *Catholicism*, 20.

[531] For a summary of the legend of the creed as written by the Apostles, see Henri de Lubac, *The Christian Faith* (San Francisco: Ignatius Press, 1986), chapter 1. This is an English translation of *La Foi chrétienne: Essai sur la structure du Symbole des Apôtres* (Aubier-Montaigne, 1969).

communio sanctorum, although of ancient origin, represents a later addition to the creed in the fourth century well after the reference to the church had been added.

The third article of the Apostles' Creed is about eschatology:

> I believe in the Holy Spirit,
> the holy catholic church,
> the communion of saints,
> the forgiveness of sins,
> the resurrection of the body,
> and the life everlasting.

The references to the resurrection of the body and life everlasting are clearly eschatological, but the references to the communion of saints and forgiveness of sin are also arguably eschatological, although they are sacramental as well. The reference to the forgiveness of sin may be an allusion to baptism, to be compared with the phrase "one baptism for the forgiveness of sins" in the Nicene Creed. The Latin for "communion of saints," *communio sanctorum,* also can refer to the eucharist or possibly to both baptism and the eucharist when it is interpreted as communion in holy things, i.e., sacraments. The continuity between the sacramental and the eschatological meanings of this article and the implications of this continuity for a theology of the church and for eschatology is precisely what I will develop in this paper.

Numerous authors have pointed out the ambiguity of the phrase *communio sanctorum,* translated in the creed as "communion of saints."[532] The Latin phrase can be either neuter plural, meaning communion in holy things, or masculine plural, meaning communion of holy people or saints. In the Apostles' Creed, the ambiguity serves the text, for it means both, and the sacramental meaning is causative of the personal meaning. Participation in Jesus Christ creates the unity of the church. Liturgical participation in the sacramental body of Christ leads to the community of persons in Christ.[533] This is not an extrinsic

---

[532] Bilaterale Arbeitsguppe der Deutschen Bischofskonferenz und der Kirchenleitung der Vereinigten Evangelisch-Lutherischen Kirche Deutschlands, *Communio Sanctorum: Die Kirche als Gemeinschafaft der Heiligen* (Frankfurt am Main: Verlag Otto Lembeck, 2000), 15; Joseph Ratzinger, *Introduction to Christianity* (New York: Herder and Herder, 1970) 257–258; Berard L. Marthaler, *The Creed* (Mystic, Conn.: Twenty-Third Publications, 1987), 347.

[533] See Henri de Lubac, "Sanctorum Communio," *Theological Fragments,* trans. Rebecca Howell Balinski (San Francisco: Ignatius Press, 1989), 19. This is an English translation of *Théologies d'occasion* (Desclée de Brouwer, 1984).

participation in sacred objects. Nor is it the result of an impersonal collectivity. The sacramental participation in Christ creates with all others in union with him an interrelationship so close and interdependent that it is best described as the communion of a "body."

Henri de Lubac's study of the phrase *communio sanctorum* uncovers two interpretations of the personal meaning of the term. According to the first, it designates "the Church in heaven, the triumphant Church within which all are permanently holy and whose only hierarchy is that of holiness."[534] According to this interpretation, the phrase is in contrast to the preceding item in the creed, "Holy Catholic Church," which refers to the "living Church on earth." However, de Lubac hastens to add that the most common view interprets "communion of saints" to refer to the network of spiritual relations woven between the living members of the church and those in heaven (as well as those suffering, if included) forming the one church.[535] He cites St. Augustine's use of this concept of communion: "We are united with angels and all blessed immortals, who help us to join them in praising God."[536]

Sacramentum tantum/res et sacramentum/res tantum

The phrase *communio sanctorum* draws together the eucharist and the communion of holy ones, but in itself it does not explicitly develop the eschatological meaning of the eucharist. For this, it is helpful to refer to the scholastic analysis of the sacraments according to which (1) the sign of the sacrament is the *sacramentum tantum*, (2) the reality of the sacrament is the *res et sacramentum*, and (3) that which is signified by the sacrament is the *res tantum* or the *res sacramenti*. In the case of the eucharist, the bread and wine is the *sacramentum tantum,* the sacramental real presence of Christ is the *res et sacramentum,* and the unity of the church is the *res tantum.* This unity, the ultimate purpose of the sacrament, is none other than the communion of saints in the mystical body.[537]

The eschatological meaning of the *res tantum* is reinforced by the parallelism between the scholastic sacramental schema *sacramentum tantum/res et sacramentum/res tantum* and the threefold meaning of Scripture interpreted through spiritual exegesis: the literal meaning, the

---

[534] de Lubac, *Theological Fragments*, 20.

[535] de Lubac, *Theological Fragments*, 20.

[536] de Lubac, *Theological Fragments*, citing *De Civitate Dei*, 1. 10, c. 25 (Corpus Christianorum, Series Latina, 47, 300).

[537] de Lubac, *Theological Fragments*, 24.

allegorical meaning, and the anagogical meaning. The literal meaning corresponds to the sacramental sign, the *sacramentum tantum*. The allegorical meaning, referring to the Christological or ecclesial meaning of the text, corresponds to the *res et sacramentum*. This is the actualization of the New Covenant that makes both Christ and the Church present under sacramental sign. The anagogical or eschatological meaning of the text corresponds to the *res tantum*, the ecclesial unity effected by the eucharist. Within this correspondence, the preceding term functions as the figure of the reality represented by the succeeding term.[538] Only the last term—the anagogical sense or the *res tantum*—is reality, but not figure.[539]

Thus the bread and wine are the figure of the real presence of Christ. But the sacramental presence of Christ is itself a figure of the church as the *totus Christus*. Similarly, in spiritual exegesis the Old Testament is a figure of the New Testament; the exodus is a figure of Christ's passion. Both Christ and the Eucharist are figures of the church viewed as the "whole Christ," with the members of the church in union with their head, Christ. Even though spiritual exegesis is not a contemporary method of biblical interpretation, it provides a framework of interpretation that is still operative in the liturgy. There it functions to express the relationship between sign and reality, between promise and fulfillment, as well as the temporal relationships of memorial, present reality, and future fulfillment. This is illustrated by the following table:

Literal sense (historical reality)	*sacramentum tantum* (bread and wine)
Allegorical sense (Christological and ecclesial meaning)	*res et sacramentum* (sacramental presence of Christ and the church)
Anagogical sense (future fulfillment)	*res tantum* (eschatological completion of the *totus Christus*, the reconciled unity of all in Christ)

The unity present in the communion of saints is also what Augustine called the *totus Christus*, the fullness of Christ in the union of the faithful

---

[538] Thomas Aquinas allows for an "allegorical" interpretation of Christ vis-a-vis his members wherein Christ the head of the body functions as a figure or sign of a later reality, the mystical body, which is the Church. See Quodibet 7. q. 6. a. 2. ad 5.

[539] See Susan K. Wood, *Spiritual Exegesis and the Church in the Theology of Henri de Lubac* (Grand Rapids, Mich.: Eerdmans, 1998), 61–62.

constituting the body of Christ with their head, Christ, although Augustine himself did not use the term *communio sanctorum* with respect to the *totus Christus*. The *totus Christus* represents the church in its eschatological dimension since the unity of the body will only be complete in the eschaton. This unity is achieved eucharistically, which leads de Lubac to say "the eucharist makes the church."[540] This phrase, however, says nothing other than "Christ makes the church," for the church is really a union in Christ even though in the second millennium interpretation of the church as a visible institutional society gained precedence over a sacramental one.[541] The unity of the body received in communion is a sign of the union of the ecclesial body. The emphasis is never on an individual's union with Christ in communion, but the union effected among individuals in Christ.[542]

This theology is developed and illustrated in Augustine's mystagogical sermons. For instance, he exhorts: "Take, then, and eat the body of Christ, for in the body of Christ you are already made the members of Christ."[543] In this same sermon: "Because you have life through Him, you will be one body with Him, for this sacrament extends the body of Christ, and by it you are made inseparable from Him."

---

[540] *Catechism of the Catholic Church,* §1396; Henri de Lubac, *Corpus Mysticum: The Eucharist and the Church in the Middle Ages,* trans. Gemma Simmonds, C.J., with Richard Price and Christopher Stephens (London: SCM Press, 2006), 88; see Paul McPartlan, *The Eucharist Makes the Church: Henri de Lubac and John Zizioulas in Dialogue* (Edinburg: T&T Clark, 1993); *Sacrament of Salvation: An Introduction to Eucharistic Ecclesiology* (Edinburg: T&T Clark, 1995); "Eucharistic Ecclesiology," *One in Christ* (22, no. 4, 1985): 314–331; J. M. R. Tillard, *Flesh of the Church, Flesh of Christ: At the Source of the Ecclesiology of Communion,* trans. Madeleine Beaumont (Collegeville, Minn.: Liturgical Press, 2001). For an Orthodox perspective, see John Zizioulas, *Eucharist, Bishop, Church: The Unity of the Church in the Divine Eucharist and the Bishop during the First Three Centuries,* trans. Elizabeth Theokritoff (Brookline, Mass.: Holy Cross Orthodox Press, 2001).

[541] See Robert Bellarmine (1542–1621), *De controversiis,* vol. 2, book 3, *De ecclesia militante;* Eric Plumer, *"The Development of Ecclesiology: Early church to the Reformation"* in *The Gift of the Church,* Peter Phan, ed. (Collegeville: Liturgical Press, 2000), 23–44; Michael J. Himes, "The Development of Ecclesiology: Modernity to the Twentieth Century," in Phan, *The Gift of the Church,* 45–67.

[542] See Henri de Lubac, *Corpus Mysticum: L'Eucharistie et l'Eglise au moyen age* (Paris: Aubier, 1948), 24, 26.

[543] Sermon 3, translation from *Selected Easter Sermons of Saint Augustine* by Philip T. Weller (St. Louis: B. Herder Book Co., 1959), 113.

At one level it would seem that Augustine is simply comparing the unity of the bread with the unity of the ecclesial body and what we have is simply a literary device, a simile, or a metaphor. The unity of the body received at the altar, however, is a sign and measure of the unity of the ecclesial body. The eucharistic sacrament is a sacrament of unity. This means that it signs, signifies, and creates the unity of the church, which is the unity of the communion of saints. Thus the bread is a sacrament of the church not just because it belongs to the church, but because it signifies the church. The sacramental realism of the real presence of Christ in the Eucharist leads to the sacramental realism of the ecclesial Christ so that Augustine can say, "there you are on the altar, there you are in the chalice."[544] Affirmation of the Christological reality leads to the affirmation of the ecclesial reality. The presence of the latter is as real as the presence of the first. When we commune with the sacramental Body of Christ, we commune with the resurrected Christ and the Church, which is also the body of Christ.

"Communion" in the Eucharist is not only incorporation in Christ, but incorporation into Christ's ecclesial body. The unity of the eucharistic body with the ecclesial body is never an extrinsic unity because the ecclesial body is not another body besides the body of Christ, but the *totus Christus*, the fullness of Christ, the head joined to the members. The *totus Christus*, the whole Christ, represents the end of the mystery and therefore represents the Church in its eschatological dimension. Since the eucharistic action is memorial, presence, and anticipation, corresponding to the literal, the allegorical, and anagogical senses of Scripture, the Eucharist signs and makes sacramentally real this fullness of Christ which will be definitively achieved only eschatologically. We anticipate a fullness and wholeness in the Eucharist, even while our experience of the body is presently one of brokenness and alienation through sin.

Importantly, this unity of the *totus Christus* is not a unity of a collectivity. To identify the kind of unity that de Lubac intends, it is important to situate this relationship within the broader framework of the problem that he addresses in the relationship between nature and grace. In this he strives to avoid both immanentism and extrinsicism.[545] The unity of a collectivity would be an example of an extrinsic relationship among individuals. Extrinsicism also would characterize the

<hr>

[544] Sermon 6 (Denzinger), translation in Weller, 109.

[545] See Henri de Lubac, *The Mystery of the Supernatural*, trans. Rosemary Sheed (New York: Herder and Herder, 1967), chapters 2 and 3; English translation of *Le mystère du surnaturel* (Paris: Montaigne, 1965).

relationship of the communion of saints if detached from the eucharistic meaning of *communio sanctorum.* Finally, it would view the Eucharist as merely a sacred object or as a sign extrinsic to its referent or *res.*

The contrary of extrinsicism—namely, the problem of immanentism—can take one of two forms. The first is a kind of horizontalism wherein the liturgical celebration of a community becomes a merely human rite cementing a community organization.[546] Parodoxically, a church in an extrinsic relationship to the Eucharist may fall victim to a form of ecclesial immanentism when reduced to only a sociological entity. It becomes closed in on itself, limited to its socio-temporal aspect. Although the second form of immanentism is not mentioned by de Lubac, I believe a unity that collapses the church into Christ without acknowledging the distinction would be an immanentism at the other extreme. The first kind would be analogous to the Christological heresies that denied the divinity of Christ. The ecclesial analogy would be a view of the church as an exclusively human institution like any other institution. The second form of immanentism is analogous to a kind of docetism, which denies the humanity of Christ. The ecclesial analogy is the church insufficiently differentiated from Christ and considered as a prolongation of the Incarnation.

The ecclesial solution is analogous to the Christological solution and is expressed in *Lumen gentium*, which speaks of the church as a complex reality comprising a human and a divine element "likened to the mystery of the incarnate Word," the social structure of the church serving "the Spirit of Christ who vivifies the church towards the growth of the body (see Eph. 4:16)."[547]

The Eucharist does not exist for itself. Nor does it exist primarily in order to make Christ present so that we may worship him in the sacramental species. It exists to transform us into the body of Christ, so that by our being united in Christ we become one body. In the language of scholastic analysis, the *res et sacramentum* does not exist for itself, but for the *res tantum.* The Eucharist is memorial, presence, and anticipation. It is the memorial of Christ's paschal mystery, the sacramental real presence of Christ, and the anticipation of final unity in Christ by the power of the Spirit. Thus the Eucharist has an eschatological *telos*, an eschatological purpose and direction inseparable from the eschatological meaning of the church and the eschatological destiny of all believers.

---

[546] de Lubac discusses the immanentism, but not the extrisicism of this relationship in "Sanctorum Communio," 28–29.

[547] *Lumen gentium*, 8.

Sacramental realism leads to ecclesiological realism, and this in turn points to eschatology. The "aesthetic form," if you will, of this sacramental, ecclesial, and individual destiny is the Incarnation, achieved in its fullness only eschatologically.[548]

The effort to describe accurately the relationship between the human and divine natures in Christ gives us the tools we need to make the necessary sacramental and ecclesial distinctions. The eschatological fullness is not only the union, although not commingling, of the societal nature of the church and its divine nature, but also the union, although not commingling, of the body of the faithful with their head, Christ. This is why eschatology can never be considered individualistically or apart from the sacraments and the church. The sacramental link to eschatology testifies that the community formed around the unity of the eucharistic table extends beyond the frontiers of death.[549] Lest the Christological emphasis of this connection to the body of Christ be considered an instance of Christomonism, we need only recall that the connection occurs in the third article of the creed. The constitution of the church as the body of Christ and the effects of the sacraments specify the work of the Spirit.

Although de Lubac developed specifically the eschatological meaning of the Eucharist, the same relationship holds true for baptism. The *sacramentum tantum* is the water bath, the *res et sacramentum* is the baptismal character that establishes an ecclesial relationship deputing an individual for the public worship of the church as a member of the baptismal priesthood of the faithful sharing in Christ's priesthood, and the *res tantum* is the sharing in the life of Christ through sanctifying grace. Thus, union with Christ in grace is the *res* of the sacrament. This is negatively expressed in the creed in the phrase "forgiveness of sins." Baptism simultaneously makes one a member of the church and establishes union with Christ through identification with his death and resurrection (Rom. 6:3-4).

Baptism and Eucharist are really two modalities of the same mystery, that of Christ's death and resurrection and our participation in that

---

[548] See Hans Urs von Balthasar, who writes in *Glory of the Lord: A Theological Aesthetics,* vol. I: "In fact, God's Incarnation perfects the whole ontology and aesthetics of created Being." Joseph Fessio and John Riches, eds.; trans. by Erasmo Leiva-Merikakis (San Francisco: Ignatius Press, 1983), 29.

[549] See Joseph Ratzinger's discussion of this in his exposition of the Apostles' Creed, *Introduction to Christianity,* trans. J. R. Foster (San Francisco: Ignatius Press, 1990), 255–260; English translation of *Einführung in das Chistentum* (Munich: K sel-Verlag GmbH & Co., 1969).

mystery through union with Christ. The eschatological meaning of baptism, therefore, is the same as the eschatological meaning of the Eucharist. What is begun both individually and ecclesially in baptism—namely, the incorporation (in the strong sense) of the church as the body of Christ—finds its fulfillment eschatologically. Eschatology is not a break from the previous order, but its completion. The community initiated in baptism is the form of salvation in the end time. Finally, baptism is related to eschatological hope because having died with Christ, we hope to rise with him (Rom. 6:2-11). Baptism orients us to a future that does not end in death even while it initiates us into a cruciform pattern of life.

Communal Eschatology and the Doctrine of Justification

These sacramental relationships are important for ecumenical dialogues between Roman Catholics and traditions issuing from the Reformation, for this is where sacramental theology, ecclesiology, and eschatology encounter the doctrine of justification. At the time of the Reformation the question regarding the effect of grace was posed in terms of the relationship between grace and sin rather than in terms of the relationship between nature and grace. One was *simul justus et peccator* rather than *simul justus et humanus.* It also was posed in individualistic terms rather than in terms of the community of grace. Finally, the doctrine of justification was largely divorced from its sacramental roots, not only from baptism, the sacrament of justification, but also from the Eucharist that contains within it the eschatolological meaning of justification as final union with Christ within the *totus Christus.*[550]

Neither the joint statement nor the Lutheran or Catholic clarifications situate this union with Christ within a communal context even though the emphasis on renewal through union with Christ is not inconsistent with the notion of the body of Christ, the sacramental theology, and the communal eschatology developed in this essay. The idea of justification establishing a community of salvation through union with Christ is simply absent from the systematic section of the "Joint Declaration." The biblical section states, however, that justification "occurs in the reception of the Holy Spirit in baptism and incorporation into the one body (Rom. 8:1f, 9f; 1 Cor. 12:12)."[551]

---

[550] See Susan K. Wood, *One Baptism: Ecumenical Dimensions of the Doctrine of Baptism* (Collegeville, Minn.: Liturgical Press, 2009), especially chapters 1 and 6.

[551] "Joint Declaration on the Doctrine of Justification" (1999), ¶11.

With this in mind, it is good to revisit the text of *The One Mediator, the Saints, and Mary*, which says:

> Lutherans hold . . . that faith does not mean individualism, but rather a being born anew into the communion of believers, the body of Christ which is the church. As members of the church, believers participate by grace in the divine trinitarian life—in a "mystical union" (*unio mystica*) that anticipates the full future glory of Christ "beheld with an unveiled face" (2 Cor. 3:18; cf 5:1-10 and Rom. 8:20-30 in the context of 8:18-39). [552]

Future work on justification needs to develop its communal dimensions and to strengthen the connection among baptism, eucharist, justification, and eschatology within a view of the church as the *totus Christus*. Such a development envisions final destiny as having a communal form. Perhaps what has been most objectionable in terms of too close of an association of the church with Christ will become less so if viewed from an eschatological perspective. Then the church in the present time will be seen as anticipated eschatology, that is, as embodying the "already but not yet completed" form of the end time.

Lumen gentium

The themes of the salvation of the whole human race, salvation as a social reality, the communion of saints, and Christian unity conceived as a body with Christ as its head also figure prominently in Chapters II and VII of *Lumen gentium*. The first describes the origins and life of the people of God and the second, its destiny. For this reason it is helpful to consider them in relationship to one another as bookends, although they are neither the first nor the final chapters in the document.

The second sentence in Chapter II makes the remarkable claim that God has willed "to make women and men holy and to save them, not as individuals without any bond between them, but rather to make them into a people who might acknowledge him and serve him in holiness."[553] According to Chapter II, this people is comprised of those elected by Christ's covenant. This new people of God, including both Jews and Gentiles, is reborn of water and the Spirit, a reference to baptism (John 3:5-6). Its destiny is the kingdom of God that will be brought to

---

[552] Lutherans and Catholics in Dialogue VIII, *The One Mediator, the Saints, and Mary*, H. George Anderson, J. Francis Stafford, and Joseph A. Burgess, eds. (Minneapolis: Augsburg, 1992), ¶50.

[553] *Lumen gentium*, 9.

perfection at the end of time. All of creation will participate in this final freedom of the glory of the sons and daughters of God (Rom. 8:21). This messianic people, even though it does not include everyone, is "a most certain seed of unity, hope and salvation for the whole human race."[554] The people, compared to a "seed" because of its limited scope, is, nevertheless, "the instrument for the salvation of all." This people of God is also called the church of Christ, identified as "the visible sacrament of this saving unity."[555] Finally, this people is a "kingdom of priests" that offers spiritual sacrifices, including the sacrifice of a holy life, the offering of the Eucharist, prayer, and the reception of the sacraments.[556]

This text indicates that salvation for individuals occurs within a community of salvation. The unity of community is a "saving unity."[557] Covenant and election are the identifiers of the community. Salvation is not limited to the people of the covenant, but extends potentially to the whole human race. The church, then, as a visible sacrament of this saving unity, has a role in the saving unity that potentially can encompass all. Evidently this role is precisely to be a sacrament, meaning that the church both signifies and effects that unity. The unity of the church is a sign of the eschatological unity that includes the whole cosmos. How it effects this unity, however, is not exactly specified. The sacramental references to baptism and the Eucharist would seem to imply that the church—and thus the people of God—itself increases such unity through these sacraments of initiation and the evangelizing work of the church. How the whole human race becomes one through the church is not explained. Nevertheless, women and men are saved, not as individuals, but as members of a people.

Chapter VII's central theme is eschatology. Here again, the whole human race and the entire universe are perfectly established in Christ at the end time. The affirmation of the church as "the universal sacrament of salvation" is repeated.

This chapter originally had a more individualistic emphasis evident in its initial title, "The Eschatological Nature of Our Calling and Our Union with the Heavenly Church." The council Fathers, however,

---

[554] *Lumen gentium*, 9.

[555] *Lumen gentium*, 9. This echoes a statement in *Lumen gentium*, 1, that declares "the church, in Christ, is a sacrament—a sign and instrument, that is, of communion with God and of the unity of the entire human race. . . ." This also has eucharistic overtones since the Eucharist is the sacrament of unity.

[556] *Lumen gentium*, 10.

[557] *Lumen gentium*, 9.

immediately criticized this individualistic approach. As a result, the title was changed to reflect a more communal and ecclesiological emphasis evident in the present title, "The Eschatological Character of the Pilgrim Church and its Union with the Heavenly Church."

Lumen gentium does not use the phrase "communion of saints," although it does use such phrases as "communion of the whole mystical body of Jesus Christ," "our communion with the saints," and "the living communion which exists between us and our sisters and brothers who are in the glory of heaven or who are yet being purified after their death."[558] It speaks of the disciples who are pilgrims on earth, those who have died and are being purified, and others who are in glory," emphasizing the union of the wayfarers with the brothers and sisters who sleep in the peace of Christ.[559] It notes that "this union is reinforced by an exchange of spiritual goods."[560] Those in heaven intercede to the Father for those on earth and "proffer the merits which they acquired on earth through the one mediator between God and human, Christ Jesus."[561] The document recommends honoring the memory of the dead and asking them for the help of their intercession. Those women and men who have faithfully followed Christ show us the way to union with Christ through their example, and in them we vividly see the image of Christ. Our communion with the saints brings us closer to Christ. In fact, "every authentic witness of love offered by us to those who are in heaven tends towards and terminates in Christ, 'the crown of all the saints,' and through him in God. . . ."[562] Our union with the heavenly church is best realized in the sacred liturgy.

Chapter VII concludes with the admonition to correct any abuses, excesses, or defects that may have crept in, reminding us that an "authentic cult of the saints does not consist so much in a multiplicity of external acts, but rather in a more intense practice of our love."[563] It affirms that "our relationship with the saints in heaven, provided that it is understood in the full light of faith, in no way diminishes the worship of adoration given to God the Father, through Christ in the Spirit; on the contrary, it greatly enriches it."[564]

---

[558] *Lumen gentium*, 50–51.

[559] *Lumen gentium*, 49.

[560] *Lumen gentium*, 49.

[561] *Lumen gentium*, 49.

[562] *Lumen gentium*, 50.

[563] *Lumen gentium*, 51.

[564] *Lumen gentium*, 51.

These texts associate the sacraments of baptism and eucharist with eschatology as does the third article of the Apostles' Creed. We can affirm that baptism, its accompanying profession of faith, and the new creation that results are not simply elements in the sanctification of an individual. Through these, an individual becomes a member of a people and a member of the body of Christ in being a member of the community of the baptized. Conversely, by becoming a member of the community of the baptized, an individual receives salvation. Thus, there is a reciprocal relationship between the justification of an individual and the constitution of a community of salvation. Aloys Grillmeir, commenting on these chapters in *Lumen gentium*, says that "all the paths of God's salvation lead to the community."[565] This community then becomes the instrument of salvation of the entire human race and even the entire cosmic order. The form of this salvation is the unity of humankind as children of the one God in Christ through the power of the Spirit.

Sacraments are fundamentally eschatological because they are oriented to a future completion. They also are eschatological in a second sense. The eschaton with its perfect unity and salvation breaks into "this world in the sacramental sign and is caught in any earthly element as in a seal."[566] In other words, there is an inbreaking of the eschaton into the present time under the aegis of sacramental sign. The perfection that is awaited in future glory exists now within sacramental sign. The sacraments are not extrinsic instruments of grace, but the form of grace under sacramental sign, effective signs making Christ present both within the sacramental sign and within the community constituted by the sign. The "form" is none other than the baptismal and eucharistic community, which is itself not a mere collection of individuals, but the unity of individuals with Christ and with each other in the body of Christ. This body of Christ is identified as the people of God throughout *Lumen gentium*.

Ecumenical Implications of a Communal Eschatology

At the end time sacraments will pass away, for the reality they signify will no longer be present under sacramental sign, but will exist in its fullness. At the present time, the unity of all in Christ through the power

---

[565] Aloys Grillmeier, "The People of God," in *Commentary on the Documents of Vatican II*, Herbert Vorgrimler, ed. (New York: Herder and Herder, 1967), 156.

[566] Otto Semmelroth, "The Eschatological Nature of the Pilgrim Church and her Union with the Heavenly Church," *Commentary on the Documents of Vatican II* (New York: Herder and Herder, 1967), 282.

of the Spirit is celebrated sacramentally. Once we step outside that sacramental and liturgical reality, however, we find ourselves enmeshed in the disunity characteristic of sin not yet vanquished, engaged in the process of praying for unity at the same time we work to build it. This is the already/not yet realized state of eschatology. At the end time, this unity will be complete.

Since the unity of all in Christ extends beyond the frontier of death, the exchange of goods within the body of Christ crosses this frontier. The saints bear testimony to the redemption that the living anticipate in faith. They do not lose their connection with their past histories for they are with "their deeds, which follow them" (Rev. 14:13).[567] These deeds give encouragement and example to those who follow them. When the community of the faithful joins together in offering praise to God, they are united with the saints in this praise. According to the ancient tradition of the church, the liturgy is a participation in the heavenly liturgy of the saints eternally offering worship to God. As we pray for one another on earth, so also do the saints in heaven intercede for us. This does not compromise the unique mediatorship of Christ, for the saints intercede only by virtue of their union with Christ. They are instruments of his mediatorship precisely as members of his body.

The Council of Trent affirmed that it is good and useful to invoke the saints and to have recourse to their prayers and help in obtaining God's benefits through Jesus Christ.[568] Vatican II said it was supremely fitting to invoke the saints and have recourse to their prayers.[569] Round VIII of the dialogue between Lutheran and Catholics did not reach agreement on the substantive issue of whether invocation of saints is legitimate and beneficial.[570] Nevertheless, in that dialogue, Lutherans were of the opinion that the practice of the veneration of the saints is not church-dividing, "provided that the sole mediatorship of Christ is clearly safeguarded and that in any closer future fellowship members would be free to refrain from the practice."[571] The Catholics affirmed that the sole mediatorship of Christ serves as the critical principle for identifying abuses in the practice of the veneration of the saints. Invocation of the

---

[567] Cited by Otto Semmelroth, *Commentary on the Documents of Vatican II*, 283.

[568] Henricus Denzinger and Adolphus Schönmetzer, eds., *Enchiridion Symbolorium, Definitionum, et Declarationum de Rebus Fidei et Morum*, 33rd edition (Freiburg, Germany: Herder, 1965), ¶1821.

[569] *Lumen gentium*, 50.

[570] *The One Mediator, the Saints, and Mary*, ¶97.

[571] *The One Mediator, the Saints, and Mary*, ¶97.

saints is not essential for full communion with the Catholic Church, although the invocation of the saints occurs in the first of the penitential rites of the Eucharist as well as in the Litany of the Saints used in the Easter Vigil and in the rites of baptism and ordination. The individual Catholic is strongly encouraged to make use of prayers invoking the saints. Thus, the Catholics in Round VIII said they could enter into a fellowship with Lutherans in a situation where Lutherans would proclaim Christ as the one Mediator and the invocation of the saints would recede with the stipulation that the Catholic tradition of worship would be respected and not impugned as idolatrous.[572] Perhaps a fair judgment would be that the consensus reached in Round VIII was rather minimal.[573]

The problem addressed by that dialogue was "how to affirm the unique mediatorship of Christ so that all the 'mediations' in his church not only do not detract from, but communicate and extol, his sole mediatorship."[574] The topic of Round XI necessarily touches on this topic again insofar as the veneration and the invocation of the saints is a topic within eschatology. This essay proposes to this present dialogue that sacramental theology with its corresponding theology of the mystical body of Christ and its account of the unity achieved sacramentally in baptism and the Eucharist offers a theology of the saints such that invocation of the saints is never an invocation of them apart from Christ, but always in virtue of their union in and with Christ. Veneration of the saints is best understood ecumenically as a way of joining the saints in their adoration of God and a way of recognizing the redemption achieved in them, a redemption for which we hope and pray for ourselves.

Finally, grace, justification, and redemption all possess a communal dimension. They create a community of salvation, a community that now exists not only sacramentally, but also eschatologically. If the sixteenth-century discussion of the doctrine of justification had been more closely connected with the doctrine and practice of baptism—namely, that faith is the effect of grace and the condition for justification—then the description of justification itself would have not been posed in almost exclusively individualistic terms. We come to faith because we have heard

---

[572] *The One Mediator, the Saints, and Mary*, ¶98.

[573] See Mark Ellingsen, "The One Mediator, the Saints, and Mary," *Lutheran Quarterly* 7 (no. 3, 1993): 345–347; also Maxwell E. Johnson, "The One Mediator, the Saints, and Mary: A Lutheran Reflection," *Worship* 67 (no. 3, May 1993): 226–238.

[574] *The One Mediator, the Saints, and Mary*, ¶70.

the gospel preached within a community of faith. Grace not only "elevates" my individual human nature, nor is it only "imputed" to me as an individual. It grafts me into union with Christ, a union simultaneous with a union with all others also in union with Christ. The effect of grace is fundamentally relational, reconciling enmity and creating unity where there had been division. The question for the dialogue is whether this relational view of sacraments, grace, and justification from an eschatological perspective constitutes a lens through which we may overcome past divisions and enact a new, more communal vision of our hope for everlasting life.

Communal Eschatology and the Communion of Saints: A Lutheran Perspective

by Cheryl M. Peterson

Can a communal dimension of eschatology be affirmed from a Lutheran theological perspective, and if so, on what basis? Susan Wood outlined a Christian account of the communal destiny of humanity with a sacramental analysis of the Third Article of the Apostles' Creed and an examination of *Lumen gentium*, Chapters II and VII. She demonstrated the continuity between the sacramental and eschatological meanings of the Creed's Third Article. Then she developed the implications for a communal eschatology rooted in a body of Christ ecclesiology.

The "Joint Declaration on the Doctrine of Justification" and Luther's sacramental realism serve as common ground for the current U.S. Lutheran-Catholic Dialogue.

Wood argues that future work on justification is needed "to develop its communal dimensions and to strengthen the connection among baptism, eucharist, and eschatology within a view of the church as the *totus Christus*." In this paper, I show that the Lutheran emphasis on personal salvation (*pro me*) in the doctrine of justification by grace through faith does not preclude a communal dimension of the "hope of eternal life," but in fact includes it. I support this thesis with an analysis of Martin Luther's explanation of the Third Article of the Apostles' Creed in the Large Catechism. Finally, I offer some brief thoughts on an understanding of communal eschatology in terms of the *totus Christus* view of the church.

The "Joint Declaration on the Doctrine of Justification" points to the Scriptural basis for an understanding of justification as "acceptance into communion with God—already now, but then fully in God's coming kingdom," and further, that this communion occurs by reception of the Holy Spirit and incorporation into the body of Christ.[575] Indeed, according to the findings of a previous dialogue, "Faith [for Lutherans] does not mean individualism, but birth into a communion of believers, the body of Christ which is the church. As members of the church, believers participate by grace in the divine Trinitarian life—in a 'mystical union' (*unio mystica*) that anticipates the full future glory of Christ 'beheld with an unveiled face' (2 Cor. 3:18; cf 5:1-10 and Rom. 8:20-30 in the context of 8:18-39)."[576]

"Any merely individualistic understanding of 'eternal life'" also is rejected by the more recent statement of the German Catholic-Lutheran Dialogue, *Communio Sanctorum*. The basis is this: Scripture contains various images of a living, eschatological communion with Christ that "express a sense of being with one another that is also constituted as an all-embracing being for one another."[577]

What resources within the Lutheran confessional tradition might support Wood's proposed understanding of a communal eschatology? An under-appreciated Lutheran resource for this communal aspect is Luther's explanation of the Third Article of the Apostles' Creed in the Large Catechism, one of the confessional writings included in the *Book*

---

[575] "Joint Declaration on the Doctrine of Justification," (hereinafter cited as JDDJ), October 31, 1999, ¶11. Justification creates a new person and brings the person into communion with God, through faith; it is not only a forensic act of "gracious exclusion" but also one of "gracious inclusion." The German text speaks of becoming righteous as well as being reckoned righteous. The JDDJ states that although justification and the renewal that follows must be distinguished, they cannot be separated. They are joined together in Christ, who is present to the believer in faith.

[576] "Common Statement: The One Mediator, the Saints, and Mary," § II.A.50, in Lutherans and Catholics in Dialogue VIII, *The One Mediator, the Saints, and Mary,* H. George Anderson, J. Francis Stafford,, and Joseph A. Burgess, eds. (Minneapolis: Augsburg, 1992), 41. This is cited hereinafter as *The One Mediator, the Saints, and Mary.*

[577] *Communio Sanctorum: The Church as the Communion of Saints,* Bilateral Working Group of the German National Bishops' Conference and the Church Leadership of the United Evangelical Lutheran Church of Germany, trans. by Mark W. Jeske, Michael Root, and Daniel R. Smith (Collegeville, Minn.: Liturgical Press, 2004), ¶219, 75.

of Concord (1580).[578] Although Luther's explanation of the first two articles has a decidedly *pro me* accent, he describes in his explanation of the Third Article a mutual relationship between the individual and the community by means of the Spirit. Thus, he views this article primarily in pneumatological rather than sacramental terms. Yet, his earlier sacramental understanding of the *communio sanctorum* is reflected indirectly in this article, especially when read in light of other sections of the Large Catechism.[579] While there is not a detailed discussion of eschatology in this article, one can find the connections between justification and ecclesiology. Whereas Wood argues for an interpretation of the Third Article that is both eschatological and sacramental, Luther draws a connection between the pnematological and eschatological meanings of the *communio sanctorum*. A sacramental meaning is indirectly inferred, however, and can be seen as complementary.

Luther's Explanation of the Third Article of the Apostles' Creed

The work of the Spirit has been interpreted by Lutherans as an application of the event of Christ's death and resurrection to individual believers. As a result, the objective work of Christ becomes subjectively applied to the believer through faith. Eilert Herms offers an extreme example of this in his theology. He describes the work of the Holy Spirit in individual terms using the category of revelation.[580] Through the external preaching of the Word, the Holy Spirit works internally in the human heart to reveal the meaning and truth of the gospel into each

---

[578] Martin Luther, The Large Catechism, *The Book of Concord*, Robert Kolb and Timothy J. Wengert, eds. (Minneapolis: Fortress Press, 2000), 435–440; cited herein after as *Book of Concord*. See also the *Constitution, Bylaws, and Continuing Resolutions of the Evangelical Lutheran Church in America*, in provision 2.06., declares: "This church accepts the other confessional writings of the Book of Concord [in addition to the Augsburg Confession], namely, the Apology of the Augsburg Confession and the Treatise, the Smalcald Articles, the Small Catechism, the Large Catechism, and the Formula of Concord, as further valid interpretations of the faith of the church."

[579] See Martin Luther, "Sermon on the Blessed Sacrament of the Holy and True Body and Blood of Christ and the Brotherhoods (1519)," *Luther's Works*, American Edition, vol. 35, E. Theodore Bachman, ed. (Philadelphia: Muhlenberg Press, 1960), 45–73.

[580] Eilert Herms, *Luthers Auslegung des Dritten Artikels* (Tübingen: J.C.B. Mohr, 1987). The concept of "revelation" only became theologically important after Luther's time, suggesting this category may not be the most appropriate to Luther's own context and concerns.

believer's heart. Without the Spirit's work, the redeeming work of the incarnate Son of God on the cross would remain hidden and unknown to the individual believer. Thus, the proper work of the Spirit is to bring an existential transformation to the believer and a new eschatological standing before God.[581] The work of the Holy Spirit may be called sanctifying in that it endows each human person with new existential knowledge about his or her redemption.[582] Herms even understands the forgiveness of sins in revelatory terms as "nothing other than recreated existence in light of the appearance of the truth of the gospel."[583]

In spite of his strong focus on the individual's appropriation of the Spirit's sanctifying work, Herms does recognize that the external means through which the Holy Spirit works occurs in the gathered community, the church. In this sense, the church is necessary for salvation, for "Outside of this community of his body, there is no access to Christ."[584] Further, Herms acknowledges that the believer is incorporated into the assembly of the saints simultaneously with her or his transferal into a new eschatological existence before God.[585]

Luther's account of the sanctifying work of the Holy Spirit, however, has a more communal emphasis than Herms acknowledges. Not only does Luther suggest a deeper, mutual relationship between the individual and community in his description of "making holy," sanctification is

---

[581] Herms, *Luthers Auslegung*, 65, 100.

[582] Herms, *Luthers Auslegung*, 74.

[583] Herms, *Luthers Auslegung*, 96. The original German reads: "… nach nichts anderes als eben die durch das Heiligungswirken des Geistes geschaffene Existenz im Lichte der erschienenen Wahrheit des Evangeliums." As Fr. Jared Wicks, S.J., emphasized in deliberations of this dialogue, the transformative work of the Holy Spirit affects the behavior of the believer, not just the believer's existential standing before God. Although the Holy Spirit works in the church through the Word and the sacraments, "anthropologically the proper locus of the Spirit is the human heart, where his work hits home and brings about a transformation." Wicks noted the paradox of this in light of the traditional Lutheran emphasis on God acting *extra nos*. See Wicks, "Holy Spirit-Church-Sanctification: Insights from Luther's Instructions on the Faith," *Pro Ecclesia* 2, no. 2 (1993): 164–168.

[584] Herms, *Luthers Auslegung*, 52. The original German reads: "Außerhalb dieser Gemeinschaft seines Leibes gibt es keinen Zugang zu Christus."

[585] Herms, *Luthers Auslegung*, 110. Fr. Jared Wicks described Luther as holding an instrumental use of the church by the Holy Spirit in the Large Catechism. According to Wicks, as early as his 1520 catechetical writings, Luther calls for pastors and believers to "envisage the church as a *communio*—necessary to salvation—of shared spiritual gifts."

more than a new existential awareness for Luther. This can be illustrated by a close reading of Luther's explanation of the Third Article of the Apostles' Creed in the Large Catechism. Following his introductory comments, his explanation falls into three sections in which he discusses sanctification in relation to: 1) the community of saints or the Christian church; 2) the forgiveness of sins; and 3) the resurrection of the body and life everlasting.[586]

> 1) In the first section,[587] Luther writes, "The Spirit first leads us into his holy community, placing us in the church's lap, where he preaches to us and *brings us to Christ*,"[588] thus stressing the church as the means by which believers are drawn to Christ. Even though individual believers are "called through the gospel," it is through the spiritual community of the church that this gospel is proclaimed. And again, "Being made holy is nothing else than bringing us to the Lord Jesus Christ to receive this blessing [the redemption won for us by Christ on the cross], to which we could not have come by ourselves."[589] Indeed, the word that Luther uses here is not *Gemeinschaft* (community) but *Gemeine* [*Gemeinde* in contemporary usage], which is perhaps closer to the English "fellowship" or "sharing or participative community."[590] The church is described further by Luther as the "mother" who begets and bears each Christian through the Word, that is as a community of new birth. The church is the means through which individuals are brought to faith by the proclamation of the gospel. In this first section, Luther understands the Spirit's work of "making holy" primarily in terms of the gift of faith, that is true knowledge of our

---

[586] The Large Catechism, *Book of Concord*, §§34-37, 435–436.

[587] The Large Catechism, *Book of Concord*, §§37-53, 435–438.

[588] The Large Catechism, Book of Concord, §37, 435–436. Italics added.

[589] Large Catechism, *Book of Concord*, §39, 436. This discussion clearly assumes and I would even say overlaps with justification (especially the first sub-section when Luther speaks about the gift of faith). In his discussion of the second article on the Son of God, it is interesting to note that Luther does not use the word justification once. He refers to it in other ways: being redeemed and released; being brought back from the devil to God, from death to life, from sin to righteousness; being Christ's own possession; and "being restored to the Father's favor and grace."

[590] See the discussion of Luther's third article of the creed in "The Church as Spiritual Communion," in *The Church as Communion: Lutheran Contributions to Ecclesiology*, LWF Documentation 42, Heinrich Holze, ed. (Geneva: Lutheran World Federation, 1997), 104–121.

redemption in Christ. The Holy Spirit reveals and proclaims this promise, illuminating and inflaming the hearts of believers "so that they grasp and accept it, cling to it and persevere in it."[591]

Luther goes on to emphasize the communal aspect of this new life that Christians receive through Christ through the sanctifying work of the Holy Spirit.[592] Believers are "incorporated" into this community by the Holy Spirit and the Word. The proclamation that brings the good news to each individual believer, therefore, cannot be understood only in terms of an individual existential experience. Through the Word, believers are incorporated into the holy community as "a part and member, a participant and co-partner in all the blessings it possesses."[593] Luther refers to this community as a "holy little flock" that the Spirit gathers in one faith, mind, and understanding under the headship of Christ to be ruled together by the one head, Christ.[594] Further, this community "possesses a variety of gifts, and yet is united in love without sect or schism."[595] Thus, in addition to the gift of faith, the Spirit also produces "fruits" in this holy community, which enable it to grow in holiness and become strong.[596] The Spirit will teach and preach the Word through this holy community, remaining with it until the Last Day.

2) In the second part of his explanation,[597] Luther explains that daily forgiveness of sins is the primary blessing that believers receive in the holy community through "the holy sacraments and absolution as well as all the comforting words of the entire gospel."[598] Luther

---

[591] Large Catechism, *Book of Concord,* §42, 436. This is the only section in which Luther uses "heart" language. He does so here three times in §§37-42, 435–436.

[592] Large Catechism, *Book of Concord*, §§47-53, 436–438.

[593] Large Catechism, *Book of Concord*, §52, 438.

[594] This is the closest Luther comes to describing the holy community as the "body of Christ" in his explanation of the third article.

[595] Large Catechism, *Book of Concord*, 438. Some have interpreted "gifts" here to be referring to the means of grace, that is, the Word and sacraments. In this context, I believe it is more likely that what Luther had in mind was the variety of spiritual gifts listed by Paul, in 1 Corinthians 12, who begs the church in Corinth to exercise their gifts in a unity of love.

[596] Large Catechism, *Book of Concord*, §53, 438.

[597] Large Catechism, *Book of Concord*, §§54-56, 438.

[598] Large Catechism, *Book of Concord*, §54, 438.

underscores the conviction that forgiveness is needed continually, because believers are never without sin in this life. While the believer experiences the gift of faith individually, this blessing is received not only individually but also communally—that is, in relationship not only to God but also the other members of the community. Luther writes that the Christian experiences new life as "full forgiveness of sins, both in that God forgives us and that we forgive, bear with, and aid one another."[599] Through our incorporation into this holy community, we experience this forgiveness and are not harmed by our sin. This, Luther says, is what it means to be "made holy"—namely, the receiving and experiencing daily the forgiveness of sins.

3) In the final section,[600] Luther connects eschatology to the process of sanctification, although it is unclear whether the growth he describes here should be attributed to individuals, the community, or both. He writes, "Meanwhile, because holiness has begun and is growing daily, we await the time when our flesh will be put to death, will be buried with all its uncleanness, and will come forth gloriously and arise to complete and perfect holiness in a new, eternal life."[601] The Holy Spirit's work continues until the eschaton. "Now, however, we remain only halfway pure and holy. The Holy Spirit must always work in us through the Word, granting us daily forgiveness until we attain to that life where there will be no more forgiveness."[602] The Holy Spirit will continue to work in us, increasing holiness on the earth through the church and forgiveness, until the last day, "when there are only perfectly pure and holy people full of integrity and righteousness, completely free from sin, death, and all misfortune, living in new, immortal, and glorified bodies."[603] On that day, the Spirit will make us perfectly and eternally holy through the resurrection of the body and the life everlasting.

In this treatment of the Third Article of the Creed, Luther uses the locus of sanctification to put forth an understanding of salvation that is, at the same time, personal and ecclesial, as well as eschatological in

---

[599] Large Catechism, *Book of Concord*, §55, 438.

[600] Large Catechism, *Book of Concord*, §§57-62, 438–439.

[601] Large Catechism, *Book of Concord*, §57, 438.

[602] Large Catechism, *Book of Concord*, §58, 438.

[603] Large Catechism, *Book of Concord*, §58, 438.

nature.[604] Grace is personally experienced by individuals but not only in individualistic terms. Individuals experience the blessings of Christ as members of a community of which Christ is the head and into which they are incorporated by the Holy Spirit. This community grows and increases in holiness (experienced through the gospel and forgiveness of sins) until the eschaton.

Thus, it would not be incorrect to say that, for Luther, justification and sanctification are both eschatological and ecclesial. Later Lutherans traditionally have affirmed the former but not always the latter.[605] For example, George Forell writes, "It is because God is coming toward us, because the 'dear Last Day' is approaching, that we can live here and now as sinners and righteous at the same time. . . . It is because history is moving toward a goal which is so controlled by God that we are enabled to live in this tension he so colorfully describes as *simil justus et peccator.*"[606] He quotes Luther in the 1535 Lectures on Galatians: "We have indeed begun to be justified by faith, by which we have also received the first fruits of the Spirit; the mortification of our flesh has begun. But we are not yet perfectly righteous. Our being justified perfectly [i.e., our being made and not only declared righteous] still remains to be seen, and this is what we hope for. Thus our righteousness does not yet exist in fact, but it still exists in hope."[607] This is why Christians must pray incessantly for the coming of the kingdom, because that day is the completion of the work God began in our justification. This is an act of God involving not only the individual but his community and his world; the future that is coming is a hope for all people, indeed for all of creation.[608] More recently,

---

[604] As Christoph Schwöbel notes, by reorganizing the Apostles' Creed into three rather than twelve articles, Luther purports the integration of a series of formerly independent articles of belief in the church, so that "the Spirit's work of sanctification is now not only related to a particular aspect of the doctrine of grace; it now comprises the whole dynamic of God's Trinitarian action. The Spirit thus becomes the common denominator of ecclesiology, soteriology, and eschatology." C. Schwöbel, "Quest for Communion," *Communio Sanctorum: The Church as the Communion of Saints,* 273.

[605] See, for example, George W. Forell, "Justification and Eschatology in Luther's Thought," *Church History,* vol. 38, no. 2 (June 1969): 164–174, as well as works of Gerhard O. Forde for eschatological understandings of justification. Robert W. Jenson affirms both the eschatological and ecclesial dimensions of justification in his theological enterprise.

[606] Forell, 169.

[607] Forell, 170.

[608] Forell 172–173.

the ecclesial reality of justification is being explored by Lutherans such as Scott Hendrix, who argues that "justification and ecclesiology articulate the same reality from different angles and explore complementary dimensions of the one new life in Christ."[609]

Communio Sanctorum

We now come to the question: Can this communal understanding of justification be affirmed in sacramental terms? In an early treatise, "Sermon on the Blessed Sacrament of the Holy and True Body and Blood of Christ and the Brotherhoods,"[610] Luther offers an understanding of the church in terms of the sacramental union with Christ.[611] In this treatise, Luther articulates an understanding of the Lord's Supper that, according to Paul Althaus, "both expresses and guarantees the reality of the church as the community of saints."[612] Partaking of the eucharistic meal incorporates the Christian into Christ's spiritual body, which for Luther is analogous to the incorporation of a citizen into a city: "And whoever is taken into this city is said to be received into the community of saints and to be incorporated into Christ's spiritual body and made a member of him."[613] Althaus regards the later Lutheran emphasis on "real presence"

---

[609] Scott Hendrix states further that "both justification and the church are best understood not as separate theological loci, but as different facets of the one new reality that embraces Christians because they believe that Jesus of Nazareth inaugurated the kingdom of God." See Scott Hendrix, "Open Community: The Ecclesial Reality of Justification," in *By Faith Alone: Essays on Justification in Honor of Gerhard O. Forde*, Joseph A. Burgess and Marc Kolden, eds. (Grand Rapids, Mich.: Eerdmans, 2004), 237.

[610] "Sermon on the Blessed Sacrament of the Holy and True Body and Blood of Christ and the Brotherhoods (1519)," *Luther's Works*, vol. 35, 45–73. The background for his concept of *communio sanctorum* is his critique of the practices of the religious brotherhoods, civic associations, and craft guilds that, in contrast, offered a self-serving model of "communion."

[611] Simon Peura, "The Church as Spiritual Communion in Luther," in *The Church as Communion*, 93–131. See also Vilmos Vajta, "The Church as Spiritual-Sacramental Communio with Christ and His Saints in the Theology of Luther," trans. Carter Lindberg, in *Luther's Ecumenical Significance: An Interconfessional Consultation*, Peter Manns and Harding Meyer, eds., in collaboration with Carter Lindberg and Harry McSorley (Philadelphia: Fortress Press, 1984), 111–122.

[612] Paul Althaus makes this point based on an evaluation of several sermons and treatises of Luther's written from 1519 and 1524. See Althaus, *The Theology of Martin Luther*, trans. by Robert C. Schultz (Philadelphia: Fortress Press, 1966), 318.

[613] *Luther's Works*, 35:51.

(including in Luther's own works) as an impoverishment to which he understood as Luther's earlier, broader interpretation of the Lord's Supper as the sacrament of the *communio sanctorum*.[614]

This has led many contemporary Lutheran theologians to suggest that Luther has a kind of "communion ecclesiology." In distinction to much of current communion ecclesiology, however, Luther describes this *communio* not in terms of Trinitarian *perichoresis*,[615] but in language that closely resembles that of the "happy exchange" in Luther's famous 1520 treatise, "On the Freedom of a Christian."[616] In that treatise, Luther speaks of an "interchange of blessings" by which Christ takes upon himself our form—that is, our sin and infirmity—and we take on his form—that is, his righteousness. This interchange has implications for the communion among members of the body of Christ. As Luther states: "Again, through this same love, we are to be changed and to make the infirmities of all other Christians our own; we are to take upon ourselves their form and their necessity, and all the good that is within our power we are to make theirs, that they may profit from it. . . . [I]n this way we are to be changed into one another and are made into a community by love."[617]

Luther also addresses the significance of this union in eschatological terms. In the sacrament, we are united with Christ. This union makes us into one body "with all the saints," Luther says,

> . . . so that Christ cares for us and acts in our behalf. As if he were what we are, he makes whatever concerns us to concern him as well, and even more than it does us. In turn we so care for Christ, as if we were what he is, which

---

[614] See Peura, 93–131, for a discussion of scholarly views on the thesis of Althaus as well as Peura's won position.

[615] This Greek term is used to describe the triune relationship between each person of the Godhead.

[616] "On the Freedom of the Christian," trans. W. A. Lambert, *Luther's Works*, vol. 31, Harold J. Grimm, ed. (Philadelphia: Muhlenberg Press, 1957), 333–377.

[617] *Luther's Works*, 35:58. Christians are called to live out this horizontal aspect of communion in both spiritual and physical ways, from bearing one another's burdens and afflictions to sharing material goods with those in need, as St. Paul writes in 1 Corinthians 11:23. Luther recognizes how difficult this calling is: "Now if one will make the afflictions of Christ and all Christian his own, defend the truth, oppose unrighteousness, and help bear the needs of the innocent and the sufferings of all Christians, then he will find affliction and adversity enough, over and above that which is his evil nature, the world, the devil and sin daily inflict on him." *Luther's Works*, 35:56–57.

indeed we shall finally be—we shall be conformed to his likeness. As St. John says, "We know that when he shall be revealed we shall be like him" [1 John 3:2]. So deep and complete is the fellowship of Christ and all the saints with us. . . . For the union makes all things common, until at the last Christ completely destroys sin in us and makes us like himself, at the last day.[618]

The question remains whether by "all saints" Luther is referring to living Christians, the blessed departed, or both. Vilmos Vajta argues that in most cases the expression "Christ and all saints" characterizes the saints in heaven and on earth and that we can interpret this phrase to refer equally to the militant and triumphant church—that is, all of those whom have been incorporated into Christ's body through Word and Sacrament.[619] True, the Lutheran Reformers redefined the term "saint" in light of the gospel of justification by faith alone as "one who is justified by faith alone and who consequently lives and acts on that basis, one who claims and desires nothing for self but lives in the light of divine grace,"[620] Lutherans in recent decades, however, have become more aware of the doxological and eschatological dimension of the church, the unity of the church militant on earth and the church triumphant in heaven.[621] This doxological link between living and deceased Christians is reflected in the Lutheran liturgical tradition, especially eucharistic prefaces and the order for the burial of the dead.[622]

Whether this early sacramental understanding of Luther is reflected in his later writing, in particular his catechisms, remains an important question. While Luther makes a direct link in his 1519 treatise between the personal and sacramental meanings of *communio sanctorum* (as the communion or community of saints, on the one hand, and communion in holy things, i.e., baptism and eucharist, on the other), the sacramental sense seems to be absent in his discussion of the "communion of saints" ten years later in his catechisms. In fact, Luther interprets the expression

---

[618] *Luther's Works*, 35:59.

[619] Vajta, "The Church as Spiritual-Sacramental Communio with Christ and His Saints in the Theology of Luther," *Luther's Ecumenical Significance*, 117.

[620] *The One Mediator, the Saints, and Mary*, ¶47, 39.

[621] *The One Mediator, the Saints, and Mary*, 125.

[622] *The One Mediator, the Saints, and Mary*, ¶199, 108.

"communion of saints"as a gloss on the "holy catholic church."[623] He sees it as a later addition to the western baptismal creed.[624] In spite of this, Simon Peura makes the argument that one can see Luther's early view of the church as a sacramental community reflected in both the Small and Large Catechisms.[625] Peura points to the motif of God's self-giving that he sees as dominant in Luther's explanation of the Creed. As Luther himself writes, "For in all three articles God himself has revealed and opened to us the most profound depths of his fatherly heart and his pure, unutterable life. For this very purpose he created us, so that he might redeem us and make us holy, and, moreover, having granted and bestowed upon us everything in heaven and on earth, he has also given us his Son and his Holy Spirit, through whom he brings us to himself."[626] In what Timothy Wengert has come to call "Luther's reverse Trinity,"[627] it is the Holy Spirit who reveals to us Jesus Christ the Son who reveals to

---

[623] *Book of Concord*, fn. 246. Paul Althaus offers a helpful explanation as to why Luther prefers "community" [*Gemeine* in the German] over "communion." See Althaus, *The Theology of Luther*, 294–297. For Luther, the idea of a transfer of merits from the treasury of Christ and the saints is replaced by serving one another (especially the living saints); we can help the faith and life of those through prayer, but Luther rejects the idea of a treasury of merits that can be drawn on (in Thesis 58, he states "no saint has adequately fulfilled God's commandments in this life." Thus their good works cannot be meritorious for anyone—themselves included.

[624] Scholarly opinion today favors the sacramental meaning, that is, as participation in Eucharist and Holy Baptism. In his historical study, Stephen Benko makes the argument that insertion of *communio sanctorum* into the Apostles' Creed resulted from a long process to find a connecting link between the holy catholic church and the forgiveness of sins in the western church: that is, the forgiveness of sins is granted through participation (*koinonia*) in the Eucharist as well as baptism (holy things). The final step in the development of this connection came with Augustine in the wake of the Donatist controversy. Previously, baptism alone had conferred participation in the body of Christ. Because baptism could not be repeated and because the question of readmission to ecclesial fellowship became critical during the Donatist controversy, restoration was effected through admission to the Eucharist. "*Communio sanctorum* is, therefore, a participation in the sacraments, within the church where, through the blood of Christ (this is the content of baptism and Eucharist), the forgiveness of sins is imparted." See Benko, *The Meaning of Sanctorum Communio*, Studies in Historical Theology, 3 (Naperville, Ill.: Alec R. Allenson, Inc., 1964), 53.

[625] Luther's Small and Large Catechisms date from 1529.

[626] Large Catechism, *Book of Concord*, §§64-65, 439.

[627] Timothy J. Wengert, *Martin Luther's Catechisms: Forming the Faith* (Minneapolis: Fortress Press, 2009), 43–44.

us the Father's heart and, thus, the self–giving of God. As Luther writes, "We could never come to recognize the Father's favor and grace were it not for the Lord Jesus Christ, who is a mirror of the Father's heart . . . but neither could we know anything of Christ, had it not been revealed by the Holy Spirit."[628]

In his explication of the Third Article of the Creed, Luther does emphasize the need for the *communio sanctorum*, through which the Holy Spirit acts to reveal the Son through the preaching of the gospel.[629] As has already been noted, the first task of the Holy Spirit is "to lead us into his holy community, placing us in the church's lap, where he preaches to us and brings us to Christ."[630]

Although Luther does not explicitly make a connection to the sacraments of baptism and the Lord's Supper, Peura argued that "there is absolutely no justification for seeing a contrast between the preaching of Christ and the sacraments as means of grace," especially in light of Luther's discussion of the sacraments in his 1528 treatise, "Confessing Concerning Christ's Supper,"[631] which is another treatment of the Creed, and in the fourth part of the Large Catechism itself.[632] According to Luther, what makes a sacrament is the Word of God (in particular, the gospel) joined to an earthly element. Although he rejects the philosophical framework of transubstantiation, he clearly holds a sacramental realism. It is by virtue of the Word of God that the water of Holy Baptism is truly "a saving, divine water" and the elements of bread and wine are truly the body and blood of Christ. In Holy Baptism, "we are initially received into the Christian community" and through which we participate in the blessings that baptism promises and brings— namely, deliverance from death and the devil, forgiveness of sin, grace, "*the entire Christ*," and the gifts of the Holy Spirit.[633]

Luther recognizes that, although Christians are born anew through baptism, they still face the struggle against sin and evil until the last day. He writes, "Therefore the Lord's Supper is given as a daily food and sustenance so that our faith may be refreshed and strengthened and that

---

[628] *Book of Concord*, §65, 439–440.

[629] Peura, 109.

[630] The Large Catechism, *Book of Concord*, §37, 435–436.

[631] *Luther's Works,* vol. 37, Robert H. Fischer, ed. (Philadelphia: Muhlenberg Press, 1961), 161–372.

[632] Peura, 111.

[633] Large Catechism, *Book of Concord*, §42, 461. Italics are mine.

it may not succumb in the struggle but become stronger and stronger. For the new life should be one that continually develops and progresses."[634] Just as he does in his explication of the Third Article, Luther in his explanation of the sacraments affirms that the Christian life is a participation in the blessings of Christ and a process that involves both struggle and growth. He makes a direct link between the Third Article of the Creed and the Lord's Supper when he writes, "Now the whole gospel and the article of the Creed, 'I believe in one holy Christian church . . . the forgiveness of sins,' are embodied in this sacrament and offered to us through the Word."[635]

Totus Christus?

In this paper, I have offered a Lutheran perspective on communal eschatology and the communion of saints, showing connections in Luther's Large Catechism between ecclesiology and eschatology that are both pneumatological and sacramental. Justification is both ecclesial and eschatological, even as it is personal (*pro me*). Therefore, the hope of eternal life is not only a hope for individuals but also for the "holy community."

What remains finally to be explored from a Lutheran perspective is Wood's proposal that the communal form of the eschaton is the *totus Christus*, interpreted eschatologically in order to avoid an immanentism that views the church as an extension of the Incarnation. She writes, "The *totus Christus* [that is, the members of the church in union with their head, Christ] represents the church in its eschatological dimension since the unity of the body will only be complete in the eschaton." Wood anticipates the objection of Christomonism. She responds by stating that the connections between sacrament and eschatology occur in the Third Article of the Creed as the work of the Spirit. Robert W. Jenson is one Lutheran theologian who has wholeheartedly embraced the Augustinian concept of *totus Christus*, interpreting it through a Barthian understanding of predestination as the election of Jesus Christ together with his people. Thus, the church originates by the will of the Father, who predestines the church in the Son; that is, the one sole object of eternal election is Jesus with his people, *the totus Christus*.[636] In this regard,

---

[634] Large Catechism, *Book of Concord*, §§23-25, 469.

[635] Large Catechism, *Book of Concord*, §32, 470.

[636] Robert W. Jenson, *Systematic Theology II: The Works of God* (New York: Oxford University Press, 1999), 175.

Jenson cites Augustine's Sermons on John (Tractate XXI, 8). His citation of this text reads: "Let us rejoice, then, and give thanks that we are made not only Christians but Christ. . . . For if He is the head, we are the members: the whole man is He and we. . . . The fullness of Christ, then, is head and members."[637] Jenson also proposes that the church is "ontologically the risen body of Christ," the object through which Christ is made personally and bodily available to the world and its own members. His view has been criticized (by Wood, among others) as coming dangerously close to collapsing ecclesiology into Christology, even though Jenson insists he is not positing ecclesiology as realized eschatology but as "anticipated eschatology."[638]

Traditionally, the concept of the "kingdom of God" has been more favored by Lutherans for picturing our eternal destiny than the "*totus Christus*." For example, while Wolfhart Panneberg describes that destiny using words such as "unending communion" and "participation in God's eternity," his central symbol is not the body of Christ, but the kingdom of God. The traditional themes of Christian eschatology are the resurrection of the dead (in which the destiny of the individual is at stake, her destiny for a life in communion with God beyond death), and the kingdom of God (that is, the social aspect of human life beyond death, a hope for all of humankind to be in communion with God).[639] In the catechism's section on the Lord's Prayer, Luther refers to the creed in his definition of the kingdom of God.[640] He says that it is through the power of God's Word that "many, led by the Spirit, may come into the kingdom of grace and become partakers of redemption so that all may remain together eternally in this kingdom that has now begun [and will be

---

[637] Jenson, *Systematic Theology II*, 81.

[638] According to Robert Jenson, "The church lives by what God will make eschatologically of it *as* the people of God, the body of Christ, and the temple of the Holy Spirit." This is possible, Jenson states, because "it is what creatures may anticipate from God that is their being." R. Jenson, *Systematic Theology II*, 171–172.

[639] Wolfhart Panneberg, "The Task of Christian Eschatology," *The Last Things: Biblical and Theological Perspectives on Eschatology,* Carl E. Braaten and Robert W. Jenson, eds. (Grand Rapids, Mich.: Eerdmans, 2002), 4.

[640] Indeed, the language of Jesus as king appears in Luther's explanation of the second article of the Apostles' Creed: Jesus is Lord and King because he showed us mercy by redeeming us and freeing us. Luther then goes on to say, "As his own possession he has taken us under his protection and shelter, in order that he might rule us by his righteousness, wisdom, power, life, and blessedness." See Large Catechism, *Book of Concord*, §30, 434.

210 | The Hope of Eternal Life

consummated]."[641] As the *totus Christus* concept includes Christ as head (and king) of the church, it would be interesting to see what kind of connections might be drawn between these two biblical motifs (body of Christ and kingdom of God) that have been used to describe the communal dimension of eschatology, and what role the Spirit might play in that connection.

---

[641] Large Catechism, *Book of Concord*, §52, 447.